Server Side Swift

with

Kitura

By Chris Bailey & David Okun

Server Side Swift with Kitura

By Chris Bailey & David Okun

ISBN: 978-1-942878-96-4

Dedications

"To the Kitura core team and community, without whom none of this would exist, and to Dave Okun who said the ominous words: 'It'll be fun, it'll only take a couple of weeks...'"

— *Chris Bailey*

"Thanks to everyone who lent me an ear when I told you that Swift was a better idea than Node.js or Java. Thanks to the Kitura team for helping me realize a true passion in my professional life. Finally, thanks to the person reading this - you're stepping outside your comfort zone, and I promise you it's worth it."

— *David Okun*

About the Authors

Chris Bailey is a co-author of this book. Chris is a software developer and architect at IBM. He's been working on programming languages and web frameworks longer than it's polite to discuss. Somewhere along that journey, he got got involved in the very early days of Swift on Linux and became the chief architect for the Kitura web framework.

David Okun is a co-author of this book. He is a mobile software developer turned developer advocate for IBM in Austin, Texas. David has been primarily focused on iOS mobile software, but is also interested in Swift on the Server, and other web technologies such as Node.js.

About the Editors

Yono Mittlefehldt is a Tech Editor of this book. He is an indie developer specializing in iOS, Backend Development, and Machine Learning. He is a co-creater of Gus on the Go, a language learning app for kids. Yono speaks 3 languages fluently and 4 more at a novice level. He has been programming since he was 7 years old, because he enjoys it. Basically, he likes languages and coding. That's his jam.

Brian Schick is a Tech Editor of this book. Brian lives in Ashland, Oregon, and is Mobile Team Lead with Beezwax in Oakland, California. Brian has mastered a wide range of technologies, from deep data to frontend UI and UX tools and approaches. Currently, he's very happily obsessed with all things Swift. When not coding, Brian can be found exploring the mountains and coast of southern Oregon, tending bamboo groves, working with wood, or hanging with a craft brew in hand.

Jerry Beers is the Final Pass Editor of this book. Jerry is co-founder of Five Pack Creative, a mobile development company specializing in iOS development. He is passionate about creating well-crafted code and teaching others. You can find his company's site at fivepackcreative.com.

About the Artist

Vicki Wenderlich is the designer and artist of the cover of this book. She is Ray's wife and business partner. She is a digital artist who creates illustrations, game art and a lot of other art or design work for the tutorials and books on raywenderlich.com. When she's not making art, she loves hiking, a good glass of wine and attempting to create the perfect cheese plate.

Table of Contents

What You Need

macOS

The examples in this book are written using Swift **5.1**. To follow along, you'll need Xcode **11.0** using macOS **Mojave (10.14.6)** or higher and have at least **8GB of RAM** in your machine.

If you haven't installed the latest version of Xcode, be sure to do that before continuing with the book. The code covered in this book depends on Swift 5.1 and Xcode 11 — you may get lost if you try to work with an older version.

You will be writing using Kitura version **2.8.1**, and we will point out which features came out in which version. This book will always use the latest version of Kitura available. However, if you would like to experiment with Kitura, you can try writing an app in Kitura **1.x** and it will still work! The Kitura team iterates on Kitura additively, and they take great care to avoid introducing breaking changes to the main APIs available in the tool.

You will also frequently make use of the command line. Terminal, provided by macOS, is sufficient for everything needed throughout this book.

iOS

This book will also walk you through some development on an iOS app, which is mostly pre-written. This iOS app will be written for iOS **13.0**. The iOS Simulator will be completely sufficient for the development of this app, but feel free to try running it on your own iOS device if you have one.

Linux / Kubernetes

Throughout this book, you will test your Kitura app in a Docker container that runs Linux and in a Kubernetes cluster that can manage multiple containers. These tools will be explained in depth in a later chapter. For now, go to https://store.docker.com/editions/community/docker-ce-desktop-mac and make sure your machine has the pre-requisites covered.

If you don't already have a login, first you'll have to create one. Then, once you're logged in, make sure you scroll down halfway through the page and install the **Stable** version. When installing, you have a choice of either the **Stable** or **Edge** version of Docker for Mac — in this book, you want to use Kubernetes support built into Docker for Mac. At the time of this writing, Kubernetes is fully included in the stable build of Docker for Mac, and we cannot guarantee that the projects in this book will work using the **Edge** version.

Book License

By purchasing *Server Side Swift with Kitura*, you have the following license:

- You are allowed to use and/or modify the source code in *Server Side Swift with Kitura* in as many apps as you want, with no attribution required.

- You are allowed to use and/or modify all art, images and designs that are included in *Server Side Swift with Kitura* in as many apps as you want, but must include this attribution line somewhere inside your app: "Artwork/images/designs: from *Server Side Swift with Kitura*, available at www.raywenderlich.com".

- The source code included in *Server Side Swift with Kitura* is for your personal use only. You are NOT allowed to distribute or sell the source code in *Server Side Swift with Kitura* without prior authorization.

- This book is for your personal use only. You are NOT allowed to sell this book without prior authorization, or distribute it to friends, coworkers or students; they would need to purchase their own copies.

Book Source Code & Forums

If you bought the digital edition

The digital edition of this book comes with the source code for the starter and completed projects for each chapter. These resources are included with the digital edition you downloaded from https://store.raywenderlich.com/products/server-side-swift-with-kitura.

If you bought the print version

You can get the source code for the print edition of the book here:

- https://store.raywenderlich.com/products/server-side-swift-with-kitura-source-code

Forums

We've also set up an official forum for the book at forums.raywenderlich.com.This is a great place to ask questions about the book or to submit any errors you may find.

Digital book editions

We have a digital edition of this book available in both ePUB and PDF, which can be handy if you want a soft copy to take with you, or you want to quickly search for a specific term within the book.

Buying the digital edition version of the book also has a few extra benefits: free updates each time we update the book, access to older versions of the book, and you can download the digital editions from anywhere, at anytime.

Visit our *Server Side Swift with Kitura* store page here:

- https://store.raywenderlich.com/products/server-side-swift-with-kitura.

And if you purchased the print version of this book, you're eligible to upgrade to the digital editions at a significant discount! Simply email support@razeware.com with your receipt for the physical copy and we'll get you set up with the discounted digital edition version of the book.

About the Cover

Naturally, the Purple Vampire Crab does carry meaning to Kitura aside from just looking really cool.

The crab is considered a creature of the sea, but it spends most of its life ashore shuffling and pinching. Swift is a language generally made for mobile apps, but, throughout this book, you'll use Swift in a different environment. This might feel like walking sideways everywhere you go at first, but we are confident that the experience will grow on you!

Additionally, the crab has a hardened shell to protect it from the outside world. Writing a REST API involves a bit of security and authentication, so you'll also learn how to ensure that you write your Kitura API safely. It will respond to a large throng of devices, so your Kitura API will have a nice hard shell by the time you finish this book!

Crabs are also delicious if prepared correctly.

Chapter 1: Introduction

David Okun

Welcome! It is awesome that you've decided to take a step into the (sometimes) weird and (often) wonderful world of Swift on the server.

Swift as a programming language has grown leaps and bounds since it was announced at WWDC 2014. For developers coming from the world of Objective-C, Swift was a breath of fresh air in a world of square brackets versus dot notation. Swift has certainly experienced bumps along the road to where it is today, but developers who write apps for Apple platforms have largely embraced its modern, streamlined and type-safe approach.

But when Swift made its debut, one thing still stuck out like a sore thumb: Much like its counterpart, Objective-C, Swift was initially confined to the worlds of the Mac and iOS. This meant that a mobile developer writing an app with Swift still had to learn Node, Python or some other server-side language to create a data back end (or find a friend who could write this wizard-like code).

Then in 2015, Apple open-sourced Swift (cue thunderous applause all around). Almost in passing, as he introduced this milestone, Craig Federighi let slip under the radar the tantalizing fact that it was now possible to compile a version of Swift on Linux. The developers who ultimately began principal development on Kitura took notice.

What's a "Kitura"?

You might wonder about the source of the word "Kitura". Etymologically, the word **Kitura** relates loosely to the Hebrew word *Keturah*, which roughly translates to "incense." So is this the true derivation of the term? Maybe! It also turns out that there's a special type of Swift bird called the *Chaetura*.

When I started working for IBM, the entire team kept me in the dark about this for some time. They went so far as to play an ongoing practical joke — deliberately using different pronunciations of the word each day and playing dumb whenever I pressed for clarity. I finally got to the bottom of this at WWDC 2019, when the co-author of this book, Chris, came clean and let me know that "Kitura" derives from the name of the bird, and that it's pronounced ki-TU-ra. Mysteries solved!

When Apple announced availability for the Linux build of Swift, IBM quickly pounced. Out of the box, there were major hurdles to overcome: The team worked to port most of Swift's core APIs, like Dispatch, to compile and pass tests on Linux. In addition to this, the team visualized a module for running a RESTful server using Swift. That module is now known as Kitura.

Why Swift on the server?

The core argument in favor of writing Swift for your server is to share code and knowledge between the front end and the back end of your app. And if you're a team of one, this streamlining is arguably even more crucial and empowering. This includes, but is not limited to, your model object code.

Given that the team who wrote Kitura came from the Node.js ecosystem, there was a conscious desire to model Kitura after Express.js, which is arguably the most popular Node.js framework for running a RESTful server. There are many facets of Express to discuss, but the **router** is one of the most important ones. You will learn more about this later in the book. Think of a router as a module that routes requests to the appropriate place. Here is an example of a route in Express.js:

```
app.get("/testing", (req, res) => {
    res.send("Hello world!")
})
```

In English, this means that, whenever someone accesses /testing on your server, you send a plain-text response that says "Hello world!" Notice that you have two parameters called req and res passed into your closure for handling the response. Compare this to how a similar route would look in Kitura 1.x:

```
router.get("/testing") { request, response, next in
    response.send("Hello world")
    next()
}
```

The two code snippets are nearly identical, except for closure syntax in Javascript versus Swift, and the need to call `next()` (something they managed to eliminate in Kitura 2.x). Not only does this provide a comfortable landing for Node.js developers interested in trying Swift, but this also means Kitura has been architected with a consistent, tried-and-true methodology that caters to performance, ease of use and code longevity.

The BFF pattern and why it matters

The BFF (Backend for Frontend) is a design pattern that will quickly become your best friend (forever?).

It's a common task for a mobile developer to interface an app with a REST API. It's also somewhat common to run into issues during this integration. This could happen for any number of reasons:

- Verbose responses

- Inconsistent error states

- Versioning issues

- Poor documentation

If you're nodding your head, you might also remember saying something along the lines of, "I wish I could have just written the server myself!"

What if there was a way to handle these issues in the same programming language you write your iOS apps in, and you could deploy this solution to the cloud separately from your mobile app? Well, that's precisely what you will learn. In this book, we will show you how the BFF pattern enables you to deploy a server written in Swift that integrates with the existing server API.

This server acts as an intermediary between your mobile app and that existing server API, and it allows the mobile developer to spend much less time integrating the app with the API. This also means that the only code your mobile app written in Swift will ever have to integrate with is also written in Swift, which insulates your mobile developers from having to work with something that may have a steep learning curve.

Picture a common scenario amongst developer teams for modern-day apps. With all due respect to DevOps and Data Science engineers, this scenario only involves two types of developers: the **front-end** developer and the **back-end** developer.

For the sake of explanation, assume the front end has two media: an **iOS app** and a **website**. You are the iOS developer. Assume you also do not know how to set up a back end in any language.

Your app must show a series of restaurants with the following properties:

- Name

- Latitude and longitude

- Address

- Rating

The back-end developer has already made this method on the server, and you can access it RESTfully with a GET method. You would need to query the server based on providing a longitude and latitude. However, the current response is a little bit verbose, and looks like this:

```
{
    "reasons": {
        "count": 0,
        "items": [
            {
                "summary": "This spot is popular",
                "type": "general",
                "reasonName": "globalInteractionReason"
            }
        ]
    },
    "venue": {
        "id": "40b13b00f964a520cff31ee3",
        "name": "North By Northwest (NXNW)",
        "location": {
            "address": "10010 N Capital of Texas Hwy",
            "crossStreet": "Stonelake",
            "lat": 30.391062198099544,
            "lng": -97.73859813809395,
            "labeledLatLngs": [
                {
                    "label": "display",
                    "lat": 30.391062198099544,
                    "lng": -97.73859813809395
                }
            ],
            "distance": 144,
```

```
            "postalCode": "78759",
            "cc": "US",
            "city": "Austin",
            "state": "TX",
            "country": "United States",
            "formattedAddress": [
                "10010 N Capital of Texas Hwy (Stonelake)",
                "Austin, TX 78759",
                "United States"
            ]
        }
    }
}
```

You have parsed JSON before, so the task might not be too terribly difficult to complete, but you are not the only iOS developer who will ever work on this. You might be a pro, but it would be nice to make the job easier for everyone, right? And what if this API goes down all of a sudden? You could cache data on the device if you wanted, but your users might notice a different user experience if the app is just loading data from the disk, and not able to pull data from a brand new query.

The Monolith

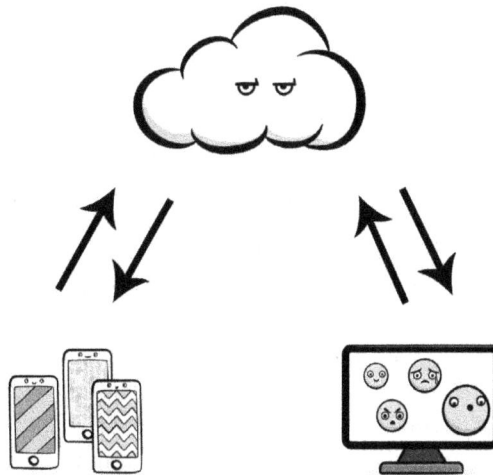

This is where the **Backend for Frontend** design pattern comes in. To this point, I have described a **Monolith** pattern, where one API is responsible for handling requests from every single possible client that may consume it. Aside from these issues, how can you be sure that the API is up to the task of fielding requests from X number of devices concurrently? We want to make their job easier too, right?

The Backend For Frontend

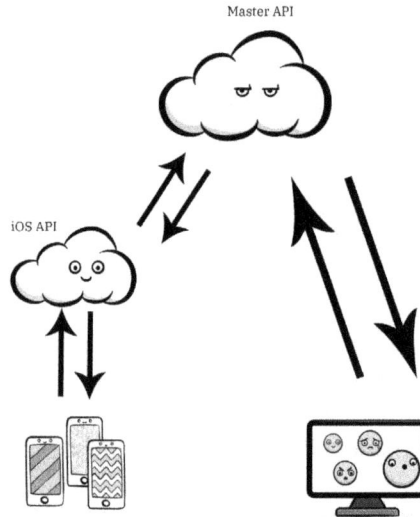

Master API

iOS API

A few reasons why this pattern works in this particular use case:

1. You can be sure that the only devices that make requests from this API will be iOS devices. This means you can be less worried about balancing request load.

2. You have more control over what data goes in a response to an iOS device. Before this, you may have waited for the back-end developer to eventually get around to helping you, and conditionally trimmed response data based on a User-Agent header. Now, you can let the back-end developer work uninterrupted, and solve your problem by parsing response data down to only what your BFF device needs.

3. In our specific use case, you can save responses for queries one user might make into a database before sending a response. This means that, if someone else requests restaurants in the same exact location, and the stored data is new enough to satisfy your refresh policy, you do not even have to send a query to the master server! You can just send the cached data and trust that it is fresh enough for your users.

4. You can accomplish 1–3 in the language you already know how to write code in — Swift!

This is a micro-service friendly approach that SoundCloud and ThoughtWorks pioneered in 2015. Imagine a workplace where you are free to "make your app work" without having to depend on another developer potentially blocking you. Thanks to this design pattern, you do not have to imagine it anymore. Throughout this book, you will create a full-stack app that follows this pattern, has both an iOS app and a web client, and a back end that uses Kitura.

EmojiJournal

Social networks are a little crazy these days — it would be nice if you could use a social network focused on your feelings, right? By the time you finish this book, you'll have written your own social network called **EmojiJournal**!

To do this, you'll write a Kitura server that serves a REST API that interacts with both an iOS app and a web client to let users record what emoji they feel like at a given time. Users will be able to view emoji entries, add new ones, delete old ones and make friends through the network.

Each chapter of this book includes work that is additive in nature to the project, so each chapter will provide you both a starting point and an ending point in the files you can download when you purchase this book. We recommend you go start to finish to get the whole experience. But you can also jump into any chapter at any time and pick up wherever you want.

Chapter 2: Hello, World!

Chris Bailey

While Kitura is a fully featured web framework with which you can build a number of rich web apps, chat engines, RESTful APIs and all manner of other server apps, it's traditional to first build a "Hello, world!" app.

In this chapter, you'll do just that, learning about some of the tools and fundamental concepts of building server-side Swift apps as you go.

In this chapter, you'll:

- Create a project and manage dependencies with Swift Package Manager.

- Build a web server that listens on port 8080.

- Learn to handle web requests and build responses.

- Run your server on Linux using Docker.

In essence, by the end of this chapter, you'll have taken your first steps toward becoming a backend Swift engineer.

Creating your project

All server-side Swift projects manage their dependencies using Swift Package Manager — Apple's package management tooling that's part of Swift itself.

You can work with Swift Package Manager using either the the Swift **package** command line option, which provides a number of functions and capabilities, or directly through Xcode.

First you'll see how to create a new Swift Package Manager project using the command line, and then you'll work with that project through Xcode.

To create your "Hello, world!" project using the command line, you'll use the **swift package** command with the following options:

- **init**: Creates a new Swift Package Manager project.

- **show-dependencies**: Displays a graph of your project's dependency tree and the versions that your project is using.

- **generate-xcodeproj**: Builds an Xcode project file.

> **Note**: Although the `generate-xcodeproj` option is still present, this command — and the `.xcodeproj` file it creates — are no longer necessary in Xcode 11, as we can now open the project by opening the `Package.swift` file!

To create a new project, you'll use the **init** command. Before doing so, you'll need to create a new directory for your project. This is required, as Swift Package Manager will use the name of the current directory as the name of the project.

The **init** command also accepts a **--type** option. This allows you to request that an empty, executable, library or system module project be created. Since you are going to run your project directly, you'll create an executable project.

Let's get started!

Open **Terminal** and navigate to the location of your choice — where you'd like your first Kitura project to live. Then, enter the following:

```
mkdir hello-world
cd hello-world
swift package init --type executable
```

With these commands, you've created a clean project folder and navigated to it. You then invoked Swift Package Manager to create a new project for you, creating the following structure for your project:

```
Package.swift
README.md
.gitignore
Sources/
Sources/hello-world/main.swift
Tests/
Tests/LinuxMain.swift
```

```
Tests/hello-worldTests/
Tests/hello-worldTests/hello_worldTests.swift
Tests/hello-worldTests/XCTestManifests.swift
```

You can now run **open Package.swift** in your Terminal window to open your new project in Xcode.

Notice that you're opening Package.swift directly, and *not* an Xcode project file (.xcodeproj) as usual. As mentioned earlier, this is because Xcode 11 no longer requires an .xcodeproj file for server-side projects. You'll see this pattern in our Emoji Server project throughout this book, and in fact, we'll *never* need an Xcode file for our server project!

You can open any project without an .xcodeproj file in one of three ways:

1. Enter open Package.swift in Terminal (from within the project directory).

2. Double click on the project's Package.swift file in Finder.

3. In Xcode, choose Open and then select the project folder.

This shows the following contents in the Project navigator view:

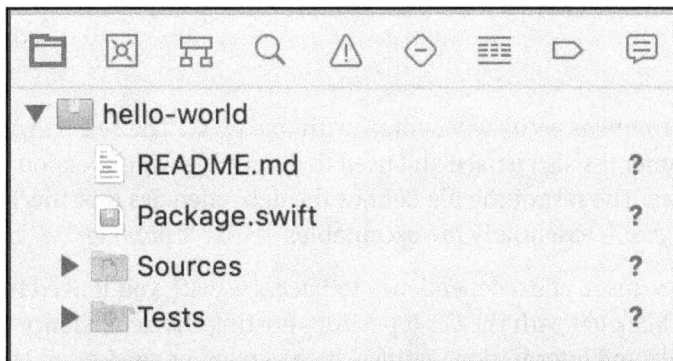

Let's focus on Package.swift. This is the Swift Package Manger's configuration file. You'll update this file repeatedly throughout this book to manage your Kitura project dependencies.

You'll see that it contains the following:

```
// swift-tools-version:5.1
// The swift-tools-version declares the minimum version of Swift
required to build this package.

import PackageDescription

let package = Package(
  name: "hello-world",
  dependencies: [
    // Dependencies declare other packages that this package
depends on.
    // .package(url: /* package url */, from: "1.0.0"),
  ],
  targets: [
    // Targets are the basic building blocks of a package. A
target can define a module or a test suite.
    // Targets can depend on other targets in this package, and
on products in packages which this package depends on.
    .target(
      name: "hello-world",
      dependencies: []),
    .testTarget(
      name: "hello-worldTests",
      dependencies: ["hello-world"]),
  ]
)
```

Package.swift complies with Swift syntax, with one twist: The `swift-tools-version:` comment is also parsed and used to determine which version of Swift this package will use. The rest of the file defines the dependencies that this package relies on and the targets — essentially the executables — that it provides.

Whenever you want to add a dependency to Package.swift, you'll need to provide Swift Package Manager with the Git repository hosting the dependency (it can be remote or local), and information stating which version or versions of the dependency to use.

Your "Hello, world!" project will depend on Kitura, so you'll update Package.swift `dependencies` array to include this information.

In your text editor, replace the boilerplate text in your `dependencies` array with the following:

```
.package(url: "https://github.com/IBM-Swift/Kitura.git",
         .upToNextMajor(from: "2.8.1")),
```

This adds a dependency on Kitura, specifying a minimum version of 2.8.1, which is the latest version at the point of this writing.

Swift Package Manager projects are expected to follow Semantic Versioning (SemVer), in which:

- The first digit denotes a Major version, which can contain breaking API changes.

- The second digit specifies a Minor version, which can contain non-breaking feature enhancements.

- The third digit provides a Fix version, which can contain fixes only.

Here, using `.upToNextMajor(from: "2.8.1")` tells Swift Package Manager to use the latest version between 2.8.1 and the next Major version, which would be 3.0.0. This means that feature and fix updates can be included, but not breaking changes. Swift Package Manager also provides support for specifying other version levels, including `.upToNextMinor()`, `.exact()` and `.branch()`.

In addition to specifying the Kitura dependency's location and acceptable versions, you also need to add it as a specified dependency to each target that will use Kitura. You'll want to use Kitura in both your `hello-world` app and in your tests.

Add an entry of `"Kitura"` in the `dependencies` array for both of those targets. Your **Package.swift** file should now look similar to this:

```
// swift-tools-version:5.1
// The swift-tools-version declares the minimum version of Swift
required to build this package.

import PackageDescription

let package = Package(
  name: "hello-world",
  dependencies: [
    .package(url: "https://github.com/IBM-Swift/Kitura.git",
    .upToNextMajor(from: "2.8.1")),
  ],
  targets: [
    // Targets are the basic building blocks of a package. A
target can define a module or a test suite.
    // Targets can depend on other targets in this package, and
on products in packages which this package depends on.
    .target(
      name: "hello-world",
      dependencies: ["Kitura"]),
    .testTarget(
      name: "hello-worldTests",
      dependencies: ["hello-world", "Kitura"]),
```

```
    ]
  )
```

Great! With these changes, you've added your dependency on Kitura to your Swift package!

You'll see several new folders begin to appear in the left-hand Project Navigator as Xcode 11 retrieves Kitura — along with all its dependencies. When this is finished and all the progress indicators are gone, make sure your mac is selected as the build device. Then run your project by clicking the **Build and then run the current scheme** button to run your app.

This will build and run your app. Once the app runs, you'll see "Hello, world!" printed in the console:

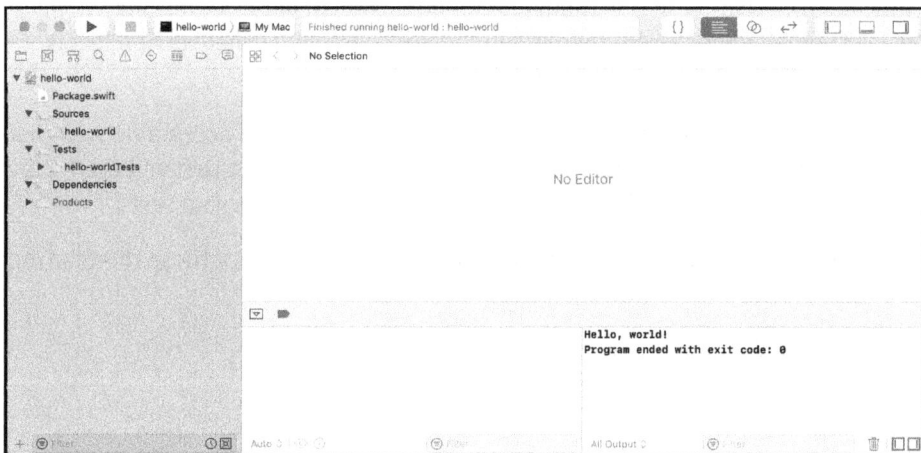

> **Note:** Even though you didn't write any code to create this output, Swift Package manager generated the project with `print("Hello, world!")` in main.swift for you. You'll learn more about this in the next section.

Huzzah! But let's not get too excited just yet. This isn't yet a server-side Swift app that's able to respond to web requests. To achieve this, you'll need to create a Kitura Server. Let's make it so!

Creating a Kitura server

In Swift Package Manager projects, each defined target has its own sub-directory within the Sources directory, and each executable target has a corresponding main.swift file inside that sub-directory.

Since your project has an executable target called hello-world, it therefore also contains Sources/hello-world/main.swift. This file acts as the entry point for the hello-world executable and is invoked when your app is started.

Open **main.swift** in Xcode. It currently contains:

```
print("Hello, world!")
```

This was automatically added when you ran **swift package init --type executable**, and is the reason "Hello, world!" was printed to the console. You'll now update this file to create a Kitura server that will handle incoming requests and return "Hello, world!" responses.

Remove the existing contents of the file, and add the following:

```
import Kitura
```

This gives you access to Kitura functions, which you'll use to create a web server and route incoming web requests to methods you create to handle those requests.

Next, add the following:

```
let router = Router()

Kitura.addHTTPServer(onPort: 8080, with: router)
Kitura.run()
```

Here, you instantiate a Kitura router, create an HTTP server that uses this router and listens on port 8080, and, finally, you run the new server.

And that's it! With just these three lines of code, you've just completed your first Kitura web server!

Build and run the project to start your server. After your app starts, you may see a macOS prompt asking you to allow incoming network connections:

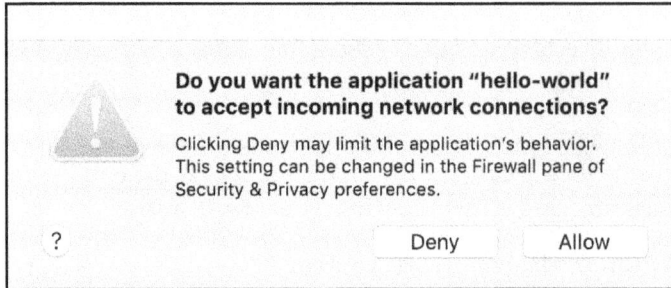

Click **Allow**. Then, open your browser and go to http://localhost:8080.

Kitura should receive your browser request and display the default Kitura splash screen:

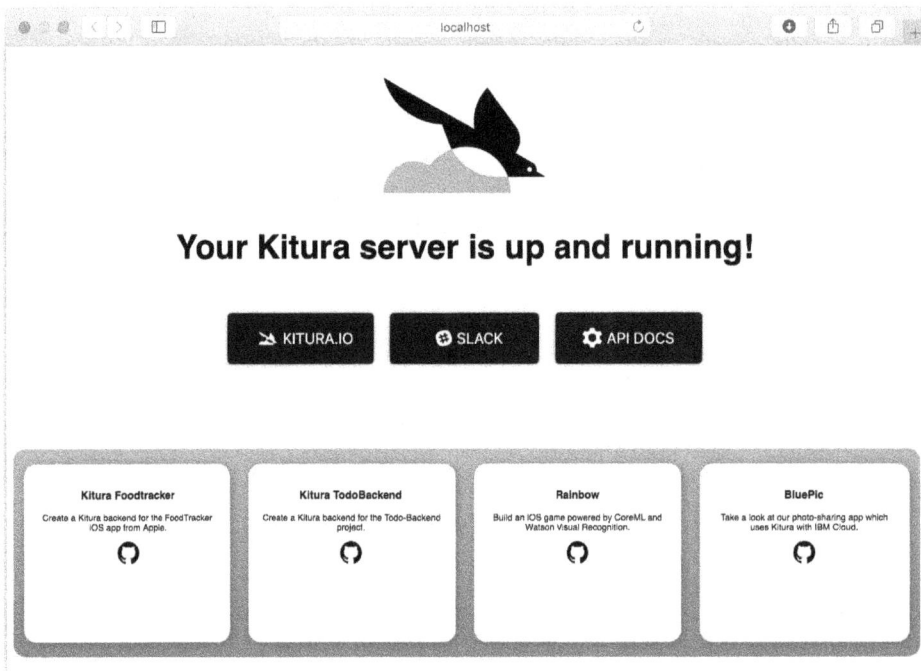

Nice! Now that you have a running Kitura server, it's time to teach your app to respond to web requests with a friendly "Hello, world!" message!

Creating a "Hello, world!" response

The heart of any Kitura-based application is the `Router` object. When Kitura receives an incoming request, it uses the router to determine which handler functions have been registered to handle it. If a matching handler function is found, it's passed a `RouterRequest` object representing the contents of the HTTP request and prepared to respond via a `RouterResponse` representing the HTTP response to be returned.

The method used to register handler functions with the router takes this form:

```
router.<HTTP Method>(<url>, <handler>)
```

Requests from web browsers use the GET HTTP method. To register a handler function for GET requests with no additional path, add the following to your **main.swift** file immediately after you create your `router`:

```
router.get("/", handler: helloWorldHandler)
```

This will route any incoming HTTP GET requests on the root path to the `helloWorldHandler` function. Since you haven't yet created this, you'll see an Xcode error complaining that you've used an unresolved identifier. You'll fix this now.

Add the following function to the top of **main.swift**, right after the `import` statement:

```
func helloWorldHandler(request: RouterRequest,
    response: RouterResponse, next: () -> ()) {
      response.send("Hello, world!")
      next()
}
```

Your main.swift file should now look like this:

```
import Kitura

func helloWorldHandler(request: RouterRequest,
    response: RouterResponse, next: ()->()) {
      response.send("Hello, world!")
      next()
}

let router = Router()
router.get("/", handler: helloWorldHandler)

Kitura.addHTTPServer(onPort: 8080, with: router)
Kitura.run()
```

Build and run the project to start your server, and select **Allow** if prompted to allow incoming network connections. Open your browser once again to http://localhost:8080.

This time, instead of the default Kitura splash screen, you should see your "Hello, world!" message displayed in all its minimalist glory.

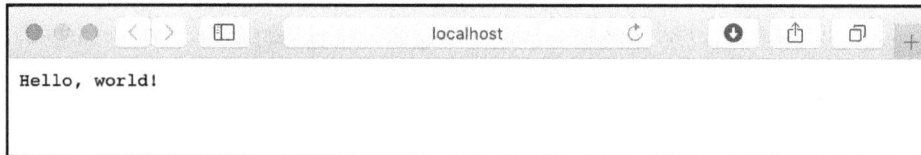

Congratulations! You've just built your first server-side Swift app with Kitura! Easy, right?

A fully featured "Hello, world!" Kitura project

You now have a basic Kitura web server running "Hello, world!" Of course, your ultimate goal will be to build fully featured server apps and microservices. And you want these to not only provide desired functionality, but do this gracefully at scale with capabilities such as logging and monitoring. Kitura has your back here, too.

In order to help you to create production-ready apps, Kitura provides a command line interface (CLI) tool as well as a macOS app that provides starter templates. These are similar to **swift package init --type executable** in that they provide a template project for you to extend that puts the basic structure and requirements in place for you.

In this section, you'll use these tools and a starter template to rebuild your "Hello, world!" app. You'll build on top of that for the next several chapters.

Installing the Kitura macOS App and the Kitura CLI

The Kitura macOS App and the Kitura CLI can both be installed by following the instructions in the > GET STARTED section of the Kitura.io website:

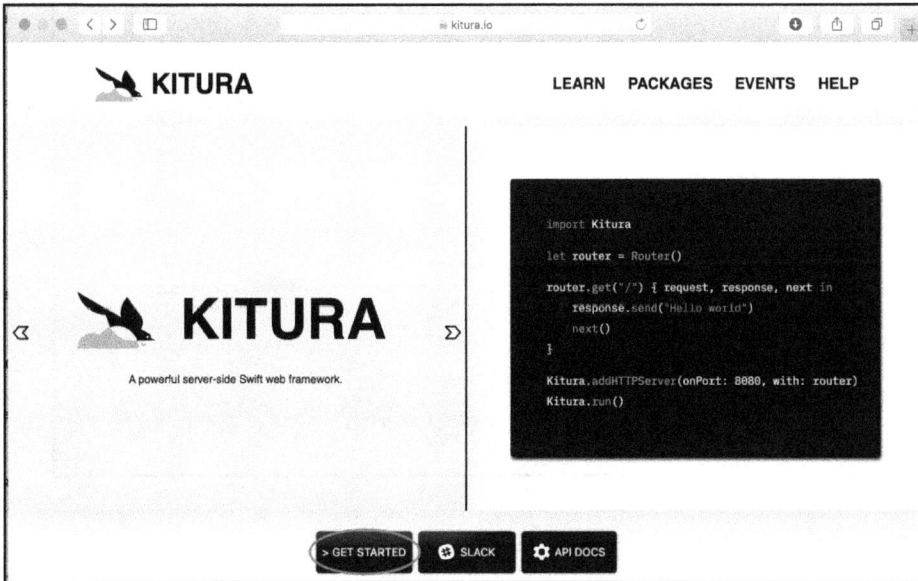

This opens the Kitura Docs in your browser window and takes you to the "Hello world example".

To locate the macOS App download, click on the "Create a server" link in the left hand contents list, and then click on the **macOS App** link.

You'll now see a page entitled "Create a server with the Kitura macOS app". Find and click **Download** link to download the Kitura mac app, and then install it on your mac.

The Kitura macOS App provides the ability to create a number of template Kitura projects. Open it now. You'll see the following, showing you three types of template Kitura applications that you can create a server from:

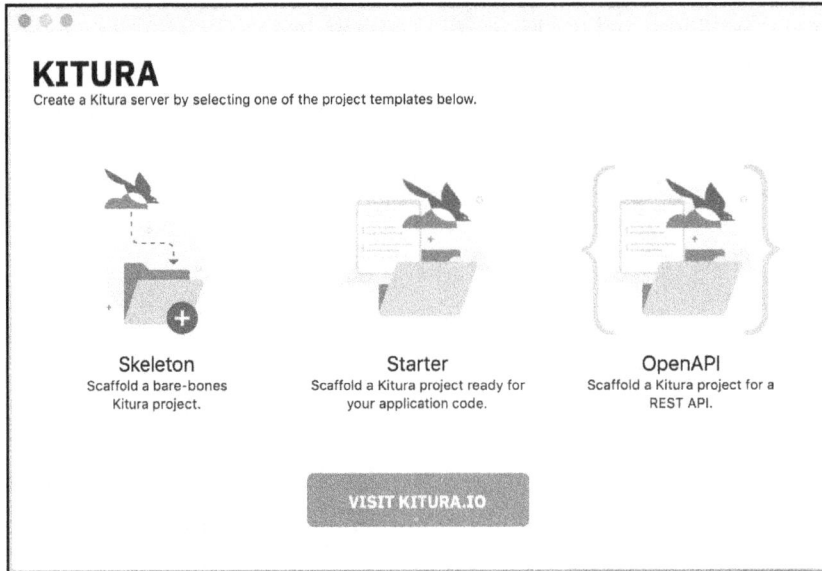

> **Note**: If your security settings prevent the app from opening, right-click on the app and choose **Open**.

Great! Next, you'll install the Kitura CLI. In addition to providing template Kitura projects, this also performs several key functions including:

- Building and running your apps in Docker.

- Creating Client SDK libraries for iOS, Android and web for your Kitura server.

The Kitura CLI tools are installed using Homebrew. To check to see if you have Homebrew installed, open your preferred terminal app and run:

```
brew
```

If Homebrew is installed, your should see usage information printed to the terminal. If you see an error message instead, follow the instructions at http://brew.sh to install Homebrew. Do this before proceeding.

Next, you'll install Kitura's Homebrew tap. This installs resources needed to access Kitura's package repository. To do this, run the following command:

```
brew tap ibm-swift/kitura
```

Now you're ready to install Kitura CLI itself. Run:

```
brew install kitura
```

Once this completes, enter the command **kitura**. This should display a screen providing basic usage information:

```
Usage: kitura [options] [command]

Kitura command-line interface

Options:
  -V, --version  output the version number
  -h, --help     output usage information

Commands:
  build          build the project in a local container
  create         interactively create a Kitura project
  idt            install IBM Cloud Developer Tools
  init           scaffold a bare-bones Kitura project
  kit            print Cocoapods boilerplate for KituraKit
  run            run the project in a local container
  sdk            generate a client SDK from an OpenAPI/Swagger spec
  help [cmd]     display help for [cmd]
```

Creating a Kitura project with the macOS App

Now that you have these core tools installed, open the macOS App. This presents you with three basic templates that you can use to start a new Kitura project:

- Skeleton: A very basic app. This does little more than add the Kitura dependencies to the Package.swift file.

- Starter: This builds on top of Skeleton and provides a full-fledged server framework that includes logging, monitoring and health checks. It also provides configuration files for Docker, Kubernetes and more.

- OpenAPI: This builds on top of Starter and provides additional support specifically for building RESTful APIs, including backend APIs for an iOS mobile app.

Select the **Starter** template and click on **Create**.

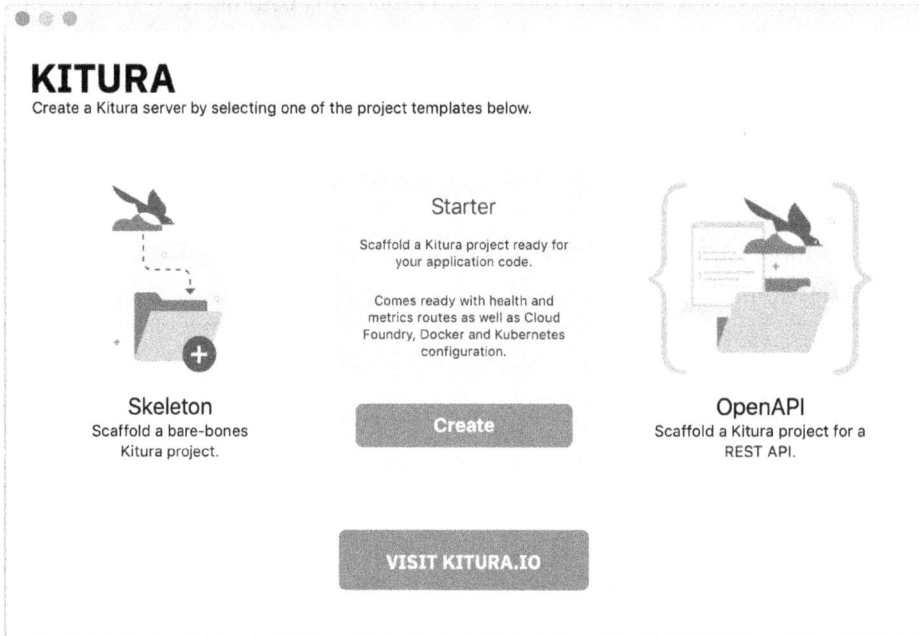

You're choosing this since you want a fully featured server, but you're not specifically building RESTful APIs. (By the way, this is the same template that's used when you create a project using the **kitura init** command with the Kitura CLI.)

Next, select a folder and a name for your project. Since you'll use this to build your EmojiJournalServer over the next several chapters, name it **EmojiJournalServer**, and click **Create**.

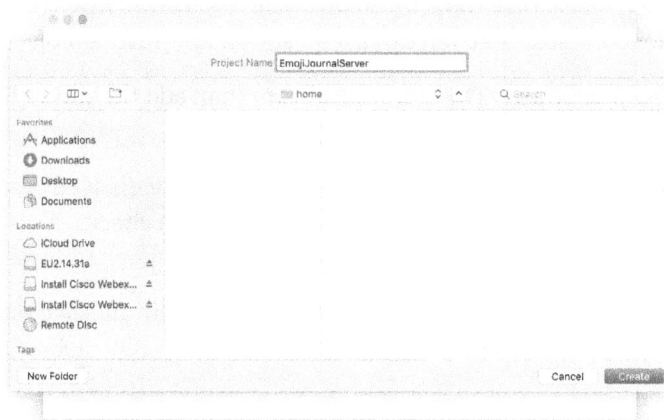

This will create a new sub-folder for your project, add a template project with the latest dependencies, build an Xcode project and open Xcode for you.

Understanding your Kitura project

The created Kitura project provides a fully working Kitura app out of the box. It offers several features you're likely to need for any app running in a production environment, including:

- Logging for informational, warning and error messages using HeliumLogger.

- Dynamic configuration lookup and settings using CloudEnvironment.

- App health status checking and reporting using Health.

- App and Kitura framework metrics and monitoring using SwiftMetrics.

Each of these has been added to the project via Package.swift dependencies along with the boilerplate code needed to initialize and enable them in the app itself.

Open **Package.swift** to see these added dependencies.

Your Package.swift should look similar to the following (these are the latest package levels at the time of this writing):

```
// swift-tools-version:5.0
import PackageDescription

let package = Package(
  name: "EmojiJournalServer",
  dependencies: [
    .package(url: "https://github.com/IBM-Swift/
Kitura.git", .upToNextMinor(from: "2.8.1")),
    .package(url: "https://github.com/IBM-Swift/
HeliumLogger.git", from: "1.7.1"),
    .package(url: "https://github.com/IBM-Swift/
CloudEnvironment.git", from: "9.0.0"),
    .package(url: "https://github.com/RuntimeTools/
SwiftMetrics.git", from: "2.0.0"),
    .package(url: "https://github.com/IBM-Swift/Health.git",
from: "1.0.0"),
  ],
  targets: [
    .target(name: "EmojiJournalServer", dependencies:
[ .target(name: "Application"), "Kitura" , "HeliumLogger"]),
    .target(name: "Application", dependencies: [ "Kitura",
"CloudEnvironment","SwiftMetrics", "Health",]),
    .testTarget(name: "ApplicationTests" , dependencies:
[.target(name: "Application"), "Kitura","HeliumLogger" ])
```

```
    ]
)
```

Note: Since the Kitura app generates this file for you, and it generates it with the latest version numbers for dependencies, your versions will likely be different than those shown above. The Kitura team takes great care to not introduce breaking changes, but if you run into any issues, try changing the versions in your Package.swift to match the ones above.

As you can see, there are four new entries in the Package dependencies array — each corresponding to one of the new packages in your project.

Additionally, you'll find a significant change in targets. Your initial project contained a single target (plus a test target), whereas the Kitura template generated two non-test targets: EmojiJournalServer and Application.

One last thing: Take note of the EmojiJournalServer target. This provides the entry point responsible for providing a wrapper to load and start the Application target. This is where all your app code resides.

For this reason, the EmojiJournalServer package target contains a dependency on the Application target. It also depends on the HeliumLogger package to log any errors.

As you've already seen, each target's dependencies are listed using an array of package names or (in the case of a dependency on another target) a .target(name:) method. The EmojiJournalServer's dependency on Application uses that method, like this:

```
.target(name: "Application")
```

You might be wondering how to determine which names to use for each package dependency. As it turns out, this is defined by each dependency itself. For example, the Package.swift file of the https://github.com/IBM-Swift/HeliumLogger.git project defines that it provides a HeliumLogger target.

To see this, open your browser to https://github.com/IBM-Swift/HeliumLogger.git and then open the Package.swift file, where you should see something like this:

```
import PackageDescription

let package = Package(
  name: "HeliumLogger",
  ...
```

As you can see, the Package's name property is **HeliumLogger**. In addition to using this name when declaring dependencies as you've just seen, you'll also use this package's name to import it into individual .swift files in your app.

Back in your EmojiJournalServer project, the `Application` target depends on the libraries exposed by the other dependencies: Kitura, CloudEnvironment, SwiftMetrics and Health.

Remember, each target in a project has its own sub-directory within the Sources directory. Since the EmojiJournalServer project has both an EmojiJournalServer target and an Application target, it has sub-directories that match both these names.

The app sub-directory contains the following structure:

```
Sources/Application/Application.swift
Sources/Application/InitializationError.swift
Sources/Application/Metrics.swift
Sources/Application/Routes/HealthRoutes.swift
```

Application.swift contains lifecycle handling for your app, providing the core `init()` and `run()` methods used by main.swift in the EmojiJournalServer target to start the app. Open **/Sources/Application/Application.swift** in Xcode to see what it does:

```swift
import Foundation
import Kitura
import LoggerAPI
import Configuration
import CloudEnvironment
import KituraContracts
import Health

public let projectPath =
  ConfigurationManager.BasePath.project.path
public let health = Health()

public class App {
  let router = Router()
  let cloudEnv = CloudEnv()

  public init() throws {
    // Run the metrics initializer
    initializeMetrics(router: router)
  }

  func postInit() throws {
    // Endpoints
    initializeHealthRoutes(app: self)
  }

  public func run() throws {
    try postInit()
    Kitura.addHTTPServer(onPort: cloudEnv.port, with: router)
    Kitura.run()
  }
}
```

```
    }
```

The App object provides two core properties that you'll rely on as you build your own apps: `router` (which you've already seen) and `cloudEnv`. The `cloudEnv` instance is used to manage any configuration the app requires. It provides a location outside the app's code from which you can set configuration, using environment variables or configuration files.

Out of the box, the `cloudEnv` instance is only used to determine the port Kitura listens on, using `cloudEnv.port`. By default, this is set to 8080, but you can change this by setting any of the following:

1. The PORT environment variable.

2. The --PORT value on the command line.

3. The PORT value in a config file passed to the `CloudEnv` initializer, like this: `let cloudEnv = CloudEnv(cloudFoundryFile: "config/local-dev.config")`

Give this a try now. Select **Product ▸ Scheme ▸ Edit Scheme...** from Xcode's menu. Make sure the EmojiJournalServer scheme is selected, then select **Run** in the left-hand pane and then choose the **Arguments** tab.

Now, add a new Environment Variable by clicking on the section's + button, entering a Name of **PORT** and a Value of **8090**.

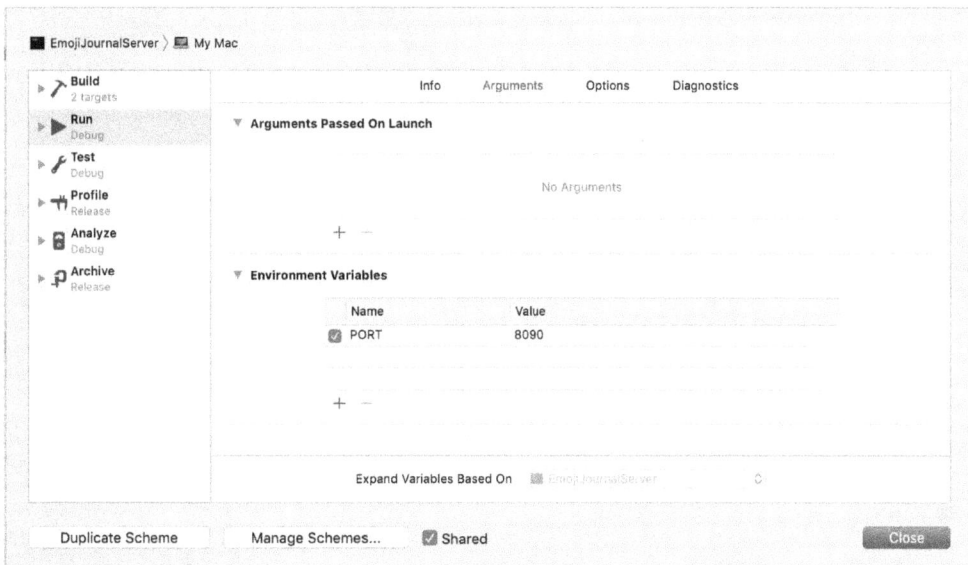

Click **Close** to exit, and then build and run the project. You'll see the following message printed to the console:

```
[2018-09-29T01:43:33.673+01:00] [INFO] [HTTPServer.swift:195
listen(on:)] Listening on port 8090
```

In your browser, go to http://localhost:8090. Once again, you see the Kitura splash screen, demonstrating that your Kitura app is now running on port 8090. Nice!

You've now gotten a glimpse of how cloudEnv can be used for configuration management. You'll now focus on these two functions:

- initializeHealthRoutes
- initializeMetrics

The first of these, initializeHealthRoutes, adds a route to the app that serves as a "health endpoint" or "liveness probe." This provides a mechanism other services can call to determine whether your Kitura app is "healthy" (i.e., if it's "live") or needs to be restarted.

Open your browser now to http://localhost:8090/health (remember that you're still using port 8090!). You should see data similar to the following:

```
{"status":"UP","details":[],
  "timestamp":"2018-09-29T00:57:19+0000"}
```

This type of health or liveness checking is common in many cloud deployment environments. You'll use this in Chapter 15, "Kitura Going Live."

The second of the these functions, `initializeMetrics`, adds metrics and monitoring capabilities to your app. These are exposed in two forms:

- A built-in monitoring dashboard that's self-hosted by your app.

- A metrics endpoint that can be used by the Prometheus open-source monitoring tool.

Open your browser to http://localhost:8090/swiftmetrics-dash to see the built-in monitoring dashboard:

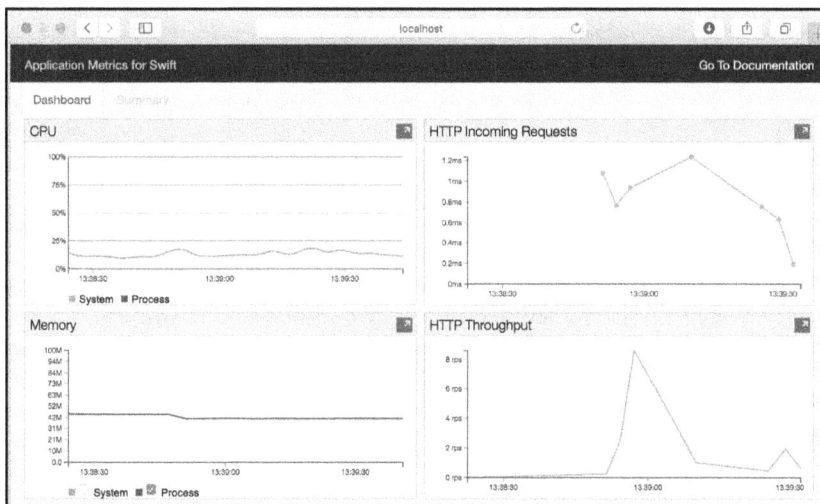

The dashboard provides four views under the Dashboard tab:

- CPU

- Memory

- HTTP Incoming Requests

- HTTP Throughput

The CPU and Memory views provide real-time information on CPU and Memory usage of both your app (labeled Process) and the machine it's running on (System).

The HTTP Incoming Requests view shows the responsiveness of incoming requests in milliseconds. Where there are large numbers of requests, the points on the graph represent a summary of a number of requests that occurred at the same time. Each point on the graph also provides a tooltip, which gives additional information describing what the point represents, including the URL, number of requests, average and longest durations.

The HTTP Throughput view shows the volume of requests occurring at any point in time using a Requests Per Second (RPS) metric.

Additionally, the built-in dashboard also provides a top **Summary** tab. Click on this, now:

As you can see, this provides a table view of HTTP endpoint and Resource usage data, along with information on the environment the application is running in. Environmental data includes the command line used, the hostname of the machine and its number of processors.

All data displayed in the built-in dashboard is also available via a "metrics endpoint." Open your browser to http://localhost:8090/metrics to see what is provided.

This endpoint displays its data as a series of key-value pairs. For example, the CPU data shown previously in the built-in dashboard is available here as process_cpu_used_ratio and os_cpu_used_ratio. These represent the percentage of the

CPU used by your application process, and by the overall operating system (OS) as a value between 0 and 1.

Kitura's metrics endpoint is designed primarily to be machine-readable rather than directly human-readable. In a later chapter, you'll look in more depth at how this data can be consumed by the Prometheus open-source monitoring tool, available at https://prometheus.io.

Adding "Hello, world!" to your Kitura project

Let's tie up a few loose ends on your project.

The macOS App has generated and configured a fully featured Kitura server that already follows several best practices. Now, you'll need to add your handler method to the provided router as you did previously in order to provide your "Hello, world!" response to requests.

First, in Xcode, edit the **EmojiJournalServer** scheme once again, and remove the PORT environment variable you set previously, so that your app will once again listen on the default 8080 port.

Next, select **Application.swift** and add the following to your `postInit` method:

```
router.get("/", handler: helloWorldHandler)
```

By doing this, you've registered a `helloWorldHandler` on GET requests on /. Because you haven't yet created this handler method, you'll see a temporary error.

To resolve this, add `helloWorldHandler` in your App class, after `postInit`:

```
func helloWorldHandler(request: RouterRequest,
    response: RouterResponse, next: ()->()) {
      response.send("Hello, world!")
      next()
}
```

Build and run the project to start your server, once again selecting **Allow** if you're asked to allow incoming network connections.

Now open your browser to http://localhost:8080. Kitura should receive your browser request and return a response of "Hello, world!":

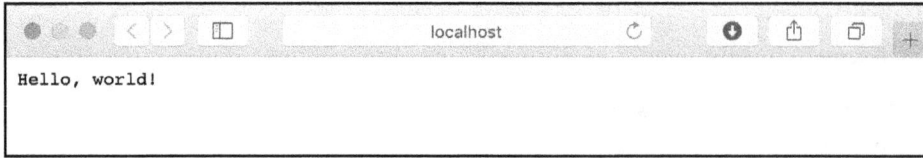

Congratulations! Your GET route is up and running, and you now have a full-fledged Kitura "Hello, world!" server! In the upcoming chapters, you'll continue building on what you've done here as the basis of your EmojiJournalServer project.

Running your app on Linux using Docker

You've already built a simple Kitura server that runs on your Mac. In this section, you'll build your app on Linux using Docker.

> **Note:** To learn more about Docker, there is an excellent tutorial at https://www.raywenderlich.com/9159-docker-on-macos-getting-started.

Docker and Kubernetes are central to Kitura deployments, and they provide major performance and scaling benefits. Later in this book, you'll deploy your EmojiJournalServer as a full-fledged scalable app running in Linux-based Docker images deployed to Kubernetes.

If you're not sure what that means, don't worry, you'll learn along the way.

Time to get started. First, in Xcode, **Stop** your current project if it's still running.

Next, make sure Docker for Desktop is installed on your Mac. You'll use this to build, manage and run Docker images on your Mac.

Installing Docker Desktop

> **Note:** If you've previously installed Docker Desktop, you can skip to the next section.

If you don't have Docker Desktop installed, go to https://www.docker.com/products/docker-desktop and select **Download for Mac**:

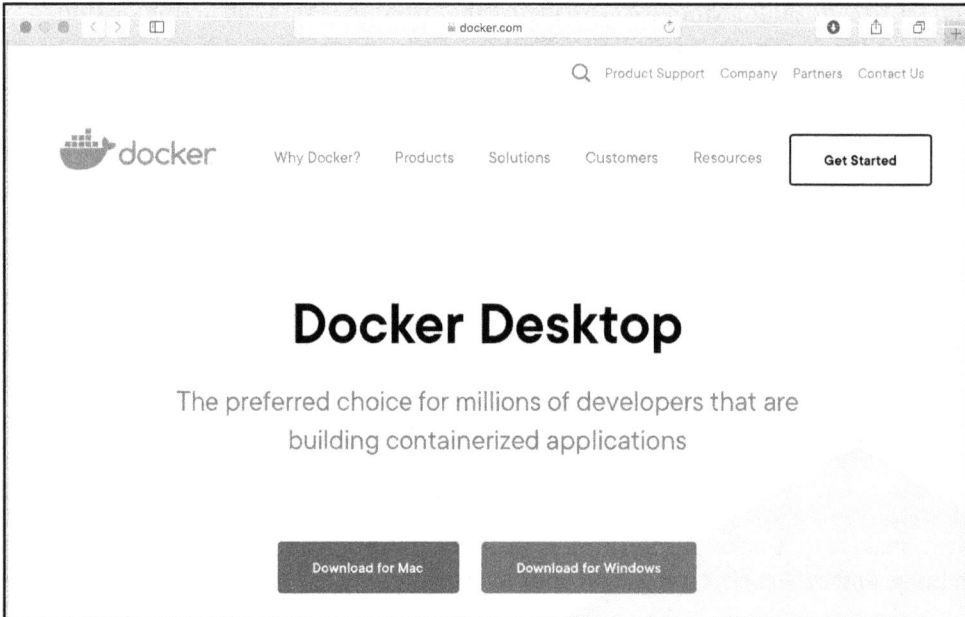

Create a Docker ID. Then, sign in and download Docker for Desktop as a .dmg file using the **Get Docker** button:

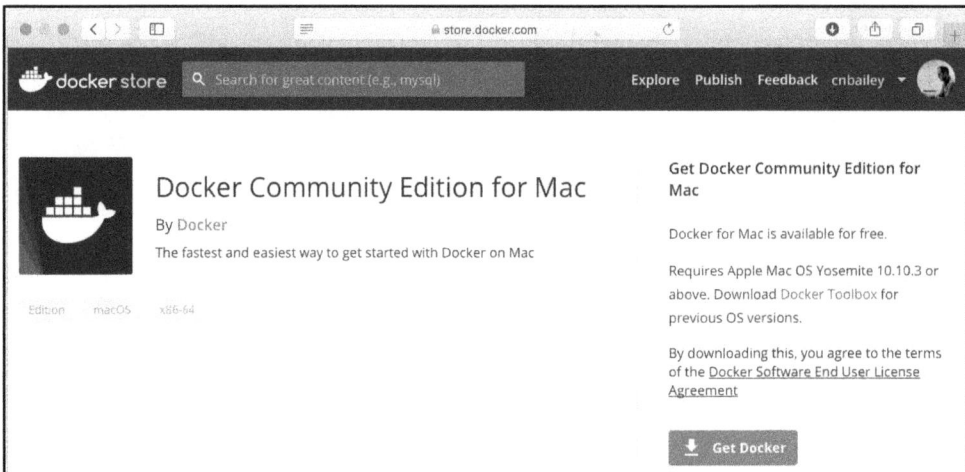

Install the .dmg file and launch Docker. This will display a dialog while it's starting, and then become an icon in your Mac menu bar:

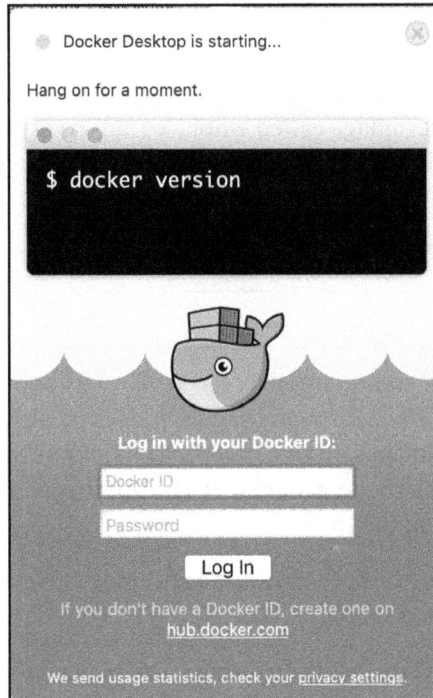

Docker's menu bar item can come in handy for quickly configuring and updating Docker. That said, you'll likely work with Docker primarily in Terminal via the docker command.

Using your project with Docker

When you used Kitura's macOS App to create your project, it automatically added Dockerfile and Dockerfile-tools files to your project. These configuration files are used by Docker to package your apps into an "image." This image consists of your app and all of its dependencies, including a copy of the Linux OS on which it will run.

For now, you'll use the default files to build and run a Docker image for your app.

You can do this most easily using the Kitura CLI, which offers two commands: one that builds your app and a second that runs it using Docker. These are the aptly named build and run commands. Both of these use the docker command under the covers to ask it to build the "image" for your project, and to then run that image in a "container."

Make sure **Terminal** is open and that your working directory is the root folder of your EmojiJournalServer project. Run the command **kitura idt**. This will initialize your CLI environment, ensuring that underlying support tools are properly installed on your Mac.

Now that your environment is initialized, run **kitura build**. This will take a few moments to build a Docker image called emojijournalserver-swift-tools from the settings in your Dockerfile-tools file.

One the build process is complete, run **docker images** command to view the image created:

```
REPOSITORY                       TAG       IMAGE ID       CREATED          SIZE
emojijournalserver-swift-tools   latest    0bad1c4e2fc0   11 minutes ago   1.75GB
ibmcom/swift-ubuntu              5.0.1     18eca5b589e0   6 weeks ago      1.68GB
```

This displays two images: emojijournalserver-swift-tools and ibmcom/swift-ubuntu. Why two images? One of Docker's many capabilities is its ability to build images that depend on other Docker images. In this case, your emojijournalserver-swift-tools image has been built using the ibmcom/swift-ubuntu image, which contains Swift and an Ubuntu distribution of Linux.

Now run **kitura run**. This builds then runs a emojijournalserver-swift-run image optimized for production usage.

Once this command completes, Terminal should display similar messages to those you saw earlier in your Xcode console:

```
Logs for the emojijournalserver-swift-run container:
[2018-12-24T21:59:24.599Z] [WARNING] [ConfigurationManager.swift:261 load(url:deserializerName:)] Unable to load
data from URL /swift-project/config/mappings.json
[Mon Dec 24 21:59:24 2018] com.ibm.diagnostics.healthcenter.loader INFO: Swift Application Metrics
[2018-12-24T21:59:24.740Z] [INFO] [Metrics.swift:20 initializeMetrics(router:)] Initialized metrics.
[2018-12-24T21:59:24.745Z] [INFO] [HTTPServer.swift:195 listen(on:)] Listening on port 8080
```

Your Kitura app is up and running as a Docker image. Open your browser to http://localhost:8080/ to see it running:

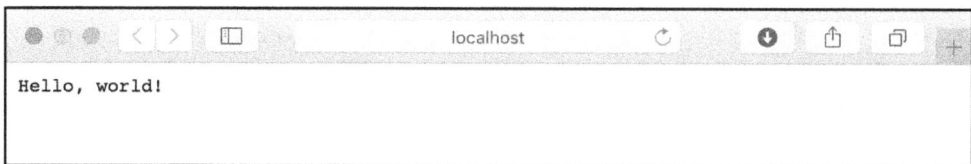

Woo hoo! Let's wrap things up. Back in Terminal, press **Control-C** to terminate your running app, and then run the command **docker images**:

```
REPOSITORY                         TAG       IMAGE ID       CREATED            SIZE
emojijournalserver-swift-run       latest    c995fef7c8b2   About a minute ago  474MB
emojijournalserver-swift-tools     latest    0bad1c4e2fc0   14 minutes ago     1.75GB
ibmcom/swift-ubuntu-runtime        5.0.1     296103103ca5   6 weeks ago        311MB
ibmcom/swift-ubuntu                5.0.1     18eca5b589e0   6 weeks ago        1.68GB
```

As you can see, there are now two additional images displayed. The emojijournalserver-swift-run image is an optimized production image of your project based on the ibmcom/swift-ubuntu-runtime image. Notice that it's almost 1GB smaller than the emojijournalserver-swift-tools image. In Chapter 15, "Kitura Going Live," you'll learn more about the differences between the "tools" and "run" images.

Congratulations! You now have a full development environment allowing you to develop your application on your Mac, and run it on Linux. In the next chapter, you'll start building the logic of EmojiJournalServer itself.

If you ran into any difficulties along the way, feel free to check out the final project for this chapter.

Chapter 3: RESTful APIs

Chris Bailey

Your EmojiJournal project will feature two front-end apps: an iOS app and a web app. Your EmojiJournalServer will provide a set of RESTful APIs that both your front-end apps will use to store, retrieve, update and delete journal entries.

Before you get started building those RESTful APIs, in this chapter, you'll learn about RESTful APIs themselves, including their architectural approach and design principles.

By the end of this chapter, you will:

- Understand RESTful API characteristics.

- Learn how RESTful APIs can be built with HTTP.

- Learn to build best-practice RESTful APIs.

This will provide you with the knowledge you'll need to design and implement best-practice RESTful APIs for your apps.

REpresentational State Transfer (REST)

REpresentational State Transfer (REST) is an architectural style — or design pattern — for APIs. An API is said to be RESTful if it conforms to a set of constraints laid out by Dr. Roy Fielding, PhD, in his 2000 dissertation, *Architectural Styles and the Design of Network-based Software Architectures*.

Fielding set out the following six constraints:

1. Client-server

RESTful APIs provide clear separation between the client and the server, allowing the client and server to be developed independently of each other. This separation makes it possible to implement multiple clients for the same server, as you'll do when you create iOS and web app clients for your EmojiJournal.

2. Stateless

RESTful APIs should be stateless. Each request should be self-contained and should not depend on any session context from previous requests being stored on the server.

3. Cacheable

Since RESTful APIs are stateless and self-contained, it's therefore possible to cache the results of requests to RESTful APIs. This can be done either by a client or by an intermediary such as a web proxy.

A well-designed RESTful API should encourage the storage of cacheable data where possible, with responses to requests implicitly or explicitly labeled as cacheable, cacheable up to a certain time (expires-at) or non-cacheable.

4. Layered system

RESTful APIs may be layered, so that the client is unaware of whether it is connected directly to the API itself or indirectly via a proxy or load balancer. Additionally, the API itself may be composed and built from several layers or sources inside the server system itself.

5. Code on demand (optional)

RESTful APIs may provide functionality that can run directly on the client. In practice, this is typically limited to JavaScript or Java Applets running in the browser.

6. Uniform interface

One of the most important concepts of RESTful APIs is the use of resources. A resource may be any object the API can provide information about, such as the JournalEntry resource you'll work with.

RESTful APIs providing a Uniform Interface must meet these four constraints:

1. Requests must identify the resources they act on.

2. Requests and responses must use a representation of a resource.

3. Messages must be self-descriptive, self-contained and only use standard operations.

4. Resources must connect to other resources through links.

These bedrock concepts of the Uniform Interface are crucial to building solid RESTful APIs. You'll revisit these concepts in much more detail later in this chapter.

Notice also that there has been no mention of HTTP and web requests. While RESTful APIs are most commonly implemented using HTTP, this is not required. That said, we'll only cover how to build RESTful APIs using standard HTTP operations, here, and we'll briefly explore HTTP itself next.

HyperText Transfer Protocol (HTTP)

The HyperText Transfer Protocol (HTTP) is a client-server, request-response based protocol that is the foundation for websites and web-based traffic. Because of this, it's universally supported by clients and servers.

A browser client making a request of a server hosting a website is the most common use case. This consists of the browser making an HTTP request of the server, which returns an HTTP response containing HTML to be rendered in the client browser.

While this is typical of how HTTP is used for common website requests, HTTP itself is far more flexible and capable, as we'll now see.

HTTP-based RESTful APIs

URLs as resources

The first requirement of the Uniform Interface is that requests identify the resources that they act upon. In HTTP, this is achieved via RESTful APIs using the URL of the request.

In your EmojiJournalServer, you're going to provide a RESTful API for interacting with journal entries. To do this, you'll provide a request URL that represents JournalEntry resources.

While it would be possible to use virtually any URL imaginable, to make it obvious which resource the URL represents, you'll provide the following URL to allow the clients to interact with the journal entries:

```
/entries
```

URL-Encoded identifier for specific resources

You'll also want to expose API endpoints to work with specific journal entries. You'll do this via the same /entries URL — along with the help of encoded identifiers.

For example, in order to provide an API to access a specific JournalEntry resource in your EmojiJournalServer, you'll provide an /entries/<identifier> URL where the <identifier> is an identifier for a specific entry.

Putting this together, you'll provide these URLs to enable clients to interact with *all* journal entries and a *specific* journal entry:

```
/entries
/entries/<identifier>
```

URL encoded query parameters for groups of resources

You might also want to provide APIs that work with a subset of a resource. This is again done through the URL, this time using URL query parameters.

URL query parameters begin with the ? identifier. They can pass any additional information about the resource using key-value pairs in a <key>=<value> format. Multiple key-value pairs can be aggregated and passed using the & separator between key-value pairs.

For example, if you wanted to provide an API to work with journal entries having a specific emoji, you'd provide an /entries?emoji=<emoji> URL. Similarly, an API for all journal entries having a specific emoji and a certain date, you'd provide an /entries?emoji=<emoji>&date=<date> URL.

You can also support multiple URLs for a given resource. If you wanted to allow the clients to interact with all entries, a filtered subset of entries based on emoji and date, and a specific entry, you'd provide the following:

```
/entries
/entries?emoji=<emoji>&date=<date>
/entries/<idenfifier>
```

Hierarchical URLs for hierarchical APIs

RESTful URLs can also be hierarchical. In your EmojiJournal app, you're only going to support users having a single EmojiJournal. But let's say that you wanted to support users having multiple journals, with each journal having its own journal entries. A hierarchical API would be just the ticket.

To do this, you'd first create a /journals URL to represent the users journals, along with the /journals/<identifier> URL to represent a specific journal:

```
/journals
/journals/<identifier>
```

Then, you'd provide APIs to interact with the JournalEntry resources in each journal by adding the journal entry APIs onto the /journals URLs:

```
/journals
/journals/<identifier>
/journals/<identifier>/entries
/journals/<identifier>/entries?emoji=<emoji>&date=<date>
/journals/<identifier>/entries/<identifier>
```

Your API would now allow users to interact hierarchically both with all journals, specific journals, and journal entries owned by specific journals. For example, a client request to the following URL would interact with entry 20 in journal 2:

```
/journals/2/entries/20
```

Resource representations

Recall that the second concept of the Uniform Interface was that requests and responses should use a representation of a resource. This is achieved in HTTP-based RESTful APIs by encoding the representation of the resource in HTTP body data.

HTTP messages, whether for a request or a response, essentially consist of two parts: a set of headers and the body data. For completeness, responses additionally contain a status code that reports the status of the request.

HTTP headers and body data

HTTP headers provide additional metadata for requests and responses. Headers are transmitted at the start of the request or response and are stored as key-value pairs, with some headers allowing for multiple values.

You can use HTTP headers to store any additional information you wish. You should be aware of both formally defined standard headers, see https://www.w3.org/Protocols/rfc2616/rfc2616-sec14.html (defined by formal core RFC specifications), as well as less formal but widely-used non-standard headers, see https://en.wikipedia.org/wiki/List_of_HTTP_header_fields#Common_non-standard_request_fields.

Standard headers are used to pass information such as Cookies, Authorization, Content-Type (which describes the media type of the body data) and Content-Length (which describes the length of the body data in bytes).

The HTTP message body contains the data associated with the request or the response. In the case of a response to a request for a web page, the body data contains the source of the web page itself. Take a look at the HTTP response generated by a request to the *Hello, World!* app you created in the previous chapter.

> **Note**: Server-side Swift projects rely on Swift Package Manager to retrieve and assemble frameworks they depend on, as specified in a project's Package.swift file. The EmojiJournalServer code in the starter and final projects for each chapter follow this convention. Prior to Xcode 11's direct integration of Swift Package Manager, it was always necessary to first assemble the resources defined in Package.swift in terminal before opening the project in Xcode.
>
> Throughout this book, we'll take advantage of Xcode 11's SPM integration. Because of this, you'll open projects directly in Xcode, and then allow Xcode itself to assemble these resources for you.

Open the project in Xcode, making sure that your mac is selected as the build target. Build and run the project.

Now return to Terminal and run:

```
curl -i http://localhost:8080/
```

This command sends an HTTP GET request to your server app and prints the headers, body data and response code returned, like so:

```
HTTP/1.1 200 OK
Date: Mon, 05 Nov 2018 16:49:02 GMT
Content-Length: 13
Connection: Keep-Alive
Keep-Alive: timeout=60

Hello, world!
```

Take a closer look at this: The first line shows the version of the HTTP protocol being used — in this case 1.1 — along with an HTTP response code of 200 OK. HTTP response codes range from 100 and 600 and are grouped like this:

Code	Category / Class
1xx	Information
2xx	Success
3xx	Redirect
4xx	Client Error
5xx	Server Error

200 OK is the most common response for a successful HTTP request, but other, more specific, success codes are also commonly used. For example, 201 Created is used when a request results in the creation of a new resource.

Common client errors include 404 Not Found for requests to resources that do not currently exist, 401 Unauthorized where authorization has failed, and 403 Forbidden where the request is authorized but does not have access to that specific resource.

Continuing with the results of your cURL command, the next four lines show the HTTP headers returned. And, last, the final line presents the body data returned.

As you can see, the HTTP headers in the response include Date, Content-Length, Connection and Keep-Alive timeout. Note, however, that it does not (yet) include a Content-Type header, which means that the client who makes the request is unable to determine how to process the body data. Even though this header is missing, clients will almost certainly treat the body as plain text, so, for this simple example, you likely wouldn't encounter problems.

That said, you can improve your Hello, World! app to include a Content-Type header. You'll set the media type to "text/plain," which is the standard value for text responses.

In Xcode, open **Sources/Application/Application.swift**. Add the following at the top of your helloWorldHandler method:

```
response.headers.setType(MediaType.TopLevelType.text.rawValue)
```

This uses the setType convenience method to set the Content-Type header to the text media type, using the rawValue, which is "text/plain."

> **Note**: The header's structure is essentially a dictionary, which means you can also set any header directly by adding a key-value pair. For example, you could also set the Content-Type header like this: response.headers["Content-Type"] = "text/plain" (don't do this now).

Build and run in Xcode to include your code changes.

Now, return to Terminal and run the same curl command once again:

```
curl -i http://localhost:8080/
```

You'll see a response similar to this, confirming that your Content-Type header is now set correctly:

```
HTTP/1.1 200 OK
Content-Length: 13
Date: Mon, 05 Nov 2018 18:16:51 GMT
Content-Type: text/plain
Connection: Keep-Alive
Keep-Alive: timeout=60

Hello, World!
```

> **Note**: The order of the headers is not important. If you see a different order than above, that's OK. But you should see each of the same headers.

Resource representations in body data

As described earlier, RESTful APIs encode the representation of a resource in the HTTP body data returned. Body typically consists of three parts:

1. The Content-Type header

    The Content-Type header denotes the encoding used to represent the resource in body data. The most commonly-used approach is to encode the representation using JavaScript Object Notation (JSON) and set the Content-Type header to application/json. Other examples of body data encoding sometimes used with RESTful APIs include Protobuf, Thrift and Avro.

2. The Accepts header (requests only)

    The Accepts header indicates the encodings the client will accept responses in. This is most commonly application/json, but it can also contain a list of encodings. For example, if a client accepted responses in both JSON and Protobuf, this value might be set to: application/json; application/protobuf.

3. The encoded body data

    Finally, the resource itself is encoded into body data using the encoding as set in the Content-Type header. In the most common application/json scenario, this is a JSON representation of the resource. The details of the JSON depend on the model of the specific resource. For example, a bit later in this book, the resource for your `JournalEntry` will contain `id`, `emoji` and `date`, similar to this:

```
{
  "id":"1",
  "emoji":"☺",
  "date":"2018-09-18T00:07:01Z"
}
```

Self-descriptive messages

You've learned about the identification and representation of resources, but how do you operate on those resources?

The third tenet of the Uniform Interface addresses this. It specifies that both requests and responses should be self-descriptive, and that they only use standard operations understood by both client and server.

In HTML-based RESTful APIs, this is achieved by using specific HTTP methods.

RFC 2616 outlines eight HTTP methods: OPTIONS, GET, HEAD, POST, PUT, DELETE, TRACE and CONNECT.

One additional method, PATCH, was added by RFC 5789. Of those nine methods, RESTful APIs typically make use of these five:

Method	Usage
GET	Access a representation of a resource or resources
POST	Create a new resource from a resource representation
PUT	Replace a resource with a new resource representation
PATCH	Update a resource with a partial resource representation
DELETE	Remove a resource or resources

Each of these operations invokes a complete representation of the resource. Well, almost. The exception here is the PATCH method, which allows an existing resource to be updated with a partial representation of a resource. For this reason, many RESTful implementations avoid use of PATCH, preferring to use PUT instead, so that all methods contain complete resource representations.

Connecting resources through links

The fourth and final concept of the Uniform Interface is that resources should connect to other resources through links.

As you've seen, HTTP-based RESTful APIs use URLs and URL-based identifiers to provide access to resources and to specify individual resources. The links between resources are therefore just further RESTful URLs and URL-based identifiers linked to a connected resource.

There are two common scenarios where a URL or identifier to a resource is needed:

1. A requested resource references another (child or related) resource.

2. You need to know the identifier for a resource.

In the first scenario, the resource representation is expected to contain a RESTful URL link to the referenced resource. A good example of this can be seen using the Star Wars API hosted at https://swapi.co, wherein the people resource with an id of 1 represents Luke Skywalker.

Open this link in your browser to see the JSON resource representation for Luke Skywalker: https://swapi.co/api/people/1/:

```
{
    "name": "Luke Skywalker",
    "height": "172",
    "mass": "77",
    "hair_color": "blond",
    "skin_color": "fair",
    "eye_color": "blue",
    "birth_year": "19BBY",
    "gender": "male",
    "homeworld": "https://swapi.co/api/planets/1/",
    "films": [
        "https://swapi.co/api/films/2/",
        "https://swapi.co/api/films/6/",
        "https://swapi.co/api/films/3/",
        "https://swapi.co/api/films/1/",
        "https://swapi.co/api/films/7/"
    ],
    "species": [
        "https://swapi.co/api/species/1/"
    ],
    "vehicles": [
        "https://swapi.co/api/vehicles/14/",
        "https://swapi.co/api/vehicles/30/"
    ],
    "starships": [
        "https://swapi.co/api/starships/12/",
        "https://swapi.co/api/starships/22/"
    ],
    "created": "2014-12-09T13:50:51.644000Z",
    "edited": "2014-12-20T21:17:56.891000Z",
    "url": "https://swapi.co/api/people/1/"
}
```

As you can see, several resources related to Luke Skywalker are provided as absolute links. For another example, open https://swapi.co/api/planets/1/:

```
{
    "name": "Tatooine",
    "rotation_period": "23",
    "orbital_period": "304",
    "diameter": "10465",
    "climate": "arid",
    "gravity": "1 standard",
    "terrain": "desert",
    "surface_water": "1",
    "population": "200000",
    "residents": [
        "https://swapi.co/api/people/1/",
        "https://swapi.co/api/people/2/",
        "https://swapi.co/api/people/4/",
        "https://swapi.co/api/people/6/",
        "https://swapi.co/api/people/7/",
        "https://swapi.co/api/people/8/",
        "https://swapi.co/api/people/9/",
        "https://swapi.co/api/people/11/",
        "https://swapi.co/api/people/43/",
        "https://swapi.co/api/people/62/"
    ],
    "films": [
        "https://swapi.co/api/films/5/",
        "https://swapi.co/api/films/4/",
        "https://swapi.co/api/films/6/",
        "https://swapi.co/api/films/3/",
        "https://swapi.co/api/films/1/"
    ],
    "created": "2014-12-09T13:50:49.641000Z",
    "edited": "2014-12-21T20:48:04.175778Z",
    "url": "https://swapi.co/api/planets/1/"
}
```

Here, you can see that Luke's home world was Tatooine with a population of 200,000.

The second scenario where you need to access a resource's URL or identifier is when you need to know the identifier for a given resource. An example of this is where you have just created a new resource using a POST request.

There are two commonly used mechanisms for providing the URL or identifier for a newly created resource. Both are returned in response to a successful POST (Create) Request:

1. The HTTP Location header returns either the identifier or the URL. Either can then be used to access the newly created resource on the server.

2. Since RESTful POST requests should return a representation of the resource just created, the newly created resource's identifier or URL is simply embedded within this representation.

This second approach is the model used by the Star Wars API, wherein every resource representation contains a url field that is a reference to its own absolute URL.

Building RESTful APIs

OK! That's a lot of theory, but the good news is that we've now covered everything you need to build and work with RESTful APIs in this book.

As you've seen, you build RESTful API's by using a combination of HTTP methods, headers, body data and response codes. In practice, there are effectively seven different types of APIs you can provide for any resource.

Here are all the RESTful APIs you could implement as part of your EmojiJournalServer:

Action	Method	Path	Query Allowed	Request Body	Response Body	Success Status
Create a resource	POST	/entries	Yes	Yes	Yes	201 Created
Get resources	GET	/entries	Yes	No	Yes	200 OK
Get a resource	GET	/entries/{id}	No	No	Yes	200 OK
Replace a resource	PUT	/entries/{id}	No	Yes	Yes	200 OK
Update a resource	PATCH	/entries/{id}	No	Yes	Yes	200 OK
Delete resources	DELETE	/entries/	Yes	No	No	204 No Content
Delete a resource	DELETE	/entries/{id}	No	No	No	204 No Content

By now, you've learned all the basics. As you learn more about designing and implementing RESTful APIs, you'll find that there are additional best practices beyond the scope of what we've covered here. This include setting the correct Content-Type and Accepts headers, setting the Location header for successful creates and setting the correct HTTP status code for any failures in the request.

Additionally, the request and response bodies need to be encoded and decoded, most commonly to and from JSON. This used to be a laborious task. Swift makes working with JSON elegant and painless, thanks to the powerful Codable protocol.

In the next chapter, you'll learn how Codable works, and see how to use it in your Kitura app to effortlessly convert your data structures and classes to JSON and back again.

Chapter 4: Introduction to Codable

David Okun

The Codable protocol is one of the most powerful features of the Swift programming language. In a sentence: When you extend an object to conform to Codable, you enable that object to automatically serialize in to and out of any externally readable format — such as JSON, XML or protocol buffers.

As you work on almost any app that utilizes the Swift programming language, you'll need to parse data from a web service. And most often, that data will be structured as JSON — JavaScript Object Notation. As you work on EmojiJournal, it will be helpful to understand some of the underlying basics of how data that's transferred RESTfully between your client and your server is converted back and forth between JSON and a Swift-native context.

Throughout this chapter, you'll work with JSON exclusively. But remember that you can also use the Codable protocol to work with any external representation you may encounter.

Kitura contains several excellent features that greatly minimize the effort you'll need to work with raw data over the wire. In day-to-day use, you'll typically be able to work almost exclusively in a native object context when working with Kitura. In this chapter, however, you'll dive beneath the surface to explore the inner workings of Codable. By reading this chapter and working through the accompanying Xcode Playground, you will:

- Understand how objects convert to and from JSON using the Codable protocol.

- Use a custom date encoding/decoding strategy and dive into the world of ISO8601.

- Apply an example of custom coding keys to override Codable's standard behavior.

Although the majority of this book will focus on the creation of the EmojiJournal app, this chapter will use a free-standing Xcode playground that illustrates the capabilities of the Codable protocol. The playground requires no external dependencies and should run out of the box.

This chapter will not comprehensively cover all aspects of the Codable protocol, but it will give you enough information to be able to complete this book and EmojiJournal along with it.

The bare necessities

Open up **intro-to-codable.playground** from this chapter's starter directory. At the top of the file, you'll see a declaration for a simple struct containing three simple required properties:

```
// 1
public struct Animal: Codable {
  var name: String
  var age: Int
  var friendly: Bool
}
```

Take a peek under the hood: Hold down the **Command** and **Control** keys on your keyboard, and **click** on Codable (or you can hold down just the Command key, click on Codable and select "Jump to Definition"). You will be presented with a file in the Swift Standard Library describing what Codable actually is:

```
public typealias Codable = Decodable & Encodable
```

Although Codable itself is the protocol you'll be most concerned with, it's important to know that it's merely a typealias that composites two protocols related to object serialization:

- **Encodable**, which enables an object to be **encoded** into JSON.

- **Decodable**, which enables an object to be **decoded** from raw data sent as JSON.

This also means that, depending on your needs, you'll have the ability to conform any object that you create to only one of these underlying protocols for the sake of access control and safety! That said, you'll use Codable throughout this book to make it easy to encode and decode all objects you'll work with.

OK, now that you've taken a quick peek at Codable itself, navigate back to your playground once again. Immediately, beneath the struct declaration you just reviewed, notice the instantiation of one instance of this type:

```
// 2
let baloo = Animal(name: "Baloo", age: 5, friendly: true)
```

As you work through this chapter, you'll update this line as you add further properties to this type declaration. For now, though, this is just fine as is.

Next, look below the instantiation:

```
// 3
let encoder = JSONEncoder()
let decoder = JSONDecoder()
```

This might initially seem strange, since, as you just saw, your struct already conforms to the Codable protocol. But with Codable, you also need a dedicated object to handle the specific action of *encoding* an object into data or *decoding* some data into a native object. That's where your encoder and decoder will come in.

Now, take a look at the encoder object at work:

```
// 4
let encodedBaloo = try encoder.encode(baloo)
if let balooString = String(data: encodedBaloo, encoding: .utf8)
{
  print(balooString)
}
```

The first line takes your instantiated baloo object and converts it into encodedBaloo, which is of the type Data. The next bit just prints out the contents in a human-readable format. Notice that the output is structured as pure JSON:

```
{"name":"Baloo","age":5,"friendly":true}
```

Nice! Next, it's the decoder object's turn to convert your encodedBaloo back into a native object:

```
// 5
let decodedBaloo = try decoder.decode(Animal.self,
    from: encodedBaloo)
print(decodedBaloo)
```

Because your type conforms to Codable (more specifically Decodable, in this case) it only takes one line of code to convert raw JSON data to a native object!

It's hard to overstate what an immense improvement this approach is from previous versions of Swift. To get a flavor of this, here's what used to be required to take your baloo on this same journey without Codable using the JSONSerialization class. At the time of this writing, this is still valid code that compiles:

```
let balooJson: [String: Any] =
```

```
    ["name": baloo.name, "age": baloo.age,
     "friendly": baloo.friendly]
let balooJsonData =
  try JSONSerialization.data(withJSONObject: balooJson,
    options: .prettyPrinted)
if let oldBalooString = String(data: balooJsonData,
  encoding: .utf8) {
    print(oldBalooString)
}

let balooJsonObject =
  try JSONSerialization.jsonObject(with: balooJsonData,
    options: .allowFragments) as! [String: Any]
if let name = balooJsonObject["name"] as? String,
  let age = balooJsonObject["age"] as? Int,
  let friendly = balooJsonObject["friendly"] as? Bool {
    let oldDecodedBaloo =
      Animal(name: name, age: age, friendly: friendly)
    print(oldDecodedBaloo)
}
```

Ouch! That's pretty awful to read and write, even with such a simple example. In practice, this older manual approach to encoding and decoding would get exponentially more painful to implement and maintain in real-world apps. In short: Adopting the Codable protocol is a major key to happiness!

Expanding your type declaration

So far, your type declaration only contains required properties. As it turns out, one especially nice feature of Codable is how easily it handles optional properties.

Update your type description by making the age property optional, like so:

```
public struct Animal: Codable {
  var name: String
  var age: Int?
  var friendly: Bool
}
```

In all honesty, *The Jungle Book* is so old that it's impossible to really know how old all the characters are! Now, take a look at the output of your playground: You'll see that this has slightly changed as well:

```
Animal(name: "Baloo", age: Optional(5), friendly: true)
```

Next, directly beneath your declaration of baloo, create another instance of your type, setting its age to nil:

```
let bagheera = Animal(name: "Bagheera",
  age: nil, friendly: true)
```

Scroll down to your try/catch block, and perform the same operation with bagheera as you do with baloo:

```
let encodedBagheera = try encoder.encode(bagheera)
if let bagheeraString =
  String(data: encodedBagheera, encoding: .utf8) {
    print(bagheeraString)
}
```

After your playground compiles and runs, you'll see the output:

```
{"name":"Bagheera","friendly":true}
```

Sweet! Even after updating the nullability of one property, everything still "just works."

Next, just like you did with baloo, convert bagheera back into a native object:

```
let decodedBagheera = try decoder.decode(Animal.self,
  from: encodedBagheera)
print(decodedBagheera)
```

Just like before, notice the printed output:

```
Animal(name: "Bagheera", age: nil, friendly: true)
```

Although this corner case is simple in nature, it's nice to know that our encoder and decoder stood up to the task!

Now we'll consider another corner case. What if the JSON you send across the wire needs to conform to a different schema than it does internally within your app? For example, assume that you need to update your JSON to read like the following:

```
{"name":"Baloo","age":5,"is_friendly":true}
```

Until now, the names of your properties have directly matched the JSON payload the object encodes into. Don't change your playground just yet, but note that one way to accomplish this would be to update the friendly property, like so:

```
var is_friendly: Bool
```

While you *could* do this, snake_case variable names (is_friendly) are generally frowned upon in Swift in favor of camelCase (isFriendly). Because sending JSON payloads with snake_case is a common need, Codable offers a nice way of automagically converting between the two formats!

Update your object declaration to look like this:

```
public struct Animal: Codable {
  var name: String
  var age: Int?
  var isFriendly: Bool
}
```

Your playground will stop compiling. To resolve this, change the constructors for both baloo and bagheera to match the new name for friendly, like so:

```
let baloo = Animal(name: "Baloo", age: 5, isFriendly: true)
let bagheera = Animal(name: "Bagheera",
  age: nil, isFriendly: true)
```

Everything should once again run after you've done this. Take a look at your output below:

```
{"name":"Baloo","age":5,"isFriendly":true}
{"name":"Bagheera","isFriendly":true}
```

That's good, but it doesn't accomplish your goal yet. Scroll up to the declaration of encoder and add the following directly beneath it:

```
encoder.keyEncodingStrategy = .convertToSnakeCase
```

JSONEncoder objects contain multiple "encoding strategy" properties that you can override. We'll cover the others shortly, but note that this immediately changes your output, like so:

```
{"name":"Baloo","age":5,"is_friendly":true}
{"name":"Bagheera","is_friendly":true}
Error occurred: The data couldn't be read because it is missing.
```

You're close! Your data encodes into snake_case JSON correctly, but the reverse operation of bringing this JSON payload back into a native context is now failing. This should make sense, because you haven't told your decoder to look for snake_case!

Scroll back up to the line where you declared your JSONDecoder and add this directly underneath it:

```
decoder.keyDecodingStrategy = .convertFromSnakeCase
```

Poof! All your errors should now vanish. Codable now handles the round trip transition from snake_case to camelCase and then back again effortlessly on your behalf! Being the curious sort, you may be wondering, "What else can my encoders and decoders do?" I'm glad you asked!

Date formatting and the ISO8601 standard

I've never met a developer who was particularly *thrilled* to undertake a date-formatting task, whether it has to do with the UI of an app or parsing underlying JSON. That said, using dateDecodingStrategy on a JSONDecoder is probably the most fun you'll ever have handling dates! At the top of your playground, add a fourth property to your struct directly underneath your isFriendly property:

```
var birthday: Date
```

Next, scroll down to where you created baloo and bagheera and update their constructors to include a birthday:

```
let baloo = Animal(name: "Baloo", age: 5,
   isFriendly: true, birthday: Date())
let bagheera = Animal(name: "Bagheera", age: nil,
   isFriendly: true, birthday: Date())
```

Everything in your playground should be running again. Take a look at the first two lines of output, which show the encoded values of your new "birthday" property:

```
{"age":5,"name":"Baloo","is_friendly":true,
   "birthday":561991096.16503203}
{"name":"Bagheera","is_friendly":true,
   "birthday":561991096.170838}
```

These values may not look like dates at first glance, but they're actually numbers in reference to an **epoch**.

The standard definition of an epoch is **an instant in time chosen as the origin of a particular era**, so this number in your encoded JSON represents the amount of time that has elapsed since some reference point in time.

This is where things get interesting: In Swift, the epoch of choice is January 1, 2001 AD. But Unix in general chooses a different point in time — January 1, 1970 AD — as its epoch.

It's unclear why these epochs are different. The documentation of the Swift `Date` class implicitly acknowledges the awkwardness of having mismatched epochs through the existence of computed properties like these:

```
/// The number of seconds from 1 January 1970
/// to the reference date, 1 January 2001.
public static let timeIntervalBetween1970AndReferenceDate:
  TimeInterval

/// The interval between 00:00:00 UTC on 1 January 2001
/// and the current date and time.
public static var timeIntervalSinceReferenceDate:
  TimeInterval { get }
```

Whatever moment in time you're experiencing, your goals are first, to make the birthday property more readable in the encoded JSON, and, second, to maintain the Swift representation of the date without doing anything funky. This is where ISO8601 comes in.

ISO8601 is an international standard for reading dates and times, and is purposely meant to **provide an unambiguous and well-defined method of representing them**. Take a look at this example of a date in ISO8601 format:

```
2019-01-19T18:24:17.345Z
```

From left to right, the components of the date read like so:

- Year (*2019*)

- Month (*01*)

- Day (*19*)

- The letter **T** (*used as a delimiter*)

- Hour (*18, using 24 hour formatting*)

- Minute (*24*)

- Second (*17*)

- Milliseconds (*.345*)

- The letter **Z** (*used to specify the UTC time zone*)

In addition to these required components, there are some others that can be modified and added as well:

- A time zone other than UTC can be specified by appending +0100 to the time instead of Z. For example, 18:00:00Z and 20:00:00+0200 are the exact same times.

- Different systems have different levels of granularity for the amount of digits after the seconds component. Most commonly, you will see 0, 3 or 7 decimal places to gauge the second — all three are acceptable within the standard.

Given that ISO8601 is such a universal standard, it's reasonable to format the date in our serialization that way. Thankfully, JSONEncoder can do this for us in just one line of code.

Scroll up to your declaration of your encoder object, and beneath your current keyEncodingStrategy line, add the following:

```
encoder.dateEncodingStrategy = .iso8601
```

Notice your new output:

```
{"age":5,"name":"Baloo","is_friendly":true,
  "birthday":"2018-10-23T13:21:10Z"}
{"name":"Bagheera","is_friendly":true,
  "birthday":"2018-10-23T13:21:10Z"}
Error occurred: The data couldn't be read because it isn't in
the correct format.
```

You'll clean up that error in a moment. But notice that, already, without touching a single DateFormatter object, you now have a human-readable and fully ISO8601-compliant representation of your encoded dates. Woohoo!

OK, now to resolve the decoder error. Underneath the line where you declared your keyDecodingStrategy, type the following:

```
decoder.dateDecodingStrategy = .iso8601
```

Take a look again at the output. Your error should be resolved, and the last two lines of your output should now be:

```
Animal(name: "Baloo", age: Optional(5), isFriendly: true,
    birthday: 2018-10-23 13:23:37 +0000)
Animal(name: "Bagheera", age: nil, isFriendly: true,
    birthday: 2018-10-23 13:23:37 +0000)
```

Well done! Now you know how to leverage Codable's ability to format dates for you.

You can do even more with dates in Codable: In addition to built-in strategies that come packaged with `JSONEncoder` and `JSONDecoder`, you can specify any kind of date format you might need via a `DateFormatter`.

For example, if you wanted to encode your dates to a long friendly format, you could simply add the following (feel free to try this if you'd like):

```
let formatter = DateFormatter()
formatter.dateStyle = .long
encoder.dateEncodingStrategy = .formatted(formatter)
```

This would give you these results:

```
{"age":5,"name":"Baloo","is_friendly":true,
    "birthday":"October 23, 2018"}
{"name":"Bagheera","is_friendly":true,
    "birthday":"October 23, 2018"}
```

Since you won't use a custom date decoding strategy in this chapter, delete these lines if you just tried them out. And don't worry — you'll make use of a similar strategy later in the development of EmojiJournal.

Nested objects and custom coding keys

Now it's time to see how we handle nested data. You'll start by adding an array of songs each character can sing. Scroll to the top of the playground. Directly beneath your declaration of the `birthday` property, add a property to display some song titles:

```
var songs: [String]
```

Once again, your playground will stop compiling when you make this change, since your instantiated objects no longer comply to your struct.

To fix this, scroll down to the instantiations of `baloo` and `bagheera` and update them to include a song in an array:

```
let baloo = Animal(name: "Baloo",
                   age: 5,
                   isFriendly: true,
                   birthday: Date(),
                   songs: ["The Bare Necessities"])
let bagheera = Animal(name: "Bagheera",
                      age: nil,
                      isFriendly: true,
                      birthday: Date(),
                      songs: ["Jungle's No Place For A Boy"])
```

Notice that Codable handles all of this perfectly right out of the box, and your output at the bottom of the playground reflects this change:

```
{"age":5,"songs":["The Bare Necessities"],"name":"Baloo",
 "is_friendly":true,"birthday":"2018-10-23T13:55:10Z"}
{"songs":["Jungle's No Place For A Boy"],"name":"Bagheera",
 "is_friendly":true,"birthday":"2018-10-23T13:55:10Z"}
Animal(name: "Baloo", age: Optional(5), isFriendly: true,
   birthday: 2018-10-23 13:55:10 +0000,
   songs: ["The Bare Necessities"])
Animal(name: "Bagheera", age: nil, isFriendly: true,
   birthday: 2018-10-23 13:55:10 +0000,
   songs: ["Jungle\'s No Place For A Boy"])
```

Nice! It's great that Codable handles arrays so well right out of the box. Still, let's not get too excited just yet. A simple array works great if all we need to know about Baloo's and Bagheera's songs are their titles. But what if you need to convey more specific information about these songs than simply their title in the JSON you send?

Scroll to the very top of your playground, and underneath the line where you `import` `Foundation`, add a new type to capture this information:

```
public struct Song: Codable {
   var title: String
   var length: Double
}
```

Now that you have a new way to represent a song, update your original `Animal` type to use this new `Song` type for your `songs` property:

```
var songs: [Song]
```

Unsurprisingly, this temporarily breaks your playground. Update `baloo` and `bagheera` to make use of your new `Song` type:

```
let baloo = Animal(name: "Baloo",
                   age: 5,
                   isFriendly: true,
                   birthday: Date(),
                   songs: [Song(title: "The Bare Necessities",
                                length: 180)])
let bagheera = Animal(name: "Bagheera",
                      age: nil,
                      isFriendly: true,
                      birthday: Date(),
                      songs: [Song(title: "Jungle's No Place For
A Boy",
                                   length: 95)])
```

Your playground should once again compile and run, and you should see:

```
{"age":5,"songs":[{"title":"The Bare Necessities",
  "length":180}],"name":"Baloo","is_friendly":true,
  "birthday":"2018-10-23T14:02:51Z"}
{"songs":[{"title":"Jungle's No Place For A Boy",
  "length":95}],"name":"Bagheera","is_friendly":true,
  "birthday":"2018-10-23T14:02:51Z"}
Animal(name: "Baloo", age: Optional(5), isFriendly: true,
  birthday: 2018-10-23 14:02:51 +0000,
  songs: [__lldb_expr_4.Song(title: "The Bare Necessities",
  length: 180.0)])
Animal(name: "Bagheera", age: nil, isFriendly: true,
  birthday: 2018-10-23 14:02:51 +0000, songs:
  [__lldb_expr_4.Song(title: "Jungle\'s No Place For A Boy",
  length: 95.0)])
```

Great! Now consider your last corner case of this chapter: Earlier, you were able to change the text style of your `isFriendly` property to be snake_case when encoded into JSON, but what if you have to make a change that doesn't just involve a style of string?

Imagine that due to external requirements outside your control, your JSON payload now needs to look like this:

```
{
  "age": 5,
  "songs": [
    {
      "song_title": "The Bare Necessities",
      "song_length": 180
    }
  ],
```

```
  "name": "Baloo",
  "is_friendly": true,
  "birthday": "2018-10-23T14:02:51Z"
}
```

Ouch! That doesn't match your internal structs at all! Whether or not this seems practical, this kind of external change happens all the time in the real world, and it's important you be able to handle this type of shift elegantly and, wait for it... Swiftly!

The great news here is that Codable enables you to specify a set of `CodingKeys` for any object. This gives you the ability to map a property to any node you'd like in your external object representation.

Scroll back up to the Song type, and add the following code immediately below the length property declaration, making sure this is *within* your Song struct's declaration:

```
enum CodingKeys: String, CodingKey {
  case title = "song_title"
  case length = "song_length"
}
```

After adding this, your playground should re-run, and take a look at your output:

```
{"age":5,"songs":[{"song_title":"The Bare Necessities",
  "song_length":180}],"name":"Baloo","is_friendly":true,
  "birthday":"2018-10-23T14:14:34Z"}
{"songs":[{"song_title":"Jungle's No Place For A Boy",
  "song_length":95}],"name":"Bagheera","is_friendly":true,
  "birthday":"2018-10-23T14:14:34Z"}
Error occurred: The data couldn't be read because it is missing.
```

Those first two lines look great! But once again, as the pattern in this chapter goes, you have to make sure you match these keys back into your native object. This time, though, you might notice that you've put yourself into a bit of a Catch 22.

Notice that, for your song objects to be properly serialized, you are specifying the CodingKeys enum specifically in snake case. Scroll back to where you set up your decoder.

Remember that you previously defined a keyDecodingStrategy to accept anything that comes as snake_case and convert it to camelCase earlier in this chapter?

It turns out that Codable applies decoding strategies first. Following your specified decoding strategy, `song_title` is converted to `songTitle` in this step. After this, Codable checks if any custom coding key behaviors are set, and in your case, it looks for the `title` property with the key `song_title`.

Here's our Catch 22: Your `decoder` has already changed this value to the camelCase `songTitle`. And this means that your custom coding key cannot find the `song_title` key it's looking for, and an error is thrown!

There are many ways to solve this problem. Given the strategy you are following here, update your `CodingKeys` strings to follow camelCase instead of snake_case:

```
case title = "songTitle"
case length = "songLength"
```

Your playground should automatically pick up the changes, and everything should compile just fine!

To quickly review, the whole round trip process now looks like this:

When your object is *decoded* from JSON, the decoder's keyDecodingStrategy will first convert snake case property names into camel case (so song_title becomes songTitle). Then, the camel case CodingKeys you enter are used to convert these values into your native property names (e.g., songTitle then becomes simply title).

When your object is *encoded* into JSON, the encoder will first look to the CodingKeys, turning your title property into songTitle in your JSON. Then, your encoder's keyEncodingStrategy will kick in, converting all camel case key names into snake case, and giving you the desired keys in your JSON!

As you can see, the two processes are mirror images of each other.

Where to go from here?

By now, you should feel reasonably comfortable working with objects that conform to Codable for the rest of this book. Codable is an extremely powerful protocol, and there is so much more to be done with it, but this playground should give you enough to go on to finish EmojiJournal!

In the next chapter, you'll first learn a bit more about how routing works in Kitura, and then you'll dive right into making use of what you learned in this chapter by taking Codable Routing for a drive!

Chapter 5: Codable Routing

Chris Bailey

Codable Routing is a feature — introduced as part of Kitura 2.0 — that incorporates the full power of Codable directly into Kitura's `Router` object.

Codable Routing enables automatic conversion between your app's structs and classes and body data used in HTTP requests and responses in a fully type-safe way. It vastly reduces the code you'll need to write as you build route handlers and it enables Kitura to perform data validation and error handling on your behalf.

In this chapter, you'll learn about:

- Raw Routing and Codable Routing.

- How to build a Raw route.

- The power of Codable Routing.

- How to build POST, GET and DELETE APIs with Codable Routing.

As you're learning these things, you'll create a `JournalEntry` data structure and build RESTful APIs enabling your iOS and web clients to save and retrieve journal entries.

By the end of this chapter, you'll be well on your way to building out your EmojiJournalServer's API.

Raw Routing and Codable Routing

Routing refers to how a web app handles a request. In Kitura, you typically register handlers (functions or closures you write) to be called for specified HTTP methods and paths (URI's) when they match a given route request from the client. Route definition takes this form:

```
router.METHOD(PATH, handler: HANDLER)
```

Here, `router` is an instance of the Kitura Router, `METHOD` is an HTTP request method in lowercase, `PATH` is a string representing the URL path on the server and `HANDLER` is the function or closure to execute.

Kitura 1.x supported Raw Routing only. Route handlers were called via `RouterRequest` and `RouterResponse` objects representing the incoming HTTP request from the client and the HTTP response being built by the handler, respectively.

While this approach provided flexibility and control, its downside was that it required you both to understand the inner structure of requests and to interpret HTTP request headers correctly and verify data yourself. In short, it was technically powerful but cumbersome — especially for typical routes.

With Codable Routing, router handlers are able to act much like methods you might define elsewhere in your code. They take struct or class types as parameters and respond with struct or class types via a completion handler, with just an additional requirement that those types implement `Codable`.

Codable Routing isn't suitable for every use case and scenario, so Raw Routing is still available where you need the full power and flexibility of accessing the raw HTTP request and response directly. But in the vast majority of typical cases — including for your EmojiJournalServer app — Codable Routing is the best tool for building RESTful APIs.

In order to understand better how these two approaches compare, you'll first build a RESTful API to store a representation of a journal entry using Raw Routing. Then you'll change this API to using Codable Routing, giving you a clear view of the differences between and benefits of each approach.

Building a RESTful API to store a journal entry

Before you can build a RESTful API to store a journal entry, you'll first need to create a Codable data structure for your journal entry data.

Your JournalEntry is going to store two items of data: a Date field for your journal entry date, and an Emoji field to contain its emoji. You'll also need an Identifier field storing a unique identifier for each entry.

Creating a JournalEntry struct

Whether you're starting where you left off previously or you're beginning with this chapter's starter project, start by opening your EmojiJournalServer project in Xcode.

To get started, add a new group within `Sources/Application` and name it **Models**. Then create a new Swift file within your new Models group and name it **JournalEntry.swift,** making sure its target is **Application**. You'll use this new file to define your `JournalEntry`.

Replace the initial contents of this file with this:

```
import Foundation

struct JournalEntry: Codable {
}
```

Here, you add `Foundation` so you can make use of `Codable`, and then your `JournalEntry` struct immediately puts this to good use by conforming to the protocol.

Next, add the following to your `JournalEntry` struct:

```
var id: String?
var emoji: String
var date: Date
```

With this code, you add three properties to your `JournalEntry` data structure:

- A `date` field represented as a `Date`.

- An `emoji` field that's stored as a `String`.

- An `id` field stored as an **Optional** `String`.

By the way, the reason id is declared as an Optional is that, when a client requests to store (POST) a new journal entry, that request won't contain an id. Your server will assign the identifier once the new entry been stored. Making id optional allows for this needed flexibility.

Congratulations! You now have a JournalEntry data structure to store your journal entries, which, because of the use of Codable, will be easily convertible into a JSON representation for use in your RESTful APIs.

Next, you'll build your first RESTful API to use this.

Creating a POST API with Raw Routing

The first API you'll create will enable clients to create a new JournalEntry resource. In Chapter 3, you learned that this means implementing the following:

Action	Method	Path	Query Allowed	Request Body	Response Body	Success Status
Create a resource	POST	/entries	Yes	Yes	Yes	201 Created

Select the Routes group (within Sources/Application) then create a new Swift file named **EntryRoutes.swift**. You'll use this for all of the routes you'll build to implement RESTful APIs for your JournalEntry resource.

Replace the file's default contents with:

```
import Foundation
import LoggerAPI
import Kitura
```

Foundation will be used to encode and decode your JournalEntry struct, LoggerAPI to add logging to your code, and Kitura to add some of the Kitura types.

Next, add a function called initializeEntryRoutes(), like so:

```
func initializeEntryRoutes(app: App) {
  Log.info("Journal entry routes created")
}
```

This will be used to register your route handlers on /entries and provide a log message when the routes have been created.

Finally, open **Application.swift** and add the following to postInit() just before its call to router.get():

```
initializeEntryRoutes(app: self)
```

Great! Now, it's time to start on your first journal entry route handler, which will store your `JournalEntry` structures.

Open `EntryRoutes.swift` once again.

Insert this line at the top of your `initializeEntryRoutes()` function:

```
app.router.post("/entries", handler: addEntry)
```

By doing this, you've registered a handler function called `addEntry` for POST requests on the "/entries" URL. (You'll get a temporary error, since you haven't yet added the `addEntry` method.) Requests using the HTTP **POST** method to the / **entries** URL will result in the **addEntry** function being called.

Now, it's time to create your `addEntry` handler function itself. As promised, you'll initially do this using Raw Routing.

Your function will take three parameters: a `RouterRequest` called `request`, a `RouterResponse` called `response` and a next function. The `RouterRequest` and `RouterResponse` structures represent the HTTP request received and the HTTP response being created, respectively.

The `next()` function is called when your handler completes. Raw Routing allows multiple handlers to be registered for the same route. When `next()` is called, it causes any other handler that is also registered for the same HTTP method and URL to be run.

Add a new `addEntry` function after `initializeEntryRoutes`, like this:

```
func addEntry(request: RouterRequest, response: RouterResponse,
    next: @escaping () -> Void) {
    response.send("Hello, World!")
    next()
}
```

For simplicity, you'll simply return the familiar "Hello, World!" message at first.

OK. Build and run. Now, it's time to test that your route is working.

Open Terminal and make a POST request by executing:

```
curl -i -X POST http://localhost:8080/entries
```

These options are similar to the ones you used previously in Chapter 3, with the addition of –X POST. As you might suspect, the **-X** option lets you specify which request method to use rather than using the default GET method, in this case a POST request.

You should receive the following result:

```
HTTP/1.1 200 OK
Date: Mon, 12 Nov 2018 13:23:00 GMT
Content-Length: 13
Connection: Keep-Alive
Keep-Alive: timeout=60

Hello, World!
```

Huzzah! You now have a working POST handler for your /entries route! This gives you a solid starting point for building out your RESTful API for storing your JournalEntry structures.

Your next step to building out a fully RESTful API is to accept and validate the incoming data associated with the POST request. You'll start by validating that the incoming request has an HTTP Content-Type header set to application/json, showing that it is sending JSON encoded data.

Return to Xcode, and add the following at the start of your addEntry function:

```
guard let contentType = request.headers["Content-Type"],
  contentType.hasPrefix("application/json") else {
    response.status(.unsupportedMediaType)
    response.send(["error":
      "Request Content-Type must be application/json"])
    return next()
}
```

Notice that this checks that the Content-Type header *starts with* "application/json". This is because the header value may contain a semi-colon at the end, and may also specify a character set, for example the Content-Type header could be set to:

```
application/json; charset=utf-8
```

Notice also that if the Content-Type header is not set to application/json, an HTTP status code of "415: Unsupported Media Type" is set on the response. This is because the Content-Type is set to a media type that your POST handler doesn't know how to handle.

Build and run your EmojiJournalServer project once again.

In Terminal, run the same **curl** command that you used previously:

```
curl -i -X POST http://localhost:8080/entries
```

You should now see a response similar to this:

```
HTTP/1.1 415 Unsupported Media Type
Content-Length: 58
Content-Type: application/json
Date: Mon, 12 Nov 2018 13:52:06 GMT
Connection: Keep-Alive
Keep-Alive: timeout=60

{"error":"Request Content-Type must be application\/json"}
```

As you can see, your route (correctly!) returned a status code of "415 Unsupported Media Type". It did this because the incoming request didn't have a Content-Type header set to application/json. You'll fix this now, using the curl utility's -**H** option to add a header to your request:

Still in Terminal, execute this request:

```
curl -i -X POST http://localhost:8080/entries -H 'Content-Type:
application/json'
```

You should now see successful response similar to this:

```
HTTP/1.1 200 OK
Content-Length: 13
Date: Mon, 12 Nov 2018 13:57:51 GMT
Connection: Keep-Alive
Keep-Alive: timeout=60

Hello, World!
```

Sweet! It's time to take things up a notch. Next, you'll need to:

- Read the HTTP body data associated with the request.

- Validate that it's a representation of a JournalEntry struct.

- Create an instance of a JournalEntry from this.

Most of this can be accomplished simply by leveraging Codable features (remembering that the JournalEntry structure you created earlier conforms to Codable). Kitura also provides a Raw Routing API that reads a request's body data directly as a Codable type and propagates any errors thrown by the decoder if this fails.

Back in Xcode, add the following to your addEntry() function right before your existing call to response.send("Hello, World!"):

```
var entry: JournalEntry
do {
  try entry = request.read(as: JournalEntry.self)
} catch {
  response.status(.unprocessableEntity)
  if let decodingError = error as? DecodingError {
    response.send("Could not decode received data: " +
      "\(decodingError.humanReadableDescription)")
  } else {
    response.send("Could not decode received data.")
  }
  return next()
}
```

With this code, you first attempt to treat the request as an instance of JournalEntry. If there is an error, you set an HTTP status code of "422 Unprocessable Entity" (signifying that the information encoded in the body data failed to meet your API's requirements) so that you return a meaningful error message.

Build and run your EmojiJournalServer project, then return to Terminal and run the **curl** command you used previously:

```
curl -i -X POST http://localhost:8080/entries -H 'Content-Type:
application/json'
```

This now returns an error response:

```
HTTP/1.1 422 Unprocessable Entity
Date: Mon, 12 Nov 2018 14:15:36 GMT
Content-Length: 75
Connection: Keep-Alive
Keep-Alive: timeout=60

Could not decode received data: The JSON appears to be
malformed. No value.
```

Here, the response's status code is correctly set to "422 Unprocessable Entity" and the error message is set to "Could not decode received data: The JSON appears to be malformed. No value." Unsurprisingly, "No value." tells you that no (JSON) data was sent with the request.

The curl command provides the **-d** option to enable sending data along with a request.

Execute this updated curl command, which sends JSON via the -d option that's intentionally **invalid** (it contains *only* an emoji):

```
curl -i -X POST http://localhost:8080/entries -H 'Content-Type:
application/json' -d '{"emoji":"😄"}'
```

This yields this error response:

```
HTTP/1.1 422 Unprocessable Entity
Date: Mon, 12 Nov 2018 14:20:42 GMT
Content-Length: 66
Connection: Keep-Alive
Keep-Alive: timeout=60

Could not decode received data: The required key 'date' not
found.
```

This time, notice that the error message reads "Could not decode received data: The required key 'date' not found." Exactly as you'd hope, this message informs you clearly that the data you provided was unprocessable because the required Date field was not present.

Now, run this curl command containing a complete JSON representation of a `JournalEntry`:

```
curl -i -X POST http://localhost:8080/entries -H 'Content-Type:
application/json' -d '{"emoji":"😄", "date":
563725805.57661498}'
```

Nice! Your route returns a **200 OK** response.

Your final task is to return the created `JournalEntry` along with the correct Content-Type header as part of the response. Once again, Kitura provides a Raw Routing API so you can send a response's body data as JSON directly from a `Codable` type. It also sets the correct Content-Type header for you.

Return to Xcode. At the end of `addEntry`, just before the final `next()` call, replace the current `response.send("Hello, World!")` with this:

```
response.status(.created)
response.send(json: entry)
```

Here, in addition to returning a much more meaningful response containing a JSON representation of your newly-created object, you also first set an HTTP response code of "201 Created" to meet best-practice RESTful API guidelines.

Your final `addEntry` function should look as follows:

```
func addEntry(request: RouterRequest, response: RouterResponse,
  next: @escaping () -> Void) {
    guard let contentType = request.headers["Content-Type"],
            contentType.hasPrefix("application/json") else {
      response.status(.unsupportedMediaType)
      response.send(["error":
        "Request Content-Type must be application/json"])
      return next()
    }
    var entry: JournalEntry
    do {
      try entry = request.read(as: JournalEntry.self)
    } catch {
      response.status(.unprocessableEntity)
      if let decodingError = error as? DecodingError {
        response.send(
          "Could not decode received data: " +
          "\(decodingError.humanReadableDescription)")
      } else {
        response.send("Could not decode received data.")
      }
      return next()
    }
    response.status(.created)
    response.send(json: entry)
    next()
}
```

Build and run your project once again, then return to Terminal and make the same POST request you did previously:

```
curl -i -X POST http://localhost:8080/entries -H 'Content-Type:
application/json' -d '{"emoji":"🤓", "date":
563725805.57661498}'
```

Your route now returns an HTTP status code of "201 Created" and at the bottom, there's your shiny new JournalEntry object echoed back to you as JSON!

```
HTTP/1.1 201 Created
Date: Mon, 12 Nov 2018 15:00:25 GMT
Content-Type: application/json
Content-Length: 42
Connection: Keep-Alive
Keep-Alive: timeout=60

{"emoji":"🤓","date":563725805.57661498}
```

Creating a POST API with Codable Routing

Great work completing that! Now it's time to do this the easier way with Codable Routing.

As we discussed earlier, Codable Routing is designed to enable automatic conversion between your app's data types and body data in HTTP requests and responses in a fully type-safe way. It also implements RESTful API best practices, so you need *a lot* less code to build your APIs.

In Xcode, remove the entire existing addEntry function you painstakingly assembled in the last section, and replace it with the following:

```
func addEntry(entry: JournalEntry, completion:
  @escaping (JournalEntry?, RequestError?) -> Void) {
    completion(entry, nil)
}
```

Build and run your app. Then, in Terminal, run the same curl command you used previously.

```
curl -i -X POST http://localhost:8080/entries -H 'Content-Type:
application/json' -d '{"emoji":"😄", "date":
563725805.57661498}'
```

As you can see, you get the identical response from before!

```
HTTP/1.1 201 Created
Content-Type: application/json
Content-Length: 42
Date: Mon, 12 Nov 2018 15:03:48 GMT
Connection: Keep-Alive
Keep-Alive: timeout=60

{"emoji":"😄","date":563725805.57661498}
```

Sweet, right? You've just implemented the same RESTful API as in the previous section. But you've saved yourself twenty lines of code and therefore twenty lines of code that might contain bugs! Needless to say, as you multiply this kind of savings out over all the routes of a complete API, it makes writing, debugging and updating your API oodles nicer. It really pays to use Codable Routing whenever you're able to!

Now that you've seen how much simpler Codable Routing is, lets look at how it works and what it does on your behalf.

A unique feature of Codable Routing is that it only requires you to define the values you expect to receive from the request in your handler function, along with the values that you'll add to the response through the completion handler.

One very nice feature is that these parameters can have any name that you like: Your `JournalEntry` does not have to be called `journalentry` and your `completion` handler doesn't need to be called `completion`.

If you like, go ahead and change the use of `journalentry` to `entry` to see this in action. (Then change it back again so your project stays in sync).

By creating a handler that receives a parameter that conforms to `Codable` (in your case the `JournalEntry` you created earlier), Kitura's Codable Router will try to create a corresponding parameter from the body data of the request. It does this in two steps:

1. It reads the Content-Type header to determine encoding.

2. It attempts to decode the body data using this encoding type.

> **Note**: At the time of writing, Kitura only supports decoding from application/ json. This means that, in practice, Content-Type currently must always be set to application/json. The Kitura team plans, however, to support other encoding types in upcoming releases.

Once Kitura has created the requested data type from the body data of the HTTP request, it passes this through to your function. If, for any reason, it cannot decode the data (e.g., if the media type is unsupported or the entity data is invalid) it sets the correct HTTP status code and error message and then creates an appropriate error response on your behalf.

Kitura also passes a completion handler to your function to be used to complete the request and build the response. For a POST request, the completion handler typically takes two Optional values:

1. The data you'd like to use in your response body (for `addEntry`, this is a representation of `JournalEntry`).

2. Any `RequestError` you might wish to respond with.

> **Note**: RequestError maps to whatever HTTP status code and message you'd like to use, so it's possible to return a RequestError of .ok if you wish to!

You can also use a second type of completion handler with POST requests in which the body data field is a Tuple. This can be very helpful in cases in which you want to set the **Location** HTTP header to provide an identifier or URL for the created resource. In your API, you'll include the created resource's identifier inside the JournalEntry struct's id field, so you'll use the first type of completion handler.

Adding a GET API to retrieve all JournalEntry data

Now, it's time to extend your API by adding a route to retrieve all the JournalEntry resources. In Chapter 3, you learned that this means implementing the following:

Action	Method	Path	Query Allowed	Request Body	Response Body	Success Status
Get resources	GET	/entries	Yes	No	Yes	200 OK

In Xcode, register a new handler at the beginning of your `initializeEntryRoutes` method (once again, you'll get a temporary error until you create the matching handler function):

```
app.router.get("/entries", handler: getAllEntries)
```

Codable Routing lets you register two types of handlers for GET requests. Both types take no body data parameters. The difference is whether their completion handlers return:

- An array of entries.
- An array of tuples, with each tuple element containing the entry itself as well as its identifier or URL.

Here, since your API uses an id field for the identifier stored in the JournalEntry struct itself, you'll use the first of these types.

At the bottom of your file, add a new `getAllEntries` function:

```
func getAllEntries(completion:
  @escaping ([JournalEntry]?, RequestError?) -> Void) -> Void {
    completion([JournalEntry](), nil)
}
```

As just described, this function receives no body data parameter, since RESTful GET requests don't provide body data. It (temporarily) returns an empty `JournalEntry` array because your EmojiJournalServer currently has no store of `JournalEntry` structs. You'll add this soon.

Build and run. In Terminal, run this curl command to make a GET request on /entries:

```
curl -i -X GET http://localhost:8080/entries
```

Your EmojiJournalServer should return a response like this:

```
HTTP/1.1 200 OK
Content-Length: 2
Date: Tue, 13 Nov 2018 16:54:43 GMT
Content-Type: application/json
Connection: Keep-Alive
Keep-Alive: timeout=60

[]
```

Note the response of "200 OK" indicating a valid request, and "[]", JSON representation of your currently empty `JournalEntry` array.

Now, it's time to add a way to store `JournalEntry` items. To do this, you'll add a field called `entries`, which will store an array of `JournalEntries`.

In Xcode, add this below your import statements, just before you declare your `initializeEntryRoutes` function:

```
var entries: [JournalEntry] = []
```

Now, in `getAllEntries`, update the call to your completion handler so that it returns your `entries` array:

```
completion(entries, nil)
```

That's good, but `addEntry` doesn't yet store anything into the `entries` array. You'll fix that now.

Update your `addEntry` handler to match this:

```
func addEntry(entry: JournalEntry, completion:
  @escaping (JournalEntry?, RequestError?) -> Void) {
    var storedEntry = entry
    storedEntry.id = entries.count.value
    entries.append(storedEntry)
    completion(storedEntry, nil)
}
```

Build and run, then run the following two curl commands in Terminal to first create and then retrieve, a new `JournalEntry`:

```
curl -i -X POST http://localhost:8080/entries -H 'Content-Type:
application/json' -d '{"emoji":"😄", "date":
563725805.57661498}'
curl -i -X GET http://localhost:8080/entries
```

In response to your second command, you'll see a response similar to:

```
HTTP/1.1 200 OK
Content-Length: 53
Date: Tue, 13 Nov 2018 17:23:26 GMT
Content-Type: application/json
Connection: Keep-Alive
Keep-Alive: timeout=60

[{"id":"0","emoji":"😄","date":563725805.57661498}]
```

As you can see, a new `entries` array element was created in response to your first request. It was assigned an `id` of `0`, since it's the first (zeroth) entry in your new array.

Adding a DELETE API to remove a journal entry

Things are taking shape nicely now. You'll round out this chapter by adding one final RESTful endpoint that lets users delete individual entries.

As you learned in Chapter 3, this means implementing the following:

Action	Method	Path	Query Allowed	Request Body	Response Body	Success Status
Delete resource	DELETE	/entries/{id}	No	No	No	204 No Content

Return to Xcode. Once again, register a new handler function just after your POST method's registration:

```
app.router.delete("/entries", handler: deleteEntry)
```

Delete requests do not include any body data, so your handler function doesn't take a parameter for data. Since you're going to use this endpoint to delete a single entry, it does need a parameter for the `id` of the entry to be deleted. This will be passed in the request's URL.

In Kitura, just as parameters used for the body data must conform to `Codable`, parameters for URL-encoded identifiers must conform to the `Identifier` protocol. Under the hood, `Identifier` is a typealias for `Codable`. However, `Identifier` is also used specifically by Kitura to identify that a function parameter is for a URL-encoded parameter.

Kitura extends both `Int` and `String` to conform to `Identifier`, meaning that you can use both of these types out of the box. In more advanced cases, it's possible to make any `Codable` type conform to `Identifier`, so that you can then use these as custom identifier types when needed. At the bottom of your file, add a new `deleteEntry` function:

```
func deleteEntry(id: String, completion:
  @escaping (RequestError?) -> Void) {
    completion(nil)
}
```

Your `deleteEntry` function takes an `id` of type `String` and a `completion` handler having only an Optional `RequestError` type, as DELETE requests return no data — only "204 No Content" on success or an error on failure. At present, you simply return success, as this method doesn't yet remove any data.

Build and run. Then, in Terminal, execute:

```
curl -i -X DELETE http://localhost:8080/entries/0
```

This returns a response similar to:

```
HTTP/1.1 204 No Content
Content-Length: 0
Date: Wed, 14 Nov 2018 09:28:33 GMT
Connection: Keep-Alive
Keep-Alive: timeout=60
```

Great! Your server returned the expected "204 No Content" denoting a successful DELETE request.

Back in Xcode, update your `deleteEntry` function to this:

```
func deleteEntry(id: String, completion:
  @escaping (RequestError?) -> Void) {
    guard let index =
      entries.firstIndex(where: { $0.id == id }) else {
        return completion(.notFound)
    }
    entries.remove(at: index)
    completion(nil)
}
```

With these changes, your function now iterates over the `entries` array searching for an entry whose `id` matches that encoded in the URL. If it fails to find a match, it returns a "404 Not Found" error. If an entry is found, it's deleted and a success message is returned.

Build and run once again, then run these two commands in Terminal:

```
curl -i -X POST http://localhost:8080/entries -H 'Content-Type:
application/json' -d '{"emoji":"😀", "date":
563725805.57661498}'
curl -i -X DELETE http://localhost:8080/entries/0
```

You'll see "201 Created" for the first command and a response similar to this for your DELETE request:

```
HTTP/1.1 204 No Content
Date: Wed, 14 Nov 2018 09:35:12 GMT
Content-Length: 0
Connection: Keep-Alive
Keep-Alive: timeout=60
```

Once again, the "204 No Content" response means a successful removal of the target entry. Now confirm that it was really deleted by executing:

```
curl -i -X GET http://localhost:8080/entries
```

You should see a response similar to:

```
HTTP/1.1 200 OK
Date: Wed, 14 Nov 2018 09:38:30 GMT
Content-Type: application/json
Content-Length: 2
```

```
Connection: Keep-Alive
Keep-Alive: timeout=60

[]
```

The empty array returned confirms that your entry been deleted.

Your completed RESTful API!

Congratulations are in order! Go ahead and give yourself a pat on the back — real or metaphorical as you prefer — for a job well done!

As you've worked your way through this chapter, you've built a RESTful API that complies with best practices. And your API now enables clients to create, retrieve and delete entries for your EmojiJournal app.

Where to go from here?

Of course, you're not finished. Currently, your entries are stored using a simple in-memory array. This has several problems:

1. All data is lost whenever your EmojiJournalServer is restarted.

2. Each entry's id is based simply on its index in the entries array *when it's created* Once array entries are deleted it's possible to get multiple entries with the same id value.

3. The entries array isn't thread safe. Server apps can potentially be used by 1,000s of clients at exactly the same time. This means that multiple calls to the count, append, index and remove functions of the same entries array will be occurring concurrently. In order to allow this to happen, the data store needs to be designed to make sure that the data is consistent across multiple requests.

Of course, you'll address all these issues soon. In Chapter 8, "KueryORM," you'll update your code to use a database, and, in doing so, you'll neatly resolve all of these issues.

But before you get to that, you'll first learn how to document your new RESTful API using the OpenAPI specification. You'll do that in the next two chapters as you first learn about the OpenAPI specification itself, and then learn about Kitura's specific and powerful OpenAPI-based tools.

Chapter 6: The OpenAPI Specification

David Okun

You've made some great progress so far! EmojiJournal now has routes enabling you to:

- GET all saved entries on your server.

- POST a new entry to your server.

- DELETE an entry by passing its id via the request.

In Chapter 3, you learned the core principles of RESTful communication. Time and experience have refined these principles repeatedly, and most everyone who writes a REST API these days adheres to these common standards.

However, this standard leaves considerable room for variation. Developers tend to write RESTful APIs in their own style, and understanding the specifics of how a given backend is structured can be difficult. Further, developers often take widely ranging approaches to documenting APIs, further adding to the difficulties awaiting you when encountering a new API.

In 2011, Tony Tam of the dictionary website *wordnik.com* encountered these very issues. He lamented the pain of needing to rewrite client-side SDKs every time developers updated a corresponding REST API. Necessity is the mother of invention, as the saying goes. Out of this pain the **Swagger API** project would be born and ultimately grow into the modern OpenAPI Specification.

In this chapter, you'll get a quick overview of the history of this specification, and you'll learn how you can use it to represent your Kitura API throughout the development of EmojiJournal!

By the time you finish this chapter, you'll be able to:

- Visit a user-friendly website that documents your entire Kitura back end.

- Easily test all of your routes.

- Generate an iOS SDK that *just works* with your API.

The goals of Swagger

Building on Tony Tam's trailblazing open-source project, other companies began contributing. Ultimately, the Linux Foundation assumed sponsorship of the project, changing its name to the **OpenAPI Initiative**. This broad support brings the **OpenAPI Specification** to a very prominent place in open source software development.

When Tony began working on the Swagger API project, he defined three key goals:

- API development

- API documentation

- API interaction

You might say that no one on the corner had swagger like Tony!

There's no shortage of tooling available for testing your API — one popular tool you may be familiar with is the excellent **Postman** — and there are many other excellent dedicated tools in this space as well. But the OpenAPI Initiative aimed to make the experience of developing, documenting and interacting with an API significantly easier and more predictable.

Consider an example from your EmojiJournal application: Since you already have a POST route set up, you could test this route with a simple cURL command from Terminal, like you did previously:

```
curl -X POST \
-H "Content-Type: application/json" \
-d '{"emoji":"😁", "date": 563725805.57661498}' \
http://localhost:8080/entries
```

This might feel pretty straightforward if you're comfortable with cURL. You might even envision using cURL like this with real-world team projects. But in reality, you simply cannot guarantee that everyone on your team will know how — or choose — to use cURL as you do. An ad hoc approach like this won't cut it in the real world.

The Swagger project addresses this by specifying a consistent, user-friendly user interface. By definition, an interface should always provide the following for each method available on the API:

- The specific method (GET, POST, DELETE, etc.).

- What to put in the body of the request.

- Possible responses.

Here's an example of what this might look like for a POST method using the KituraOpenAPI module:

Notice that this page achieves all three goals of the Swagger project: You can *develop* your API more quickly by *interacting* with your results as you write your code, and check its accuracy via the *documentation* it generates. This is really neat!

While you may still see your peers developing APIs manually, having these powerful tools in your back pocket makes developing your Kitura APIs faster, more reliable and even... fun!

That's pretty great, but... wait a minute! Exactly how does all of this get generated? How do the routes you create get converted to this friendly and powerful user interface? The answer lies in the specification itself.

Generating your specification

In Xcode, open the EmojiJournalServer project (from this chapter's starter project directory or from where you left off in the previous chapter). Open **Package.swift** and append the following to your list of **dependencies**:

```
.package(
  url: "https://github.com/IBM-Swift/Kitura-OpenAPI.git",
  from: "1.1.1"),
```

Next, find the `Application` target within your **targets** array and append `"KituraOpenAPI"` to its dependencies array. Your `targets` section should now look this:

```
targets: [
  .target(
    name: "EmojiJournalServer",
    dependencies: [
      .target(name: "Application"),
      "Kitura",
      "HeliumLogger"]),
  .target(
    name: "Application",
    dependencies: [
      "Kitura",
      "CloudEnvironment",
      "SwiftMetrics",
      "Health",
      "KituraOpenAPI"]),
  .testTarget(
    name: "ApplicationTests",
    dependencies: [
      .target(name: "Application"),
      "Kitura",
```

```
        "HeliumLogger"]),
]
```

Save your Package.swift file. Xcode should automatically resolve all of your dependencies for you, so sit back and watch the magic happen!

Next, go to **Sources/Application/Application.swift**. Scroll to the top of the file, and append the following after your current import statements:

```
import KituraOpenAPI
```

You may notice that Xcode doesn't auto-complete this module. You also might see a "No such module 'KituraÒpenApi'" warning from Xcode. No worries — this happens because you haven't yet built your project in Xcode itself.

Build your project now. It should build without errors, demonstrating that you've updated your project's dependencies to include the new package you specified in your Package.swift file a moment ago. Sweet!

Next, scroll down to your `postInit()` method and append this to it:

```
KituraOpenAPI.addEndpoints(to: router)
```

Build and run your project. Now, open a web browser and navigate to **http://localhost:8080/openapi**. You should see something like this:

```
{
  "schemes" : [
    "http"
  ],
  "swagger" : "2.0",
  "info" : {
    "version" : "1.0",
    "title" : "Kitura Project",
    "description" : "Generated by Kitura"
  },
  "paths" : {
    "\/health" : {
      "get" : {
        "responses" : {
          "200" : {
            "schema" : {
              "$ref" : "#\/definitions\/Status"
            },
            "description" : "successful response"
          }
        },
        "consumes" : [
          "application\/json"
        ],
        "produces" : [
          "application\/json"
        ]
      }
    },
    "\/entries" : {
      "get" : {
        "responses" : {
          "200" : {
            "schema" : {
              "type" : "array",
              "items" : {
                "$ref" : "#\/definitions\/JournalEntry"
              }
            },
            "description" : "successful response"
          }
        },
        "consumes" : [
          "application\/json"
        ],
        "produces" : [
          "application\/json"
        ]
      },
      "post" : {
        "consumes" : [
          "application\/json"
        ],
        "produces" : [
          "application\/json"
        ],
        "responses" : {
          "200" : {
            "schema" : {
              "$ref" : "#\/definitions\/JournalEntry"
```

What you're seeing is a description of the API you've built so far, following the OpenAPI Specification. What's fairly amazing is that all you needed to do to make this happen was to add a single project dependency, one import statement and one line of code. With these lightweight pieces in place, Kitura automatically took care of everything else needed to create this description of your API on your behalf!

Next, let's walk through some components of this specification to clarify how this can help you develop, document and interact with your API in practice.

Examining your specification

Start by looking at two topmost elements of your JSON spec (note that the json array does not guarantee sorting, so you may have to scroll to locate these elements):

```
{
"schemes" : [
  "http"
],
"swagger" : "2.0",
"info" : {
  "version" : "1.0",
  "title" : "Kitura Project",
  "description" : "Generated by Kitura"
},
```

This is metadata describing your project. Consider that one purpose of this specification is to allow other people to easily understand your API's structure and purpose. This is where human-readable metadata comes in handy.

Next, locate the top-level "paths" node. This contains an array of "/entries" describing each of the endpoints you've created so far. Find the "get" entry within this:

```
"get": {
  "responses": {
    "200": {
      "schema": {
        "type": "array",
        "items": {
          "$ref": "#\/definitions\/JournalEntry"
        }
      },
      "description": "successful response"
    }
  },
  "consumes": [
    "application\/json"
  ],
  "produces": [
    "application\/json"
  ]
}
```

The top of this snippet indicates that you are looking at a GET route for the path "/entries". Three sub-nodes describe this route:

- "responses" provides an array of responses a user can receive.

- "consumes" specifies the data type this method must be given.

- "produces" describes the type of data the response will contain.

Further down in the same top-level path "/entries" node, find your POST route. Note that in comparison to the GET route you just saw, this contains an additional sub-node:

```
"parameters" : [
  {
    "in" : "body",
    "name" : "input",
    "required" : true,
    "schema" : {
      "$ref" : "#\/definitions\/JournalEntry"
    }
  }
]
```

As you can see, when you write a POST route, the spec generator automatically adds information about the body of the request you need to send to yield a successful response. Take a moment to scroll through the rest of your currently available methods and take note of the similar properties and formats shared across each method. You're seeing the consistent sets of data defined by the OpenAPI Specification that will enable the generated UI to test each method you write. Now, locate the top-level "definitions" node:

```
"definitions": {
  "Status": {
    "type": "object",
    "required": ["timestamp","details","status"],
    "properties": {
      "status": {"type":"string"},
      "details": {"items":{"type":"string"},"type":"array"},
      "timestamp": {"type":"string"}
    }
  },
  "JournalEntry": {
    "type": "object",
    "required": ["emoji","date"],
    "properties": {
      "id": {"type":"string"},
      "emoji": {"type":"string"},
      "date": {"type":"number"}
```

```
        }
      }
   }
```

Focus on the `JournalEntry` node here. As you'll recall, you created your model object in Chapter 3, and then you made it representable in JSON in Chapter 4. Now, the `KituraOpenAPI` module has automatically added it to your project spec! This is a nice demonstration of how the `KituraOpenAPI` module dynamically observes the types of your `JournalEntry` object and automatically constructs references for them in your specification. You might notice that the specification represents the `date` property as a number. You covered this date representation issue in Chapter 4, so this should feel familiar.

Here's the really great thing about all this: You now have living, breathing documentation of your API, and from now on your documentation will grow and change right along with your live code. As you continue to build out your app, be sure to check back and see how this specification updates automagically!

Using the Kitura OpenAPI UI

Make sure your EmojiJournalServer app is still running in Xcode, then open a browser and go to `http://localhost:8080/openapi/ui`. You should see a page like this:

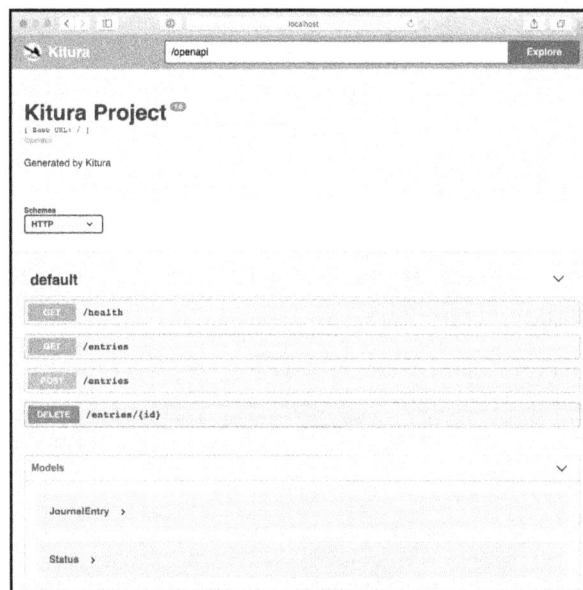

You've just learned how this information is created under the hood. Now it's time to explore and interact with your API.

Click on the **POST** route. Notice how the route's description expands:

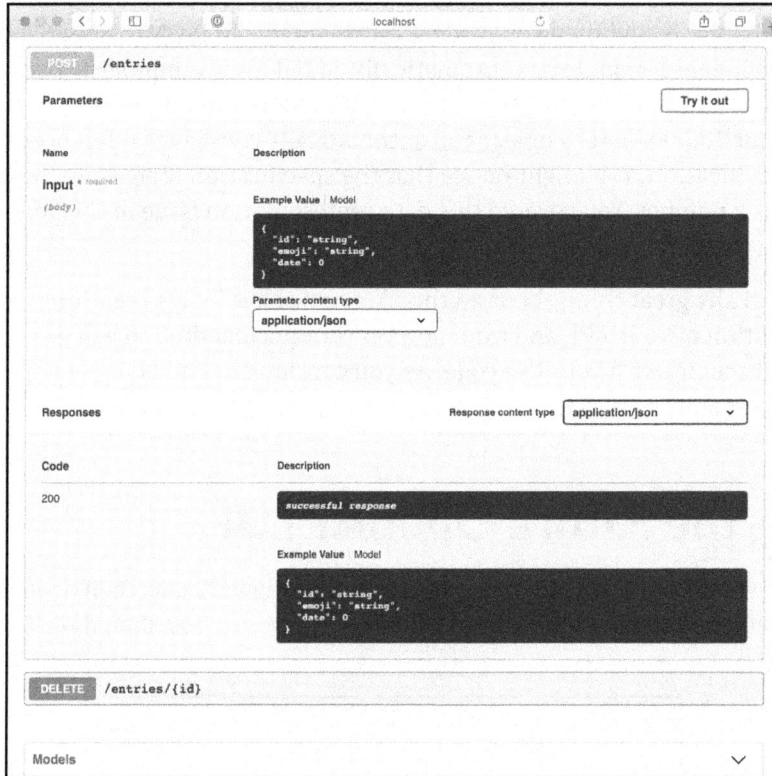

Each component of your JSON is clearly represented here. Even better, your entire API is now fully explorable!

Click the **Try it out** button at the top of this expanded page.

Because a POST route requires input, the interface pauses to let you enter this, displaying the input types required.

In the main text area (underneath the **Edit Value | Model** caption), replace the suggested text with the following:

```
{
  "emoji": "🤓",
  "date": 563725805.57661498
}
```

Before continuing, two notes about this:

1. To bring up the emoji picker on a macOS machine, press **Control + Command + Space bar**.

2. The date here is represented as a number that doesn't really seem to mean anything. Don't worry: This is just how Swift stores raw Date values under the hood. As is, this will work fine with your iOS app. In Chapter 12, you'll add a custom decoder so you can pass and view Date values as ISO8601 strings rather than raw numeric values.

Click the **Execute** button, and note how the UI updates:

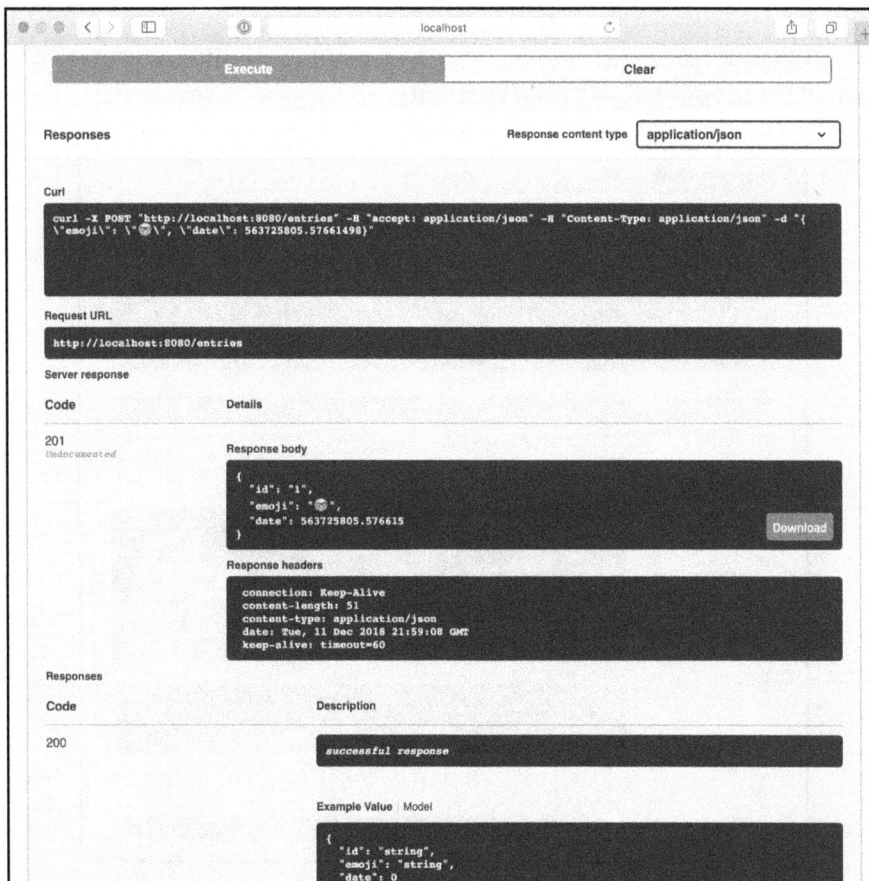

Remember that cURL command you've been using? This page shows you the exact cURL syntax needed to test any route you select! This can be very helpful in cases where you need to do a quick and dirty test — or if you just can't convince a stubborn teammate how useful this module really is!

As expected, your POST route works! You received a "201" response, and the object you created is echoed back for your inspection. You can also easily see the headers of your response, which can be very helpful if you run into issues later on.

> **Note**: The **Server response** section contains the *actual* response from the server. Just below this, the **Responses** section documents what the response is *expected* to be. At first glance, these two sections might seem a bit redundant. In practice, they each serve a complementary role, letting you easily compare the actual response you *receive* (**Server response**) with what you *expect* (**Responses**).

Now, scroll to your GET /entries route. Take a moment to familiarize yourself with the contents of the page. Now click **Try it out** and then click **Execute**:

As expected, your GET route returns the `JournalEntry` objects you created with your POST request (and your earlier cURL request). You also get other key information returned with that response in an easily digestible format. Is this UI nice or what?

Feel free to test the rest of the Kitura OpenAPI UI at your leisure. Now it's time to give your iOS app a little love!

Generating an SDK for your iOS app

The last thing you're going to do with the OpenAPI Specification is so awesome that it just might become your very favorite!

One of the auxiliary toolsets within the OpenAPI Initiative is the swagger-codegen tool, which lets you generate a client SDK in up to 30 different programming languages! I encourage you to play around with this tool and try generating some other SDKs in other languages (we'll stick with Swift here).

For the last part of this chapter, you'll need to make sure that your system has Docker up and running. The instructions in Chapter 2, "Hello, World!" should be enough to get you started. To ensure that you are ready to go, open Terminal and type in **docker version**. If you see output telling you that you are running version 18.09.0 or better, then you're all set.

> **Note:** If you'd rather install this codegen tool through Homebrew — you can! We've chosen not to go this route in this chapter so that you don't need to install Java (a requirement of the codegen tool) directly onto your machine, since Java can be a bit of a lightning rod for many developers. By installing codegen in Docker, you're shielded from having to worry about any potential harms of installing Java directly on your mac.

In Terminal, type the following command:

```
docker pull swaggerapi/swagger-codegen-cli
```

Once the image and all of its dependencies are done installing, enter this command in Terminal:

```
docker run --rm -v ${PWD}:/local \
    swaggerapi/swagger-codegen-cli langs
```

> **Note**: ${PWD} represents the path of the current working directory. If that path contains spaces, you may need quotes around the path to make it work, like `"${PWD}:/local"`.

If you're familiar with Docker, you may notice that you're specifying a volume to mount into this image. This is done so that the codegen tool has a "window" back to your local directory when it takes the parameters it needs. The output of this command should look like similar to this:

```
Available languages: [ada, ada-server, akka-scala, android,
apache2, apex, aspnetcore, bash, csharp, clojure, cwiki,
cpprest, csharp-dotnet2, dart, elixir, elm, eiffel, erlang-
client, erlang-server, finch, flask, python-flask, go, go-
server, groovy, haskell-http-client, haskell, jmeter, jaxrs-cxf-
client, jaxrs-cxf, java, inflector, jaxrs-cxf-cdi, jaxrs-spec,
jaxrs, msf4j, java-pkmst, java-play-framework, jaxrs-resteasy-
eap, jaxrs-resteasy, javascript, javascript-closure-angular,
java-vertx, kotlin, lua, lumen, nancyfx, nodejs-server, objc,
perl, php, powershell, pistache-server, python, qt5cpp, r,
rails5, restbed, ruby, rust, rust-server, scala, scala-gatling,
scala-lagom-server, scalatra, scalaz, php-silex, sinatra, slim,
spring, dynamic-html, html2, html, swagger, swagger-yaml,
swift4, swift3, swift, php-symfony, tizen, typescript-aurelia,
typescript-angular, typescript-inversify, typescript-angularjs,
typescript-fetch, typescript-jquery, typescript-node, undertow,
ze-ph, kotlin-server]
```

Until now, you've worked on the server side of the project for this book (appropriate for a book entitled *Server Side Swift with Kitura*). Now you'll take a look at the mobile app side.

The starter project directory for this chapter includes an EmojiJournalMobileApp directory to get you going. Still in Terminal, navigate to the root folder of EmojiJournalMobileApp. Create a new directory to store your generated SDK, and a local file for your specification:

```
mkdir GeneratedSDK
touch specification.json
```

Even though the specification is live for you at http://localhost:8080/openapi, the Docker container you are about to run can't easily access that URL outside of its own environment. You could monkey around with container network settings, but for simplicity you'll take a simpler approach.

Open **specification.json** in a text editor. Copy the contents of http://localhost:8080/ openapi from your browser and paste them into specification.json. Save your file.

Here comes the magic! Enter the following command in Terminal:

```
docker run --rm -v ${PWD}:/local \
swaggerapi/swagger-codegen-cli generate \
-i /local/specification.json -l swift \
-o /local/GeneratedSDK
```

Open your `GeneratedSDK` folder and take a look at its newly created contents:

Name		Date Modified	Size	Kind
▶ .swagger-codegen		Today at 12:05 PM	--	Folder
▼ SwaggerClient		Today at 12:07 PM	--	Folder
▼ Classes		Today at 12:07 PM	--	Folder
▼ Swaggers		Today at 12:07 PM	--	Folder
▼ APIs		Today at 12:05 PM	--	Folder
DefaultAPI.swift		Today at 12:05 PM	5 KB	Swift Source
▶ Models		Today at 12:05 PM	--	Folder
AlamofireImplementations.swift		Today at 12:05 PM	8 KB	Swift Source
APIHelper.swift		Today at 12:05 PM	1 KB	Swift Source
APIs.swift		Today at 12:05 PM	2 KB	Swift Source
Extensions.swift		Today at 12:05 PM	5 KB	Swift Source
Models.swift		Today at 12:05 PM	7 KB	Swift Source
.gitignore		Today at 12:05 PM	1 KB	TextEdi...cument
.swagger-codegen-ignore		Today at 12:05 PM	1 KB	TextEdi...cument
Cartfile		Today at 12:05 PM	38 bytes	TextEdi...cument
git_push.sh		Today at 12:05 PM	2 KB	Shell Script
SwaggerClient.podspec		Today at 12:05 PM	528 bytes	Document

1 of 17 selected, 2.11 TB available

Take a moment to appreciate what you're seeing. With just a single CLI command, you've created a fully functional Swift SDK that can handle all of your network communications with this specific server.

We're big fans of small commands that yield big output, and this is an especially sweet example of that! Let's take a moment to unpack the details of what codegen has created:

1. The underlying HTTP request to generate your SDK is made via Alamofire, an extremely popular Swift networking library by Matt Thompson.

2. You get both Cartfile and a .podspec files to implement this SDK. This means you can choose either Carthage or Cocoapods to integrate your SDK. Either way, you won't have to drag and drop all the files into your project over and over!

3. Everything is documented!

Just think how much time you'll save with this — and how much code you'll no longer have to write!

Open up **GeneratedSDK/SwaggerClient/Classes/Swaggers/APIs/DefaultAPI.swift** in a text editor. Locate the method entriesPost — line 93 at the time this was written:

```
public class func entriesPost(input input: JournalEntry,
    completion: ((data: JournalEntry?, error: ErrorType?)
  -> Void)) {
    entriesPostWithRequestBuilder(input: input)
      .execute { (response, error) -> Void in
        completion(data: response?.body, error: error);
    }
}
```

This method is your entry point to sending a new JournalEntry to your server! This means that you can use the following code to create a new JournalEntry object and send it to your server:

```
let newEntry = JournalEntry(id: nil, emoji: "😜", date: Date())
DefaultAPI.entriesPost(input: newEntry) { data, error in
  // handle response here
})
```

Nice and simple! This gives you a quick sample of how useful codegen can be as you develop your Kitura apps. You'll likely find that being able to automatically generate client APIs — in a very wide array of languages and directly from your server code — will be incredibly useful.

In practice, this saves time and gets you up and running quickly. It can also save errors, and prove especially helpful for folks who aren't (gasp) working in Swift!

Where to go from here?

Well, that's been a lot of fun. Hopefully, by now you can see clearly how powerful and effortless Kitura's OpenAPI support is. In practice, you'll likely find this an invaluable tool within your team, especially for testing your API. You'll also likely find these tools especially valuable to developers *outside* your team, as they seek to understand and interact with your API in a platform-neutral, standards-compliant way.

You'll make plenty of use of the Kitura OpenAPI UI throughout the rest of the book, *especially* in the next chapter. But starting in the next chapter, you'll learn that while Kitura provides fantastic tools for exploring and documenting your JSON APIs, it also shields you from working directly with these within your Swift code — via an SDK called *KituraKit*.

As you'll see, this gives you the best of both worlds: On one hand, Kitura's amazing OpenAPI support and tools make it super easy for developers of all persuasions to understand your public APIs from *outside* your app. One the other hand, thanks to *KituraKit*, *within* your app you'll be able to ignore JSON implementation details and focus directly on clean, native Swift types. It's a huge win-win!

If you ran into any difficulties along the way, feel free to check out the final projects for this chapter.

In the next chapter, you'll add more routes to your server (and your Kitura OpenAPI UI will come in handy for testing them!). You'll also integrate *KituraKit* into your iOS app to get your full stack working!

Chapter 7: KituraOpenAPI

David Okun

In the last chapter, you discovered the power of the OpenAPI specification. You learned how to add the `KituraOpenAPI` module to your EmojiJournal server and you generated a specification for your server with the module. After that, you learned to use a handy-dandy user interface designed to let you interact with, develop and document your server.

> **Note**: If you haven't already done so, please be sure you've read Chapter 6, "The OpenAPI Spec," before continuing. It introduces important background information about the OpenAPI specification that won't be explained in this chapter.

Now it's time to put all your hard work into practice! This chapter will guide you through a serious expansion of your server, as you add these new capabilities:

- Update a journal entry.

- Get a journal entry by its `id`.

- Get journal entries containing a specific emoji.

You won't stop there! You'll then dig into your iOS app and get moving with KituraKit! Your iOS app currently contains everything you need to create a nice user experience for all the people dying to use EmojiJournal. You'll focus on the networking layer by adding each operation using KituraKit in a class designed specifically for this purpose.

Here's the sweetest part: You'll do all this without having to touch raw JSON even once!

Let's dive right in, beginning with your server.

If you're continuing from previous chapters, simply open **EmojiJournalServer** in Xcode. Remember that you can do this in Xcode 11 by double clicking `Package.swift`.

Once your project opens in Xcode, build it as usual to ensure everything's indexed and in working order.

Updating a journal entry

Open the file **Sources/Application/Routes/EntryRoutes.swift** in Xcode and scroll to the `initalizeEntryRoutes` function. Underneath the registration of your DELETE route, add the following:

```
app.router.put("/entries", handler: modifyEntry)
```

This is how you register a PUT route on your server. As with the other routes you've created previously, you'll once again delegate the work for this route to a function you'll write now. Scroll down beneath the `deleteEntry` function, and add a stub for a new handler function:

```
func modifyEntry(id: String, entry: JournalEntry, completion:
  @escaping (JournalEntry?, RequestError?) -> Void) {
}
```

Notice how Codable Routing once again acts as your wingman by offering only the available parameters for autocompletion of any action. Here, it offers the `id` of the entry you're updating, as well as an `entry` object representing the incoming data. With these properties in hand, you only need to call your completion handler with your shiny new object and you'll be scot free!

Now, it's time to flesh out your handler function. Enter the following within your new `modifyEntry` function to get a reference to the existing entry:

```
guard let index = entries.firstIndex(where: { $0.id == id })
else {
  return completion(nil, .notFound)
}
```

By the way, if you find yourself wondering how sustainable this approach to a datastore is, you're thinking ahead nicely. In the next chapter, you'll overhaul your persistence layer to make it production-worthy.

Next, beneath the code you just added, create a modifiable instance of your object and set its properties, like this:

```
var storedEntry = entry
storedEntry.id = id
```

Here's what this does:

1. Since the `entry` passed in the function signature is immutable, you start by making a mutable copy of it, cleverly named `storedEntry`.

2. Since `entry` didn't contain an `id` property, you assign `storedEntry` the id from the request.

Last, add these lines to complete this function:

```
entries[index] = storedEntry
completion(storedEntry, nil)
```

This replaces the existing entry in your `entries` array with your your updated object, then ships it off to your completion handler. Easy peezy!

Build and run your server.

Now in your web browser, navigate to http://localhost:8080/openapi/ui. Open your POST route and add a new entry to your server:

```
{
  "emoji": "😀",
  "date": 563725805.576615
}
```

> **Remember**: A handy macOS keyboard command for the emoji picker is Control + Command + Space bar.

If you get a "201" response, you're in business.

Next, scroll down to your newly-minted PUT route in your UI and click the **Try it out** button. You should see a layout like so:

```
PUT   /entries/{id}

Parameters                                                    Cancel


Name                    Description

id * required
                           id
string
(path)

input * required
                        Edit Value   Model
(body)
                        {
                          "id": "string",
                          "emoji": "string",
                          "date": 0
                        }




                        Cancel

                        Parameter content type
                        application/json        ⌄


                                  Execute
```

You need to provide two values for this route: the id of the target entry and the new JournalEntry containing the updated values. Enter 0 in the id field input, then enter the following in the input field:

```
{
  "emoji": "😀",
  "date": 563725805.576615
}
```

Click **Execute**. In response, you should see this:

```
{
  "id": "0",
  "emoji": "😀",
  "date": 563725805.576615
}
```

As discussed in Chapter 6, don't worry that your date isn't very, ahem, easy on the eyes. You'll learn to decode raw Swift Dates to human-readable ISO date strings in Chapter 12.

Nice work! Now your server has the capability to update an existing entry, and you just used your automatically updating API explorer to check out the entire process! In practice, you'll likely find that while dedicated REST tools like Postman are great for heavy lifting, it's really nice to be able to examine and interact with your routes in a simple lightweight tool like this.

Retrieving a journal entry by its id

RESTful APIs commonly expect to include a route enabling users to GET a resource by its ID. Codable Routing is ready to handle this requirement out of the box.

Scroll back up to your initializeEntryRoutes function. Add the following underneath your PUT route's registration:

```
app.router.get("/entries", handler: getOneEntry)
```

If you're thinking that this looks *real* similar to the other GET route you registered, you're absolutely right. As we mentioned in Chapter 5, it's "Auto-Magic"!

Next, add the signature for this function at the bottom of this file:

```
func getOneEntry(id: String, completion:
  @escaping (JournalEntry?, RequestError?) -> Void) {
}
```

Take a look at the parameters in your new function's signature. Since you want to GET a specific journal entry, your completion handler must return either that single entry or an error. Kitura is flexible enough to handle different signatures like this as you need.

Now, add this to your new handler function:

```
guard let index = entries.firstIndex(where: { $0.id == id })
else {
  return completion(nil, .notFound)
}
completion(entries[index], nil)
```

This adds the logic needed to look up the journal entry matching the specified id and then trigger your completion handler. Take this for a spin!

Build and run your server, and then open http://localhost:8080/openapi/ui in your browser.

Just as you did previously, add a new entry via a POST request:

```
{
  "emoji": "😊",
  "date": 563725805.576615
}
```

You should see the following:

```
Server response

Code                Details
────────────────────────────────────────────────
201                 Response body
Undocumented
                    {
                      "id": "0",
                      "emoji": "😊",
                      "date": 563725805.576615
                    }                              [Download]

                    Response headers

                    connection: Keep-Alive
                    content-length: 51
                    content-type: application/json
                    date: Tue, 27 Nov 2018 11:24:47 GMT
                    keep-alive: timeout=60
```

Remember that for now, each time you restart your server all previous entries are cleared. Here, the `id` field in the response body is 0 since it's your first entry in the in-memory data store.

Now, POST a second entry to your server. This should be stored with an `id` of 1 using a different emoji and date, so that you have two total entries. For example:

```
{
  "emoji": "😎",
  "date": 558922021
}
```

Great! Now, retrieve one of the entries you've just added.

Open the GET route with the signature /entries/{id}. Click **Try it out** to inspect the route:

Enter 0 in the `id` field and click **Execute**. You'll see the first journal entry you entered. Nice!

GET   `/entries/{id}`

Parameters   Cancel

Name   Description

id * required
string   0
(path)

| **Execute** | Clear |

Responses   Response content type   **application/json**   ⌄

Curl
```
curl -X GET "http://localhost:8080/entries/0" -H "accept: application/json"
```

Request URL
```
http://localhost:8080/entries/0
```

Server response

Code   Details

200
                   Response body
                   ```
                   {
                       "id": "0",
                       "emoji": "😊",
                       "date": 563725805.576615
                   }
                   ```
                                                              Download

---

Retrieving filtered results

Now, it's time to meet a new protocol called `QueryParams`.

Currently your GET API will retrieve all the entries stored in your EmojiJournalServer. For a small number of entries, this may not be a problem. But as your EmojiJournal grows, this will eventually result in a very large set of data.

In RESTful APIs, it's possible to use URL-encoded query parameters to more easily work with groups of resources. In Chapter 3, you learned that the following URLs could be used to work with GET requests:

```
/entries
/entries?emoji=<emoji>&date=<date>
/entries/<identifier>
```

Say you want to find all entries that contain a certain emoji. To do that, you'd use a route like this, entering the desired target emoji into the <emoji> placeholder:

```
/entries?emoji=<emoji>
```

Logically, this is a different type of search than when you previously retrieved a single entry matching an `id`. Because `id` is a primary key, you could formally guarantee that either zero or one entries will match a given `id` value you passed to your route.

With emojis, however, users are free to assign any value they like — whether it's been used previously or not. This means that, for any given emoji, you might get back zero, one or several entries. For example, since your users will obviously be seriously thrilled with your EmojiJournal, you'll find oodles of entries containing the 💯 emoji!

This is where `QueryParams` offers a powerful way to filter results for you out of the box (but only when you need it to)! If you create a route hander that has a parameter type that conforms to `QueryParams`, Kitura's Codable Router will populate it from the URL query parameters in the incoming request. This provides a completely type-safe way of handling URL query parameters and delegating the verification of the fields to Kitura.

Back in Xcode, open **Sources/Application/Models/JournalEntry.swift**.

Add an import for `KituraContracts` beneath the existing `Foundation` import:

```
import KituraContracts
```

Now, create a `JournalEntryParams` struct that conforms to `QueryParams`, like this:

```
struct JournalEntryParams: QueryParams {
  var emoji: String?
}
```

Notice that you've made the sole property optional. You've done this because as your project grows, you may want to add — and filter by — more properties than just `emoji`. By making these properties optional, you pave the way for flexible future searches that are able to flexibly combine (or omit) combinations of these properties however you'd like.

Now, open **EntryRoutes.swift** and locate the function `getAllEntries`. Replace the entire function with this:

```
func getEntries(params: JournalEntryParams?, completion:
  @escaping ([JournalEntry]?, RequestError?) -> Void) -> Void {
}
```

Since the `JournalEntryQuery` parameter here is an Optional, your route handler will support *both* of the following URLs:

```
/entries
/entries?emoji=<emoji>
```

Next, locate `initializeEntryRoutes` where you register your routes. Update your GET route's registration in the first line of this function to this:

```
app.router.get("/entries", handler: getEntries)
```

So far so good: You've stubbed out and registered a new handler function. But now you'll need to address a small *gotcha*.

Consider that in the getEntries handler function you just refactored, you made
JournalEntryParams optional to enable users to flexibly search on optional
parameters. Unfortunately, this came with a side effect: This route won't work now if
you just want to get all entries, because if your parameters are nil no entries will be
found. Time to fix this.

Add this at the top of your new getEntries function:

```
guard let params = params else {
  return completion(entries, nil)
}
```

This code makes sure that if no parameters are present, the guard statement will be invoked and will send off the full array of entries in the response.

You may note that this is one of those rare cases when a guard statement acts more like a variant of if/then, rather than guarding against an error condition *per se*.

Now, complete your function by adding this:

```
let filteredEntries
  = entries.filter { $0.emoji == params.emoji }
completion(filteredEntries, nil)
```

Using some nifty Swifty moves, you search for entries matching the emoji passed in and call your completion handler to send off your filtered entries — and you're done!

Build and run your server.

Then in your browser, navigate to http://localhost:8080/openapi/ui. As before, your web app opens with a clean slate. Create a couple of new entries using your POST route, making sure to assign each a different emoji.

Now open the GET route *not* containing {id} in its signature.

Click **Try it out** and then **Execute** to see all your entries (the specific values you see will of course be those you just entered):

Now, take your spiffy emoji filtering capabilities for a spin! In this same route, enter the emoji of one of the entries you just created into the GET route's emoji field, then click **Execute** once again. This time, you should see only entries matching this emoji. Ta da!

Examining your latest OpenAPI specification

Still in your browser, navigate to http://localhost:8080/openapi. Scroll down to the node inside paths to look at the information in your spec about the get route, and notice the parameters node:

```
"parameters" : [
  {
    "in" : "query",
    "name" : "emoji",
    "required" : false,
    "type" : "string"
  }
]
```

This is how your JournalEntryParams object translates to the OpenAPI specification. Do you remember how you defined your params object as optional in this function's signature? KituraOpenAPI automatically carries this kind of information directly to your specification. In this case, because this is an optional property in code, required is automatically set to false in the specification. Your route now gracefully handles nil parameters *and* emoji values, doing exactly what you want in both cases. Sweet!

As mentioned previously, periodically checking out this specification as you develop an app is a really great way to see and understand the interrelationship between your live routing code and your API specification.

Build and run your server one more time, and leave it running on your machine for the remainder of this chapter.

Updating your iOS app

Now, it's time to beef up your mobile client to take advantage of your server's spiffy new powers. If you have the mobile app from the previous chapter, you'll still need to copy the version from the starter directory for this chapter. There are a few changes that you'll need.

Open **EmojiJournalMobileApp.xcodeproj** in Xcode. You're going to use Xcode's built-in Swift Package Manager integration to add KituraKit to your mobile app! Click the `File` menu option, then select the `Swift Packages` menu and choose `Add Package Dependency...`:

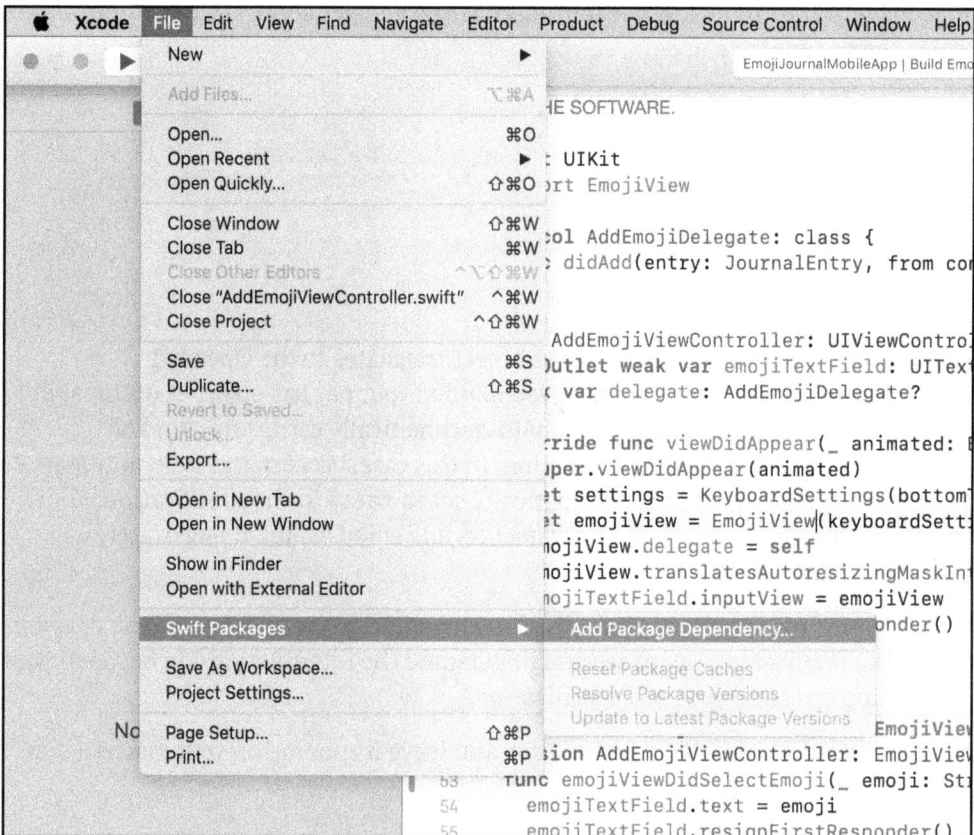

Next, enter the following repository URL in the text field prompt:

```
https://github.com/IBM-Swift/KituraKit.git
```

After Xcode verifies the link, you'll be presented with a dialog like this:

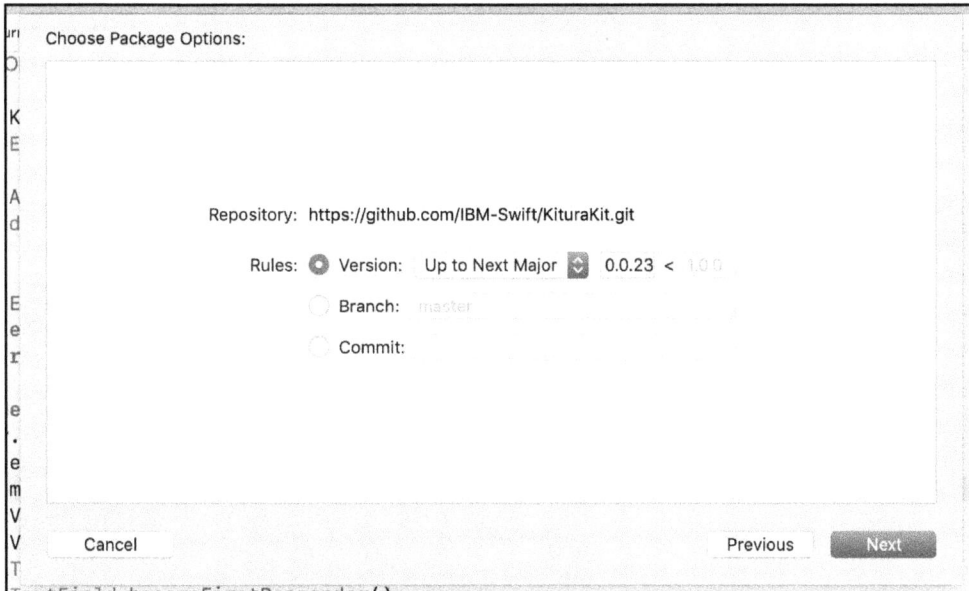

Select Exact from the menu, enter version 0.0.23 if it's not already auto-filled for you, and click Next. Xcode will now clone and build all the dependencies that KituraKit requires. Once it's done, you'll see this dialog:

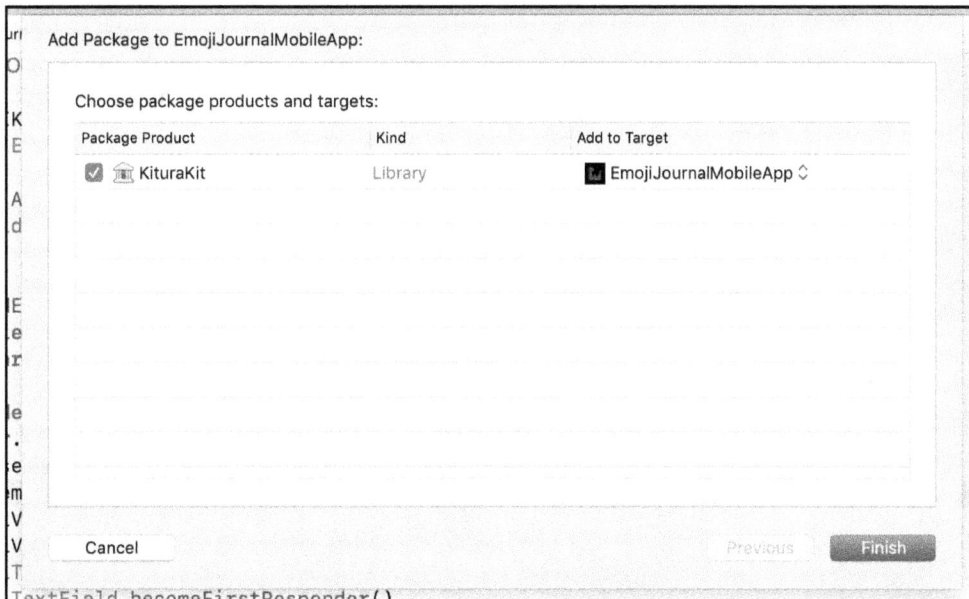

Click `Finish`. Xcode has automatically added KituraKit to your project for you — no need for a Workspace file, or even an `xcodeproj` file for that matter!

Open **EmojiJournalMobileApp/Model/EmojiClient.swift**. You'll work with this file for the duration of this chapter.

At the top of this file, add the following lines of code directly beneath `import UIKit`:

```
import KituraKit
import KituraContracts
```

Next, locate the following set of methods:

- `static func getAll(completion: @escaping (_ entries: [JournalEntry]?, _ error: EmojiClientError?) -> Void)`

- `static func get(id: String, completion: @escaping (_ entry: JournalEntry?, _ error: EmojiClientError?) -> Void)`

- `static func get(emoji: String, completion: @escaping (_ entries: [JournalEntry]?, _ error: EmojiClientError?) -> Void)`

- `static func add(entry: JournalEntry, completion: @escaping (_ entry: JournalEntry?, _ error: EmojiClientError?) -> Void)`

- `static func update(entry: JournalEntry, completion: @escaping (_ entry: JournalEntry?, _ error: EmojiClientError?) -> Void)`

Replace the contents of *each* of these methods with this:

```
guard let client = KituraKit(baseURL: baseURL) else {
  return completion(nil, .couldNotCreateClient)
}
```

Then, locate the `delete` method, and replace its contents with:

```
guard let client = KituraKit(baseURL: baseURL) else {
  return completion(.couldNotCreateClient)
}
```

Here's what you've just done: `KituraKit` provides the ability to set a `default` URL at runtime. But, in this project, you'll take this functionality on yourself. When needed, each of your routes will redirect users to a URL stored in a `static var` named `baseURL`.

As you'll see later on, this will come in especially handy when you deploy your app to the live internet!

Retrieving your journal entries on iOS

Scroll to your `getAll` method and add the following after your client declaration:

```
client.get("/entries") {
  (entries: [JournalEntry]?, error: RequestError?) in
  DispatchQueue.main.async {
    if error != nil {
      completion(nil, .couldNotLoadEntries)
    } else {
      completion(entries, nil)
    }
  }
}
```

Go ahead — do a double take! You just wrote a function for your network layer in an iOS app without referring to JSON at all! You worked directly with a clean native object — and, even better, it's the exact same object you're using on your server!

Build and run your app.

You'll notice that the previous error message goes away. If you want to cheat a little, add a couple of journal entries via the API Explorer, then refresh your iOS app's UI, reveling in the live data you'll see. Woot!

Adding a new entry on iOS

Scroll down to your add method and add the following code snippet after your client declaration:

```
client.post("/entries", data: entry) {
  (newEntry: JournalEntry?, error: RequestError?) in
  DispatchQueue.main.async {
    if error != nil {
      completion(nil, .couldNotAdd(entry))
    } else {
      completion(entry, nil)
    }
  }
}
```

Notice that, once again, even though you're working with fresh incoming data, you *still* don't have to work with JSON!

Build and run your app. Once your app launches, tap the + button in its upper right-hand corner.

You should see a view controller that looks like so:

Save the emoji, then look at your updated UI! Now you're cookin' with gas!

Filtering GET requests on iOS

Now, you'll update your two filtered GET calls. Scroll to the get(id:completion) method and add this after your client declaration:

```
client.get("/entries", identifier: id) {
  (entry: JournalEntry?, error: RequestError?) in
  DispatchQueue.main.async {
    if error != nil {
      completion(nil, .couldNotLoadEntryWithID(id))
    } else {
      completion(entry, nil)
    }
  }
}
```

Notice that in the same way that Codable Routing automatically handled your identifier as a parameter for your server's routes earlier in this chapter, KituraKit now stands ready to handle identifiers in your client app requests as well!

Locate the extension of UIApplication at the top of the file. Underneath this, add:

```
public struct JournalEntryParams: QueryParams {
  let emoji: String?
}
```

If this feels familiar from earlier in this chapter, you're paying attention! You'll make immediate use of this now.

Scroll down to the get(emoji:completion) method and add the following beneath the client declaration:

```
let query = JournalEntryParams(emoji: emoji)
client.get("/entries", query: query) {
  (entries: [JournalEntry]?, error: RequestError?) in
  DispatchQueue.main.async {
    if error != nil {
      completion(nil, .couldNotLoadEntryWithEmoji(emoji))
    } else {
      completion(entries, nil)
    }
  }
}
```

This should look very similar to what you've been adding to each method so far, with these distinctions:

1. Creating your `JournalEntryParams` struct is as simple as adding a single parameter in a struct initializer.

2. KituraKit provides an overload on `get` that allows you to include a `QueryParams` object. KituraKit will try to encode any `QueryParams` into your request, even if they are ultimately `nil`.

Build and run your app. Within the app, tap the Search icon in the upper left-hand corner, and experiment with the controls. All the hard work you've done with your server routes is really paying off now!

You can search for a single entry with a given `id`, or get all entries with a certain emoji, like so:

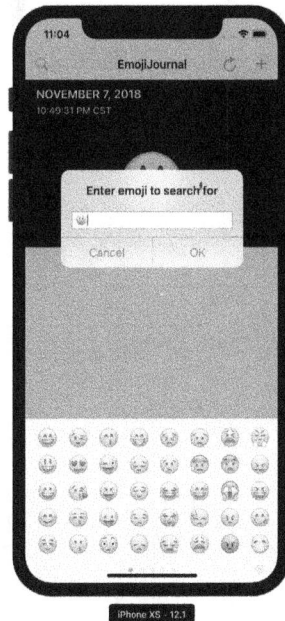

Nice work! Now try swiping one of your journal entry table view cells to the left. You'll notice that you have two options to edit a cell:

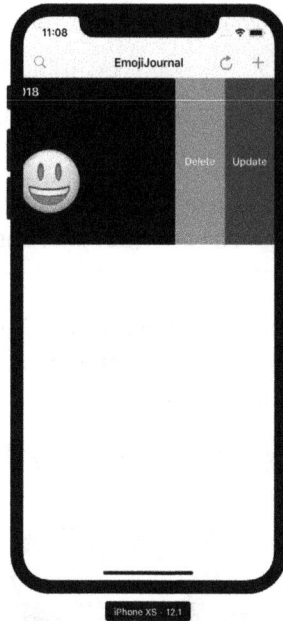

These don't do anything yet, so now you'll wire up this functionality.

Updating a journal entry on iOS

Back in Xcode once again, scroll to your `update` method. Add the following below the client declaration:

```
guard let identifier = entry.id else {
  return completion(nil, .couldNotUpdate(entry))
}
client.put("/entries", identifier: identifier, data: entry) {
  (updated: JournalEntry?, error: RequestError?) in
  DispatchQueue.main.async {
    if error != nil {
      completion(nil, .couldNotUpdate(entry))
    } else {
      completion(updated, nil)
    }
  }
}
```

Here's what's new in this code: As you may recall, you made your `JournalEntry`'s `id` property optional, and this means it's formally acceptable for an incoming request *not* to contain an `id`. But in practice, you only want to update the `JournalEntry` matching an incoming `id`.

- The guard statement you just added makes sure you only perform the update if this is the case.

- With this handled, the remaining code performs the update.

- You might also note that the PUT method's parameters are a combination of those you've recently seen when calling your GET and POST functions.

Build and run again. Swipe a journal entry to the left, tap the **Update** action, then choose a new emoji and save it. When you return to the main UI, it should now be updated! Huzzah!

Emotions are fleeting, and you need to be able to wipe the slate clean if you don't want your friends to know how you felt after all of this, so now you'll implement the final network call for this chapter.

Deleting a journal entry from the iOS app

In Xcode, scroll to your `delete` method, and add this underneath the client declaration:

```
guard let identifier = entry.id else {
  return completion(.couldNotCreateClient)
}
client.delete("/entries", identifier: identifier) {
  (error: RequestError?) in
  DispatchQueue.main.async {
    if error != nil {
      completion(.couldNotDelete(entry))
    } else {
      completion(nil)
    }
  }
}
```

Just like in your PUT request, you once again ensure that the incoming `id` isn't nil. With this done, you perform the delete function similarly to what you've previously done.

Build and run your app.

Once your iOS app launches, pick a journal entry and swipe left to delete it. Eureka!

You *may* still see some unexpected behavior, but no worries! You're quickly getting the hang of this stuff, and in the *next* chapter, you'll clean up any glitches.

Where to go from here?

You can download the finished projects in the accompanying project files for this chapter. In the next chapter, you'll learn about PostgreSQL, and use it to replace that pesky temporary `dataStore` you've been working with so far with a production database built for the real world!

Chapter 8:
SwiftKueryORM

Chris Bailey

An Object Relational Mapping (ORM) tool is designed to simplify the task of persisting data to and retrieving it from a datastore.

SwiftKueryORM lets you do just this. It enables you to store your Swift types directly in a relational database using a native, high-level API. This lets you focus on app code without having to worry about low-level database implementation details or needing to craft SQL queries to perform low-level operations on raw database records.

Even better, enabling Swift-Kuery-ORM on one of your data structs or classes is straightforward. You simply conform your data type to the Model protocol. No additional code is required. Swift-Kuery-ORM then automatically generates a table schema for you and from then on does everything needed to enable you to save, fetch, update and delete directly by calling methods on your Swift type.

In this chapter, you'll learn:

- How to enable your types for SwiftKueryORM.

- How to create, fetch and delete entries.

- How to apply filters to requests to fetch and delete entries.

In this chapter, you'll update your EmojiJournalServer to integrate SwiftKueryORM. You'll store `JournalEntry` objects in a PostgreSQL database, persist data across restarts and handle concurrent requests to add, update and delete entries.

SwiftKueryORM and the Model protocol

Codable Routing integrates Swift's `Codable` protocol into Kitura's router. This facilitates the conversion of data between native Swift types within your apps and the encoded body data in HTTP requests and responses.

This is possible because `Codable` exposes information about the names and types of fields inside the `Codable` class or struct. An `Encoder` can encode these native types and fields into a given transport format such as JSON. Conversely, a `Decoder` can convert raw encoded data from a given transport format back into native classes or structs.

For example, in Chapter 4, you saw how an instance of an `Animal` struct was created for **Baloo**:

```
public struct Animal: Codable {
  var name: String
  var age: Int
  var friendly: Bool
}

let baloo = Animal(name: "Baloo", age: 5, friendly: true)
```

This was encoded to JSON:

```
{"name":"Baloo","age":5,"friendly":true}
```

And then it was decoded back to an instance of `Animal` once again completing its round trip from native type to JSON and back again.

SwiftKueryORM's `Model` protocol relies heavily on the `Codable` protocol. Most importantly, it leverages `Codable` capabilities to:

1. Interrogate object names and field types to create database tables with fields of corresponding names and types.

2. Encode objects to create SQL queries to store, fetch, update and delete its entries.

3. Create objects to decode the results of database queries into instances of that type.

For example, the following SQL could be used to create a PostgreSQL table representing the Animal type using all of the information that you know about the type itself:

```
CREATE TABLE animal (
  name VARCHAR (255) NOT NULL,
  age INTEGER NOT NULL,
  friendly BOOLEAN NOT NULL,
);
```

This SQL query creates a table mapping directly to information about the Animal type that can be gained from Codable:

- The name column is non-optional and accepts a string.

- The age column is non-optional and accepts an integer.

- The friendly column is non-optional and accepts a Boolean.

Since the database's column types directly map to Animal, type-safety is maintained between the underlying database and your app's Swift types.

Similarly, the following SQL query could be used to store your Baloo instance in a PostgreSQL database:

```
INSERT into animal (name, age, friendly) VALUES ('Baloo', 5,
true)
```

Notice that this query contains the same information found in the JSON encoded form of the Baloo instance.

Likewise, the result of a SQL query is a set of field names and values, which can therefore be decoded to an instance. For example, the result of a SQL query to the database for a Baloo instance might look like:

```
name, age, friendly
"Baloo",5,true
```

This provides all of the information required to convert the SQL result into a native instance of Animal.

Essentially, by conforming a data struct or class in your Kitura app to Model — implicitly conforming it to Codable — SwiftKueryORM is able to use custom encoders and decoders to convert back and forth between your native Swift data types and raw SQL queries and results on your behalf.

There's one last benefit you get by doing this: Conforming to the Model protocol adds several helpful methods that come in handy for common persistence tasks. Among others, these include `createTable()`, `save()`, `delete()` and `find()`.

Enabling SwiftKueryORM in your EmojiJournalServer project

Time to put this theory into practice! You'll now use SwiftKueryORM to save your EmojiJournalServer data to a PostgreSQL database. To do this, you'll update your EmojiJournalServer project to include two new dependencies: `Swift-Kuery-ORM` and `Swift-Kuery-PostgreSQL`, which will act as connector to PostgreSQL.

Open **Package.swift** in Xcode and append these two new items to your package's `dependencies` array:

```
.package(
  url: "https://github.com/IBM-Swift/Swift-Kuery-ORM",
  from: "0.6.0"),
.package(
  url: "https://github.com/IBM-Swift/Swift-Kuery-PostgreSQL",
  from: "2.1.1"),
```

Next, within your `targets` array, append "SwiftKueryPostgreSQL" and "SwiftKueryORM" to the array of Application targets, so that your **Application** `.target` looks like this:

```
.target(name: "Application", dependencies: ["Kitura",
"CloudEnvironment", "SwiftMetrics", "Health", "KituraOpenAPI",
"SwiftKueryPostgreSQL", "SwiftKueryORM"]),
```

Save your changes to Package.swift.

Installing PostgreSQL

Now, it's time to install PostgreSQL. You'll use Homebrew to do this.

> **Note:** If you didn't install Homebrew earlier in this book, you'll need to do so now via the instructions at http://brew.sh, before you can proceed with this section.

In Terminal, execute these commands:

```
brew install postgresql
brew services start postgresql
```

The first of command installs PostrgreSQL on your Mac, while the second registers it as a background service that will automatically start whenever your restart your Mac.

> **Note:** If you'd like to stop PostrgreSQL from automatically starting when your Mac restarts, you can later run `brew services stop postgresql`. Similarly, if you'd like to remove PostgreSQL entirely at a later time, you can run `brew uninstall postgresql` at that time.

Now that you've installed and started PostgreSQL, you'll need to create a new database under the `postgres` user for your app to use. Execute this command to do this:

```
createuser postgres
createdb -O postgres emojijournal
```

Nice! You've added SwiftKueryORM and SwiftKueryPostgreSQL dependencies to your project, PostgreSQL is up and running and you've created a shiny new database ready and waiting to persist your app data. Now you can start integrated these tools into your EmojiJournalServer app!

Connecting SwiftKueryORM to PostgreSQL

Open your EmojiJournalServer project in Xcode.

Select the **Sources/Application/Models** group and create a new file with in it named **Persistence.swift**, making sure this is added to the **Application** target.

Replace the file's default contents with:

```
import Foundation
import SwiftKueryORM
import SwiftKueryPostgreSQL
import LoggerAPI
```

Next, add a `Persistence` class:

```
class Persistence {
  static func setUp() {
  }
}
```

SwiftKueryPostgreSQL provides the `PostgreSQLConnection` API for creating connections to a PostgreSQL database. The API gives you a choice of either creating a single connection using `PostgreSQLConnection` or creating a pool of reusable connections using `PostgreSQLConnection.createPool`. Since your EmojiJournalServer will need to handle concurrent requests, you'll choose `createPool`.

Both the `PostgreSQLConnection` constructor and the `createPool` method accept `host`, `port` and `options` parameters. The `options` parameter takes a set of `ConnectionOptions` that define key properties such as database name, username and password. Additionally, `createPool` provides an additional `poolOptions` parameter. This defines a set of `ConnectionPoolOptions` that include initial capacity and max capacity for each connection.

Add the following code to your `setUp()` method:

```
let pool = PostgreSQLConnection.createPool(
  host: ProcessInfo.processInfo.environment["DBHOST"]
    ?? "localhost",
  port: 5432,
  options:
    [.databaseName("emojijournal"),
     .userName(ProcessInfo.processInfo.environment["DBUSER"]
```

```
            ?? "postgres"),
        .password(ProcessInfo.processInfo.environment["DBPASSWORD"]
            ?? "nil"),
    ],
   poolOptions: ConnectionPoolOptions(initialCapacity: 10,
      maxCapacity: 50)
)
```

This code creates a connection pool with an initial capacity of 10 connections and a maximum capacity of 50 connections. Notice that host value is set to localhost by default but can be overridden using the "DBHOST" environment variable. Likewise, userName and password each have default values that may similarly be overridden. You'll later use these environment variables to override pool defaults when you deploy using Docker and Kubernetes. Last, note that your connection uses a database name of emojijournal, matching what you set up in the previous section.

Now append this to setUp():

```
Database.default = Database(pool)
```

By doing this, you've made your emojijournal database SwiftKueryORM's default. This means that unless your specify an alternative connection, any request to store, retrieve or delete Model objects will use this database. Finally, append the following code to complete this method (this will raise Xcode errors for now):

```
do {
  try JournalEntry.createTableSync()
} catch let error {
  // Database table already exists
  if let requestError = error as? RequestError,
    requestError.rawValue ==
      RequestError.ormQueryError.rawValue {
        Log.info(
          "Table \(JournalEntry.tableName) already exists")
  } else {
    Log.error("Database connection error: " +
      "\(String(describing: error))")
  }
}
```

This creates a table for your JournalEntry model. It also catches any errors, intelligently filtering trivial errors, such as if the table already exists.

Now open **Sources/Application/Application.swift** and locate your init() method. Append the following to it:

```
Persistence.setUp()
```

This causes your new database connection to be initialized along with your struct.

Making your JournalEntry conform to Model

Your existing data struct won't yet work with KueryORM. You'll fix that now.

The only thing you need to do to make your data classes or structs work with SwiftKueryORM is conform them to Model. As you now know, this implicitly conforms them to Swift's Codable as well, and means that your data types must be conformable to Codable if they aren't already.

Happily, your `JournalEntry` struct already conforms to `Codable`, so doing this will be nice and simple!

Open **JournalEntry.swift** (located in **Sources/Application/Models**).

At the top of the file, add an import for `SwiftKueryORM` after your existing import statements:

```
import SwiftKueryORM
```

Now, change `JournalEntry`'s conformance from `Codable` to `Model`, like so:

```
struct JournalEntry: Model {
```

Simply by conforming `JournalEntry` to `Model`, you've gained access to the full power of SwiftKueryORM. `JournalEntry` is now ready to be persisted to your shiny new `emojijournal` Postgres database!

Saving, fetching and deleting JournalEntry instances

Now, it's time to replace your current in-memory array and update your routes to leverage the power of SwiftKueryORM.

Open **EntryRoutes.swift** (in **Sources/Application/Routes**).

Take note of your addEntry method. Right now it looks like this:

```
func addEntry(entry: JournalEntry, completion:
  @escaping (JournalEntry?, RequestError?) -> Void) {
    var storedEntry = entry
    storedEntry.id = entries.count.value
    entries.append(storedEntry)
    completion(storedEntry, nil)
}
```

Right now, this method is designed to work with the in-memory array you created earlier. As you've seen, this approach has several major limitations that would readily fail in production. For example, you want the id field to be unique, but when entries are deleted and then new ones are added, entries.count won't produce a unique value. It's time to make those go away!

Replace your addEntry route handler with the following:

```
func addEntry(entry: JournalEntry, completion:
  @escaping (JournalEntry?, RequestError?) -> Void) {
    var savedEntry = entry
    savedEntry.id = UUID().uuidString
    savedEntry.save(completion)
}
```

With this new code, you replace your previous reliance on the in-memory array with code that leverages your new database. Note that in doing so, you now use Foundation's UUID struct to create a unique ID for each entry. You then save your entry to the database, passing in a completion handler. Let's unpack this last one a bit further:

The save method you just used came along when you conformed JournalEntry to Model. This method takes a completion handler parameter that gets called with either the saved entry or a database error. By design, this completion handler's signature matches that of the completion handler passed into your addEntry route handler. The payoff is that this handler can be passed down to the database call itself, so that the route handler can then respond directly when it gets a response back from the database.

Once again, you've made very few code changes. Your route handler now stores JournalEntry instances in the database and once again, KueryORM takes care of all the heavy lifting for you.

Next up is your getEntries method. This method needs to handle two distinct scenarios:

1. Return *all* entries.

2. Return a subset of entries (if the request `params` contains an `emoji`).

Once again, KueryORM gives you the tools to make handling both these scenarios clear and straightforward.

First, getting all records is as easy as using `Model`'s static `findAll` method, which also takes a completion handler matching the one passed in to `getEntries`, like so: `JournalEntry.findAll(completion)`. That nicely handles your first requirement.

In the second case, the incoming request will contain a target `emoji` in `params`, and, instead of fetching all records, you'll need to retrieve just the ones targeted (or none at all if no record's `emoji` matches).

SwiftKueryORM provides a clean solution for this case as well. Back when you created your `JournalEntryParams` type, you conformed it to the `QueryParams` protocol. `QueryParams` is aptly named: It's designed to be used both as URL-encoded parameters within RESTful APIs *and* within database queries.

This versatile design means that `params` can be passed directly into KueryORM, just as the completion handler is. This allows the provided completion handler to be called with either the full `entries` array when returning all entries or the `filteredEntries` that contain only matching entries.

Replace your existing `getEntries` method with this:

```
func getEntries(query: JournalEntryParams?, completion:
  @escaping ([JournalEntry]?, RequestError?) -> Void) -> Void {
    JournalEntry.findAll(matching: query, completion)
}
```

Since we've covered the basics, you'll now quickly update your remaining routes. Replace your current `deleteEntry`, `modifyEntry` and `getOneEntry` with the following:

```
func deleteEntry(id: String, completion:
  @escaping (RequestError?) -> Void) {
    JournalEntry.delete(id: id, completion)
}

func modifyEntry(id: String, entry: JournalEntry,
  completion: @escaping (JournalEntry?, RequestError?) -> Void)
{
    entry.update(id: id, completion)
}
```

```
func getOneEntry(id: String, completion:
  @escaping (JournalEntry?, RequestError?) -> Void) {
    JournalEntry.find(id: id, completion)
}
```

In each case, the parameters being passed into your handler method can be passed directly down to SwiftKueryORM, which leverages the appropriate `Model` method to satisfy the request.

Take a moment to enjoy a well-deserved sense of accomplishment! You've now updated all of your route handlers to work directly with a database through SwiftKueryORM. In the process, you've added persistence across restarts, robust concurrent data access, and significantly simplified your code.

Build and run your project.

> **Note**: In the process of development, sometimes you run into issues that require you to clean and rebuild. In Xcode you can do this using Command + Shift + K to clean the build folder.

Now, you'll take your updated RESTful API for a spin in KituraOpenAPI Explorer. Open a browser window to http://localhost:8080/openapi/ui.

Select the **POST /entries** row to expand it. In the upper `Parameters` section you're presented with the required **input (body)** parameter and given an example of the JSON data needed:

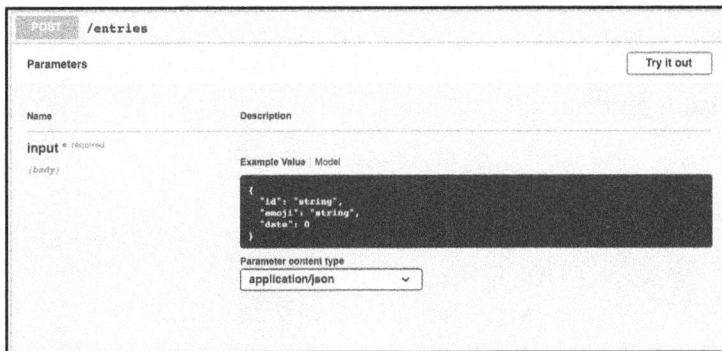

Now, click on the **Model** link; this can be hard to see because it's located to the right of the Example Value heading, just above the sample input data we just discussed. When you do, you'll see the following:

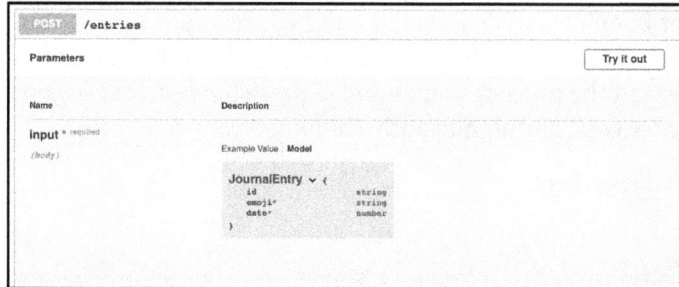

This shows that the emoji and date fields are required in the body data (since both are marked with *** required**), but that id is optional (it lacks the same *** required** mark).

Click the **Try it out** button in the upper-right corner of the route Parameters area. In the input area, enter the following body data:

```
{
   "emoji": "😂",
   "date": 563725805.57661498
}
```

Then click **Execute** (the blue button beneath the body input) to run the POST request and store your entry.

POST /entries

Parameters   Cancel

Name   Description

input * required
(body)   Edit Value Model

                              {
                                "emoji": "😀",
                                "date": 563725805.57661498
                              }

                              Cancel

                              Parameter content type
                              application/json   ⌄

Execute   Clear

This should result in a Server response with a Code of "201" and a Response body similar to the following (your id field won't match what's shown since you now assign a uniquely generated UUID as each record is created):

Next, scroll to the **GET /entries** row and click to expand it. You can see that this route accepts an optional **emoji** parameter (as you saw before, required parameters are marked with *** required**).

Earlier in this chapter, you set up this route to handle two cases. You'll first test how it functions when no **emoji** parameter is passed.

Click **Try it out** and then click **Execute**:

The Server response contains a Response body with an array containing the single entry you created a moment ago:

Now, you'll test the route's second form. Enter an **emoji** value of "😄" and once again click **Execute**:

Since your requested emoji matches the single entry stored in the database, your results will be the same as in the previous case.

Finally, repeat the same steps, this time with an **emoji** value of "😎":

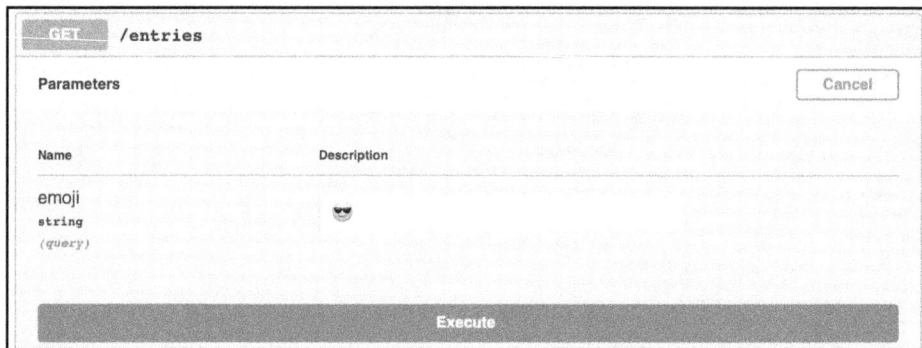

This time the server responds with a Code of "200", signifying success. Wait... what?

You might think that a request returning no matches would contain some kind of error response, but this is formally a successful response: Kitura searched the database as requested, found no matches, and it responded accordingly. The important result is the empty array that's returned this time, confirming that exactly as you'd expect, no matching entries were found for your search emoji.

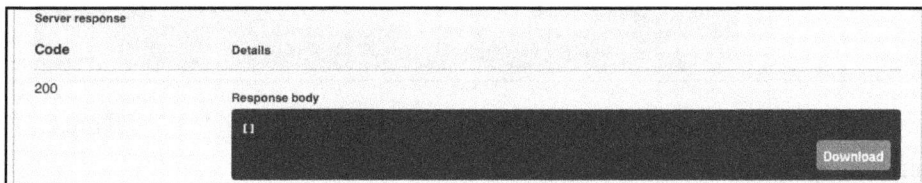

More complex database queries

As you've seen in this chapter, SwiftKueryORM makes it very easy to persist, fetch, update and delete objects from a database without having to work directly with the database or build SQL queries.

However, some apps will need to perform more complex tasks. Specifically, you'll sometimes want to be able to craft custom SQL queries. Kitura has you covered here as well.

SwiftKueryORM itself is built on a set of lower-level APIs from the SwiftKuery module — a library for building SQL queries in a type-safe manner. This means rather than creating a raw SQL query — an error-prone and potentially dangerous proposition — you can instead use native Swift tools to do this safely, with the compiler's help.

For example, instead of issuing this raw SQL:

```
SELECT id, emoji, date FROM journalentry WHERE emoji = "😄";
```

You could instead write this line of Swift:

```
let query = Select(entry.id, entry.emoji, entry.date,
    from: entries).where(entry.emoji = "😄")
```

Here's the really nice thing about this implementation: The methods added to your types when you conform them to Model use SwiftKuery in their implementations. This means that you can choose to override these methods with custom queries any time you have need to do so.

You get the convenience of SwiftKueryORM's convenience methods most of the time and the ability to easily drop down into SQL whenever the need arises!

Before continuing, return to Xcode and **stop** your server. You're doing this because, while your project runs in Xcode, it listens on port 8080. You'll need to have this port available for your Docker image to run in the next section (otherwise, attempts to run it would fail because of the port conflict).

Running on Linux in Docker

Up to this point, you've been able to build and run your EmojiJournalServer project in Docker whenever you'd like. Now that you've introduced PostgreSQL, you'll need to update your Dockerfile and Dockerfile-tools.

First, you'll need to install libpq-dev, a library Swift-Kuery-PostgreSQL needs to interact with the PostgreSQL database.

Open Finder or Terminal to the **EmojiServerJournal** directory. Open *both* **Dockerfile** and **Dockerfile-tools** in the text editor of your choice.

In *both* of these files, line 13 currently contains this identical text:

```
# RUN apt-get update && apt-get dist-upgrade -y
```

In *both* files. replace line 13 with:

```
RUN apt-get update && apt-get dist-upgrade -y && apt-get install
-y libpq-dev
```

This will run apt-get — the command line for the Linux OS' Advanced Package Tool (APT) — and ask it to update and then install libpq-dev.

The second change you'll make will be to update both these same files to configure your EmojiJournalServer with the location of your PostgreSQL instance.

You'll do this because apps running in Docker containers essentially appear to be running in their own machine. As a result, within a Docker context, connecting to localhost means connecting to itself. However, your PostgreSQL instance runs on your *machine's* (the host's) localhost, and not that of the Docker container. To resolve this, you need to configure your EmojiJournalServer to use a special address: host.docker.internal.

The good news is that when you set up your database connection, you had the forethought enable the database connection to be configured using environment variables:

```
let pool = PostgreSQLConnection.createPool(
  host: ProcessInfo.processInfo.environment["DBHOST"]
    ?? "localhost",
  port: 5432,
  options:
    [.databaseName("emojijournal"),
     .userName(ProcessInfo.processInfo.environment["DBUSER"]
       ?? "postgres"),
     .password(ProcessInfo.processInfo.environment["DBPASSWORD"]
       ?? "nil"),
    ],
  poolOptions: ConnectionPoolOptions(initialCapacity: 10,
    maxCapacity: 50)
)
```

Clever you! This makes addressing this issue in Docker a piece of cake, since environment variables can be easily set using Docker's ENV command.

Return to your **Dockerfile** and locate the comment # Command to start Swift application at line 26. Immediately before this, insert these two lines:

```
# Set the DHBOST environment variable to host.docker.internal
ENV DBHOST host.docker.internal
```

Save your changes to Dockerfile, and then return once again to **Dockerfile-tools**.

Append these lines to the very end of this file at lines 32 and 33:

```
# Set the DHBOST environment variable to host.docker.internal
ENV DBHOST host.docker.internal
```

Save your changes to Dockerfile-tools. Now you're ready to build your Docker image and run it in a Docker container.

Return to Terminal and execute these commands:

```
kitura build
kitura run
```

Once they've completed (it may take awhile to build and run your Docker container) you should see output similar to the following:

```
Logs for the emojijournalserver-swift-run container:
[2018-12-03T12:58:06.315Z] [WARNING]
[ConfigurationManager.swift:261 load(url:deserializerName:)]
Unable to load data from URL /swift-project/config/mappings.json
[2018-12-03T12:58:06.531Z] [INFO] [Persistence.swift:53 setUp()]
Table UserJournalEntrys already exists
[Mon Dec  3 12:58:06 2018]
com.ibm.diagnostics.healthcenter.loader INFO: Swift Application
Metrics
[2018-12-03T12:58:06.809Z] [INFO] [Metrics.swift:48
initializeMetrics(router:)] Initialized metrics.
[2018-12-03T12:58:06.817Z] [INFO] [EntryRoutes.swift:74
initializeEntryRoutes(app:)] Journal entry routes created
[2018-12-03T12:58:06.821Z] [INFO] [KituraOpenAPI.swift:62
addOpenAPI(to:with:)] Registered OpenAPI definition on /openapi
[2018-12-03T12:58:06.850Z] [INFO] [KituraOpenAPI.swift:105
addSwaggerUI(to:with:)] Registered SwaggerUI on /openapi/ui
[2018-12-03T12:58:06.851Z] [INFO] [HTTPServer.swift:195
listen(on:)] Listening on port 8080
```

This output demonstrates that the EmojiJournalServer project successfully loads and listen on port 8080. In short, you've successfully updated Docker to run with your new PostrgreSQL data store. Woo hoo!

Where to go from here?

Your EmojiJournalServer now provides a RESTful API for your clients, stores your data to a persistent database and provides scalability and resilience across restarts. You've made several major strides forward!

You're not done yet, however. At present, your EmojiJournalServer can still only be used effectively by a single user, since there's no way to link individual journal entries to specific users, and there's also no way of using authentication to control which entries each user can access and modify.

You'll address these issues in the next chapters as you add authentication and multi-user support to your project!

Chapter 9: Authentication

Chris Bailey

Authentication and authorization are used to identify and check access privileges for users of a system. Users are first authenticated by checking that their credentials match those in a data store or a data authentication server. Once authenticated, users can be checked for authorization to access specific resources and the level of privilege at which access is provided.

Your EmojiJournalServer currently has no authentication or authorization enabled, which means that any user can connect and create, fetch and delete journal entries.

In this chapter you'll learn:

- The different types of authentication.

- Kitura's middlewares and type-safe middlewares.

- How to add authentication to your routes.

By the end of this chapter, you'll have updated your EmojiJournalServer to be secure and enable only authenticated users to access data.

Types of authentication

Server apps can handle authentication in a variety of ways. Traditionally, users log in by providing a username and password. More recently, and with the rise of social networking, there is also delegated authentication through OAuth, in which your authentication request is delegated to an OAuth Provider such as Facebook, and federated authentication with protocols like OpenID Connect where IDs are linked.

Kitura provides the Kitura-Credentials framework (https://github.com/IBM-Swift/Kitura-Credentials), along with plugins for the framework for four different types of authentication:

- Kitura-CredentialsHTTP (https://github.com/IBM-Swift/Kitura-CredentialsHTTP)

- Kitura-CredentialsFacebook (https://github.com/IBM-Swift/Kitura-CredentialsFacebook)

- Kitura-CredentialsGoogle (https://github.com/IBM-Swift/Kitura-CredentialsGoogle)

- Kitura-CredentialsGitHub (https://github.com/IBM-Swift/Kitura-CredentialsGitHub)

There are also community-provided plugins, including CredentialsDropbox (https://github.com/crspybits/CredentialsDropbox), Kitura-CredentialsTwitter (https://github.com/jacobvanorder/Kitura-CredentialsTwitter) and Kitura-CredentialsLocal (https://github.com/NocturnalSolutions/Kitura-CredentialsLocal).

The Kitura-CredentialsHTTP plugin provides support for HTTP basic- and HTTP digest-based authentication, both of which transmit username and password information inside the HTTP headers of the request.

HTTP basic authentication

HTTP basic authentication is a very simple protocol for authentication: for every HTTP request of the server, the client transmits the username and the password for the user as a Base64 encoded value in the Authorization header of the request. The server then validates the request by checking if the client's username and password match the server's version.

The simplicity of HTTP basic authentication makes it very easy to use. However, its simplicity also means that it is only weakly secure. The primary weakness is that protocol does not provide any real privacy or authentication for the transmitted credentials as the username and password are only Base64 encoded. This means that any "man-in-the-middle" attack that intercepts the HTTP request could gain access to those details.

HTTP digest authentication

Digest authentication is an extension of basic authentication that transmits the password details using an MD5 hash of the password. The hash is one-way, meaning that although it is easy to generate the hash, it is very difficult to reverse the process and generate the original password from the hash.

The authentication process is however more complex. When the client makes a request of the server, the server responds with a request to authenticate and provides two values: a random value called a nonce and a string representing the "realm." The client then repeats the request with a hash value generated using the username, realm, password and nonce values. The server then validates the hash using its own generated version of the hash.

OAuth authentication: Facebook, GitHub, Google and more

While HTTP basic and digest methods ask the server to validate the username and password details itself, OAuth provides a mechanism to delegate authentication to a third-party provider. Here the client is typically responsible for carrying out authentication with the third-party provider and obtaining a token which is then added to HTTP requests of the server through a HTTP header. The server then contacts the third-party provider itself to verify that the token it has been provided is valid.

For example, in the case of Facebook, the client needs to set the X-token-type header to FacebookToken and then set the access_token header with the client's Facebook token.

Authentication for your EmojiJournalServer

For EmojiJournalServer you'll use the most straight-forward form of authentication — HTTP basic — in order to show the concepts.

Once you've added HTTP basic authentication to your server using the Kitura-Credentials framework and the Kitura-CredentialsHTTP plugin, you will be able to see how it's possible to switch to another authentication type without any major changes to your app code.

This is because Kitura-Credentials uses the middleware capability in Kitura.

Middlewares are essentially functions that run *in the middle* between a client request and your handler function. Middleware functions have access to the `RouterRequest` and `RouterResponse` objects and are generally used to carry out tasks that are common across multiple route handlers and/or RESTful APIs — such as user authentication for requests.

Similar to the availability of Raw and Codable forms of routing with the Codable form being type-safe, there are Router and Type-Safe forms of middlewares.

Router middlewares

Router middlewares are those that conform to the `RouterMiddleware` protocol, which requires them to implement the following method:

```
func handle(request: RouterRequest, response: RouterResponse,
    next: @escaping () -> Void) throws
```

These have full access to read and modify the `RouterRequest` and `RouterResponse`. They have the ability to redirect requests, complete responses, or to call the passed in `next()` function to allow your handler function to run.

Router middlewares then need to be registered against the routes, for which they will be called. This is done in a very similar way to the registration of normal route handlers. For example, the following code registers a `RouterMiddleware` called `authentication` to be used for all HTTP methods calling the `/entries` URL:

```
router.all("/entries", middleware: authentication)
```

Router middlewares work well in instances in which the use of the middleware is independent of the router handler, with no data or types created by the middleware being used by the route handler.

By contrast, type-safe middlewares conform to the `TypeSafeMiddleware` protocol:

```
static func handle(request: RouterRequest,
    response: RouterResponse,
    completion: @escaping (Self?, RequestError?) -> Void) -> Void
```

This again requires an implementation of a `handle` method. The method is very similar to the one in the `RouterMiddleware` protocol, but with one crucial difference: The `handle` method in `TypeSafeMiddleware` expects the method to call the completion handler with either an error or an instance of `Self`.

Type-safe middlewares are therefore designed to be used when they create data that the handler function is going to use — the instance of Self. Additionally, type-safe middlewares do not need to be explicitly registered against a route — they are implicitly registered to run when a route handler includes a parameter with the type of the type-safe middleware.

To show the difference between the two, you'll first add HTTP basic authentication as a router middleware before implementing the same function using a type-safe middeware.

HTTP basic Authentication using RouterMiddleware

To add HTTP based authentication to your EmojiJournalServer, first add a dependency on the Kitura-CredentialsHTTP package to your project.

Open your **Package.swift** file and add the following to the array of dependencies for the Package:

```
.package(url:
  "https://github.com/IBM-Swift/Kitura-CredentialsHTTP.git",
  from: "2.1.3"),
```

Next, add "CredentialsHTTP" to the dependencies array for the Application target so the target contains the following:

```
.target(name: "Application", dependencies: ["Kitura",
"CloudEnvironment", "SwiftMetrics", "Health", "KituraOpenAPI",
"SwiftKueryPostgreSQL", "SwiftKueryORM", "CredentialsHTTP"]),
```

Now save your Package.swift file, which will cause Xcode to fetch and process the new dependency.

Next, open **Sources/Application/Application.swift**. Here you will add the Credentials framework along with the CredentialsHTTP plugin into your project in order to create a middleware for your routes.

Start by adding the following `import` statements to the list of imports at the top of your file:

```
import Credentials
import CredentialsHTTP
```

Next, create a method called `initializeBasicAuth` that takes an instance of App as a parameter and add a constant instance of `Credentials`:

```
func initializeBasicAuth(app: App) {
    let credentials = Credentials()
}
```

`Credentials` already conforms to `RouterMiddeware`, providing an implementation of the `handle` method. This method checks its registered plugins to see if any of them can authenticate the incoming request. As your `credentials` instance has no plugins registered, no authorization is currently enabled.

Add the following code below your `credentials` constant:

```
// 1
let basicCredentials = CredentialsHTTPBasic(verifyPassword:
    { username, password, callback in

    // 2
    if let storedPassword = authenticate[username],
        storedPassword == password {

        // 3
        callback(UserProfile(id: username, displayName: username,
            provider: "HTTPBasic"))

    } else {

        // 4
        callback(nil)
    }
})

// 5
credentials.register(plugin: basicCredentials)
```

With this code, you:

1. Create an instance of `CredentialsHTTPBasic`, which takes a single parameter — an implementation of a `verifyPassword`.

2. Check if the password matches a stored password for the user.

3. Invoke the `callback` with a valid `UserProfile`.

4. In the case of a failure, invoke the `callback` with `nil`.

5. Finally, register the plugin with the `credentials` instance.

The `verifyPassword` implementation above does a simple lookup from a dictionary of users and passwords. Go ahead and add this dictionary to the top the `initializeBasicAuth` method to use:

```
let authenticate = ["John": "12345", "Mary": "ABCDE"]
```

This defines two users, John and Mary, whose passwords are 12345 and ABCDE respectively.

Finally, at the end of the method, register the `credentials` instance as a middleware for all HTTP method calls on `/entries`:

```
app.router.all("/entries", middleware: credentials)
```

Your overall `initializeBasicAuth` method should now look as follows:

```
func initializeBasicAuth(app: App) {
  let credentials = Credentials()

  let authenticate = ["John": "12345", "Mary": "ABCDE"]

  let basicCredentials = CredentialsHTTPBasic(verifyPassword:
    { username, password, callback in

    if let storedPassword = authenticate[username],
      storedPassword == password {
      callback(UserProfile(id: username, displayName: username,
        provider: "HTTPBasic"))
    } else {
      callback(nil)
    }
  })

  credentials.register(plugin: basicCredentials)
  app.router.all("/entries", middleware: credentials)
}
```

This short method now enables HTTP basic authentication for all of your RESTful APIs on `/entries`.

Before you can build and run, you need to make sure this setup method is called. Update the postInit() function in the App class to call it just after the other initialize functions:

```
initializeBasicAuth(app: self)
```

Build and run your project.

Using the Kitura OpenAPI UI, located at http://localhost:8080/openapi/ui, select the **GET /entries** row and click on the **Try it out** button:

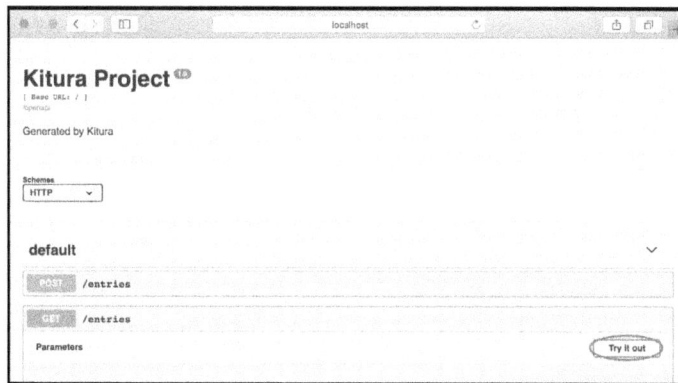

Next, click the **Execute** button to request all stored entries from your EmojiJournalServer. Previously, this returned immediately with the results. However, now you should be presented with a dialog box asking you to log in:

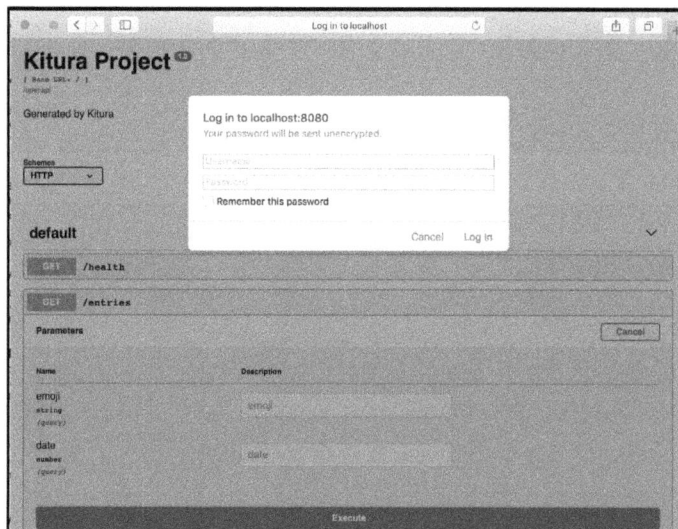

Enter the login details for either John or Mary and click **Log In**.

You should now receive a Server response with a Code of "200" and a Response body containing your stored journal entry as you did previously:

Congratulations, you have added basic HTTP authentication to your APIs!

This approach is, however, limited. `RouterMiddlewares` can only modify the `RouterRequest` and `RouterResponse` objects, which means the user data must be passed to the route handler using one of those structures. In order to enable this, Kitura treats authentication as a special case for `RouterMiddlewares`, extending the `RouterRequest` with an Optional `userProfile` field, which stores the `UserProfile` object response from the `verifyPassword` closure.

This means that the data that can be passed into the route handlers is restricted to those provided by `UserProfile` — there is no flexibility to add custom data.

Additionally, there is a separation in your code between enabling the middleware and the route handler that would make use of the data it provides. This means that bugs can easily be introduced. For example, a route handler may want access to the `UserProfile`, but no authentication middleware may have been enabled for that route.

HTTP basic authentication using TypeSafeMiddleware

Type-safe middlewares have two advantages over router middlewares:

1. They centralize your middleware logic in one place. This guarantees that routes are invoked only after any required middlewares have successfully executed and the data has been provided. If a route handler requires user data as a parameter, the middleware that creates that data is automatically added to that route.

2. They provide compile-time type safety for accessing data provided by the middleware to the route handlers. This occurs because type-safe middlewares can

return any custom type you wish to use.

To see this in action, first, remove the `RouterMiddleware` implementation of HTTP basic authentication you added in the previous steps by deleting the `initializeBasicAuth` method and the call to it in `postInit`.

Next, create a new file called **UserAuth.swift** in **Sources/Application/Models/**.

In this file, add the following code:

```
import CredentialsHTTP

public struct UserAuth {
  public var id: String
  private let password: String
}
```

The `UserAuth` struct is your custom type that will be used to store the authenticated user information passed to your route handlers as a parameter. Note that the `password` field is marked as `private`.

Next, extend your `UserAuth` struct to conform to `TypeSafeHTTPBasic`. This requires your `UserAuth` struct to implement a `verifyPassword` method that is very similar to the one used when creating the `CredentialsHTTPBasic` plugin in the `RouterMiddleware` approach previously. One crucial difference is that this `verifyPassword` implementation will respond with an instance of `Self` (in this case a `UserAuth` object), which will be passed to the route handler:

```
extension UserAuth: TypeSafeHTTPBasic {

  public static let authenticate =
    ["John": "12345", "Mary": "ABCDE"]

  public static func verifyPassword(username: String,
    password: String, callback: @escaping (UserAuth?) -> Void) {

    if let storedPassword = authenticate[username],
      storedPassword == password {
      callback(UserAuth(id: username, password: password))
      return
    }
    callback(nil)
  }
}
```

As `callback` is invoked with an instance of `Self`, the data passed to the route handlers is completely customizable according to the type.

One final task to enable the type-safe authentication is to register it with the routes that need to be authenticated. With your router middleware, this was done by registering the middleware against the routes using the router. However, in type-safe middlewares, this is done by requesting the type as one of the parameters to the route handler itself.

Open **Sources/Application/Routes/EntryRoutes.swift** and update each of your route handlers to request a parameter called `user` of type `UserAuth`:

```swift
func addEntry(user: UserAuth, entry: JournalEntry,
  completion: @escaping
  (JournalEntry?, RequestError?) -> Void) {

  var savedEntry = entry
  savedEntry.id = UUID().uuidString
  savedEntry.save(completion)
}

func getEntries(user: UserAuth, query: JournalEntryParams?,
  completion: @escaping
  ([JournalEntry]?, RequestError?) -> Void) -> Void {

  JournalEntry.findAll(matching: query, completion)
}

func deleteEntry(user: UserAuth, id: String,
  completion: @escaping (RequestError?) -> Void) {

  JournalEntry.delete(id: id, completion)
}

func modifyEntry(user: UserAuth, id: String,
  entry: JournalEntry, completion: @escaping
  (JournalEntry?, RequestError?) -> Void) {

  entry.update(id: id, completion)
}

func getOneEntry(user: UserAuth, id: String,
  completion: @escaping
  (JournalEntry?, RequestError?) -> Void) {

  JournalEntry.find(id: id, completion)
}
```

This enables HTTP basic authentication for each of your routes in a centralized way. It is immediately visible which routes are authenticated. Additionally, it is not possible for a route that needs access to the user data to discover, at runtime, that it is not available.

Build and run your project and use the Kitura OpenAPI UI, http://localhost:8080/openapi/ui, to test the **GET /entries** API.

> **Note**: You may find that you are not prompted for a username and password. This is because your browser will cache and reuse the login details that you previously used.
>
> To avoid this, open the Kitura OpenAPI UI using a private or incognito browsing window. You can do this in *Safari* by selecting the **File ▸ New Private Window**.
>
> With the new private browsing window open, enter the Kitura OpenAPI UI URL (http://localhost:8080/openapi/ui) into the URL window and the UI will open as before.

Inside the Kitura OpenAPI UI, select the **GET /entries** row and click on the **Try it out** button. Next, click the **Execute** button to run the request and receive the dialog box requesting the login details.

Enter the login details for either: 1. John with a password of 12345 or 2. Mary with a password of ABCDE. Then, click **Log In** to see a Server response with a Code of "200" and a Response body containing your stored journal entry.

That's it! You've reimplemented authentication in a more type-safe way and provided the route handlers with access to the user data. You'll use that shortly to create a multi-user EmojiJournalServer, wherein each each user only has access to their own journal entries.

Before that, you'll need to update your iOS mobile app to provide the HTTP basic authentication credentials that your EmojiJournalServer now expects.

Authentication for your EmojiJournalMobileApp

Now that your EmojiJournalServer has been updated to expect HTTP basic credentials to be provided for requests to your RESTful APIs, you'll need to update your EmojiJouralMobileApp to provide those credentials.

Luckily, KituraKit, which you're using to connect to your Kitura based server, makes this straight forward.

Go to your EmojiJournalMobileApp project in Xcode and open **EmojiJournalMobileApp/Model/EmojiClient.swift**, which contains the code that makes the connections to your server.

Inside the EmojiClient class, add a new private static field to store the HTTP basic credentials:

```
private static let credentials =
  HTTPBasic(username: "John", password: "12345")
```

This sets up HTTP basic credentials using the "John" ID from your server.

Finally, update each of the getAll, get, add, delete and update methods in the class to set the defaultCredentials on the client to your newly created credentials field.

For example, your code for getAll should look as follows:

```
static func getAll(completion: @escaping
  (_ entries: [JournalEntry]?, _ error: EmojiClientError?)
  -> Void) {

  guard let client = KituraKit(baseURL: baseURL) else {
    return completion(nil, .couldNotCreateClient)
  }

  client.defaultCredentials = credentials
  client.get("/entries") {
    (entries: [JournalEntry]?, error: RequestError?) in

    DispatchQueue.main.async {
      if error != nil {
        completion(nil, .couldNotLoadEntries)
      } else {
        completion(entries, nil)
      }
```

```
        }
      }
    }
```

Make sure that your EmojiJournalServer is running, and then build and run your EmojiJournalMobileApp project in a simulator to try it out.

Your app should then open in the simulator and successfully get the entries from your server using the credentials and display them on the screen:

You can now add and fetch entries in the app as before.

Enhancing your security

In this chapter, you've added authentication to your EmojiJournalServer and EmojiJournalMobileApp projects using HTTP basic authentication, which has enabled you to limit access to journal entries to their owners.

For any app, there's always more that can be done to enhance the level of security that's provided. In your app, three areas that you can explore include:

- **Ability to log in and store user credentials in the app**: In a real app, you would provide the ability for users to log in and you would store their credentials securely on the device. However, using an ID embedded in the code is sufficient to show how credentials work.

- **Secure storage of user passwords**: Currently, you store the user passwords inside your database in plain text. If your app's data became exposed, this would included the passwords of your users. One way to securely store the user passwords is to convert their password into a hash and store the hash in the database. To validate a user's password, you first convert their password to a hash and then compare that to the hash in your database.

- **Use of more advanced authentication types**: HTTP basic is one of the most basic forms of authentication. To move to a more advanced system, you could switch to using HTTP digest or use one of the other provided credentials middlewares. Due to the way that type-safe middlewares work, you won't have to change your RESTful APIs or your route handlers to change authentication types!

Now that your app and server are secure, in the next chapter, you'll enhance your server to become multi-user — storing journal entries tied to specific users.

Chapter 10: Multi-User Support

Chris Bailey

Your EmojiJournalServer project currently uses a static list of two users: John and Mary and your EmojiJournalMobileApp logs in as John. This is sufficient if you have two users who you want to be able to share the same emoji journal, but not if you want to extend your app so that hundreds or thousands of users can have their own emoji journals.

In this chapter, you'll add multi-user support, including:

- Adding a mechanism to dynamically add and remove users.

- Providing per-user emoji journal entries.

- Cleaning up all of a user's entries if they delete their account.

By the end of this chapter, you'll have added full multi-user support to your EmojiJournalServer.

Managing users

Before you can add support for multiple users, it's useful to have a way to add and remove users through a RESTful API so that you don't need to update your code and restart your server whenever there is a new user request.

You learned in Chapter 5, how to build a RESTful API for managing `JournalEntry` objects and, in Chapter 8, how to store those in a datastore. You'll apply that knowledge here, but to store and manage `UserAuth` objects.

Start in EmojiJournalServer by opening **Sources/Application/Models/
UserAuth.swift**. Import the `SwiftKueryORM` package and update your `UserAuth`
struct to make it conform to `Model`:

```
import SwiftKueryORM

public struct UserAuth: Model {
  public var id: String
  private let password: String
}
```

Next, open **Sources/Application/Models/Persistence.swift** and add the following
code to the end of the `setUp` method to create an additional database table for the
`UserAuth` objects:

```
do {
  try UserAuth.createTableSync()
} catch let error {
  // Database table already exists
  if let requestError = error as? RequestError,
    requestError.rawValue ==
      RequestError.ormQueryError.rawValue {
        Log.info("Table \(UserAuth.tableName) already exists")
  } else {
    Log.error("Database connection error: " +
      "\(String(describing: error))")
  }
}
```

Finally, go back to **Sources/Application/Models/UserAuth.swift** and replace the
current implementation of `verifyPassword` with the following:

```
public static func verifyPassword(username: String,
  password: String, callback: @escaping (UserAuth?) -> Void) {

  // 1
  UserAuth.find(id: username) { userAuth, error in

    // 2
    if let userAuth = userAuth {

      // 3
      if password == userAuth.password {

        // 4
        callback(userAuth)
        return
      }
    }
```

```
    //5
    callback(nil)
  }
}
```

With this code, you:

1. Call `UserAuth.find` to retrieve a single entry based on the `username` received in the HTTP basic authentication request.

2. Check that the user exists.

3. Verify that the passed in password matches the stored password.

4. Call the `callback` function with the fetched `userAuth` instance, if the passwords match.

5. Call the `callback` function with `nil`, if the passwords do not match.

Your authentication requests will now verify against a set of users stored in your PostgreSQL database. Unfortunately, you currently don't have any users stored.

You could populate the database using a static list of users by making `UserAuth.addEntry` calls as part of the `Persistence.setUp` call, but ideally you want to make it possible to add and remove users on request through a RESTful API.

To do this, add a new file to your project called **Sources/Application/Routes/UserRoutes.swift**. This file will contain your user route handlers.

Similar to the way your **EntryRoutes.swift** is structured, add the following to your **UserRoutes.swift** file:

```
import Foundation
import LoggerAPI
import Kitura

func initializeUserRoutes(app: App) {
  Log.info("User routes created")
}
```

You now have the ability to add RESTful API routes to manage your users. You'll implement two APIs:

```
POST   /user
DELETE /user/{username}
```

The first will be used to create and store a new user, and the second to remove an existing user.

Register route handlers in `initializeUserRoutes` for GET requests on /user to call `addUser` and for DELETE requests on /user to call `deleteUser`:

```
func initializeUserRoutes(app: App) {
    app.router.post("/user", handler: addUser)
    app.router.delete("/user", handler: deleteUser)
    Log.info("User routes created")
}
```

Next, provide implementations of `addUser` and `deleteUser` that stores a new user in the database table and deletes an existing user from the database table:

```
func addUser(user: UserAuth,
    completion: @escaping (UserAuth?, RequestError?) -> Void) {

    user.save(completion)
}

func deleteUser(user: UserAuth, id: String,
    completion: @escaping (RequestError?) -> Void) {

    if user.id != id {
        completion(RequestError.forbidden)
    }
    UserAuth.delete(id: id, completion)
}
```

There is no need to carry out checks to see if the user already exists before trying to store or delete the user; SwiftKueryORM will take care of that for your as part of the call to insert or delete the entry.

Notice, though, for the `deleteUser` function, you want to limit the ability to delete users to those users themselves. The code does that by requiring authentication for the API and then checking that the logged in user's id matches the id that the API is being requested to delete.

Before you can test your changes, you need to update the `postInit` function in **Sources/Application/Application.swift** to call the `initializeUserRoutes` function:

```
func postInit() throws {
    // Endpoints
    initializeHealthRoutes(app: self)
    initializeEntryRoutes(app: self)
    initializeUserRoutes(app: self)
    KituraOpenAPI.addEndpoints(to: router)
    router.get("/", handler: helloWorldHandler)
}
```

Now that you have RESTful APIs for adding and removing users, build and run your project.

Use the Kitura OpenAPI UI to check they are working correctly and can be used for authentication when adding and removing emoji journal entries.

Open a new private browsing window and visit the Kitura OpenAPI UI: http://localhost:8080/openapi/ui.

First, notice that your new APIs to add and delete users have been automatically added to the list of APIs.

Next, select the **POST /user** row and click on **Try it out** to test the API.

Set the **input** for the body data to the following in order to create a user with an id of Han and a password of Solo:

```
{
  "id": "Han",
  "password": "Solo"
}
```

Click **Execute** to run the request against the API.

This should result in a Server response with a Code of "201" and a Response body that matches the data you entered.

Now that you have created your new user, use the GET /entries API to check that you can now authenticate with your new user, and get all of the journal entries.

Select the **GET /entries** row in the UI and click on **Try it out**. As there is no request data or parameters to set, click the **Execute** button to run the request.

A login dialog box will open. Enter **Han** as the Username and **Solo** as the Password and click **Log In**.

This should successfully authenticate causing the API to respond with a Code of "200" and a Response body as follows:

Notice that, even though you haven't stored any data using your Han user, you're receiving results. This is because the entries are not yet stored against a given user, so there is no way to filter the results according to the logged-in user. You'll add that in the next section. Before you do, you need finish testing the management of users by deleting your Han user.

Select the **Delete /user/{id}** row and click on **Try it out**. Enter an id field entry of **Han** and click **Execute**.

This results in a Server response with a Code of "204" for a successfully removed resource:

Code	Details
204 *Undocumented*	**Response headers**

```
connection: Keep-Alive
content-length: 0
date: Sun, 25 Nov 2018 13:03:06 GMT
keep-alive: timeout=60
```

Now that you have built the APIs to add and remove users, the final step for providing an authenticated, multi-user emoji journal, is to store, retrieve and delete entries on a per-user basis.

Adding multi-user support

In order to provide multi-user support, where users can only store, retrieve and delete entries associated with their user ID, you'll need to restructure the way data is stored so that each journal entry is stored against the user that owns it.

To do this, you'll create a UserJournalEntry type to store the data, which is a combination of the user id for the user and the previous Journal Entry data. Additionally, you'll provide a constructor for the UserJournalEntry so that it can be created from the JournalEntry and UserAuth types that you are already using.

Open **Sources/Application/Models/JournalEntry.swift** and add the following:

```swift
struct UserJournalEntry: Model {
  var id: String?
  var emoji: String
  var date: Date
  var user: String

  init(_ journalEntry: JournalEntry, for user: UserAuth) {
    self.id = journalEntry.id
    self.emoji = journalEntry.emoji
    self.date = journalEntry.date
    self.user = user.id
  }
}
```

Note that, as you're going to use this to store the data in the database, it is marked as a Model.

Next open **Sources/Application/Model/Persistence.swift** and update the setUp function so that it creates a database table for the UserJournalEntry objects rather than the JournalEntry objects. There are two spots, where you need to replace JournalEntry with UserJournalEntry. The do-catch block should look like this, when you're done:

```swift
do {
  try UserJournalEntry.createTableSync()
} catch let error {
  // Database table already exists
  if let requestError = error as? RequestError,
```

```
      requestError.rawValue ==
        RequestError.ormQueryError.rawValue {
          Log.info("Table \(UserJournalEntry.tableName) " +
            "already exists")
    } else {
      Log.error("Database connection error: " +
        "\(String(describing: error))")
    }
  }
}
```

This provides the foundations to store, retrieve and delete user-based journal entries. However, the RESTful APIs that are exposed and the data types that they use should remain the same.

In order to do that, you'll add a set of functions to `JournalEntry` for storing, updating, fetching and deleting entries.

Each of these functions will receive a `UserAuth` parameter and will use it to filter the database requests based on the user ID. Before you can add these functions to `JournalEntry`, you'll first need to create a new type that conforms to `QueryParams` to be used for filtering.

Add the following struct to **JournalEntry.swift** that conforms to `QueryParams` and can be used to filter based on `user` field in the `UserJournalEntry`:

```
struct UserQuery: QueryParams {
  let user: String

  init(_ user: UserAuth) {
    self.user = user.id
  }
}
```

Note that the constructor makes it easy to build a `UserQuery` based on the `UserAuth` object that the route handler receives from the authentication request.

Also add a `UserJournalEntryParams`, which will be used for the `findAll` request where you will filter on entries that match both the user and the provided `JournalEntryParams`:

```
struct UserJournalEntryParams: QueryParams {
  let user: String
  let emoji: String?

  init(_ query: JournalEntryParams?, for user: UserAuth) {
    self.user = user.id
    self.emoji = query?.emoji
  }
}
```

```
}
```

As well as filtering the results from the database, the results also need to be converted from instances of `UserJournalEntry` to instances of `JournalEntry` in order to be used in responses in your RESTful APIs. To do this, add a `JournalEntry` constructor to **JournalEntry.swift**:

```swift
init(_ entry: UserJournalEntry) {
    self.id = entry.id
    self.emoji = entry.emoji
    self.date = entry.date
}
```

Now you're ready to add the `JournalEntry` functions to store, update, fetch and delete entries.

First, add the following implementation to `JournalEntry` for the save method:

```
func save(for user: UserAuth, _ completion:
  @escaping (JournalEntry?, RequestError?) -> Void) -> Void {

  // 1
  let complete = { (entry: UserJournalEntry?,
    error: RequestError?) -> Void in

    // 2
    guard let entry = entry else {
      return completion(nil, error)
    }

    // 3
    completion(JournalEntry(entry), error)
  }

  // 4
  UserJournalEntry(self, for: user)
    .save(using: Database.default, complete)
}
```

In this function you:

1. Create a new completion handler called `complete`, which will take the `UserJournalEntry` returned from a successful save request.

2. Check that the entry has a value and if it is `nil`, you call the `completion` function with the received error.

3. Call the `completion` function with a newly created `JournalEntry` from the received `UserJournalEntry`, if everything is fine.

4. Create a new instance of `UserJournalEntry` using the `JournalEntry` and the `UserAuth` and then pass in the `complete` closure you just created to the `save` method.

One `JournalEntry` function down, four more to go! Next, add the following to provide an implementation of `findAll`:

```
static func findAll(matching: JournalEntryParams?,
    for user: UserAuth, _ completion:
    @escaping ([JournalEntry]?, RequestError?) -> Void) -> Void {

  let complete = { (entries: [UserJournalEntry]?,
    error: RequestError?) -> Void in

    guard let entries = entries else {
      return completion(nil, error)
    }

    var journalEntries = [JournalEntry]()
    for entry in entries {
      journalEntries.append(JournalEntry(entry))
    }

    completion(journalEntries, error)
  }

  UserJournalEntry.findAll(using: Database.default, matching:
    UserJournalEntryParams(matching, for: user), complete)
}
```

This is very similar. You create a new completion handler that converts the returned `[UserJournalEntry]` array into a `[JournalEntry]` array. Then, you pass that into a call to `UserJournalEntry.findAll`.

Notice that an instance of your new `UserJournalEntryParams` created from the authenticated user and any `JournalEntryParams` is used to filter the results to only include matching journal entries for that user.

Now, add an implementation of `delete`:

```
static func delete(id: String, for user: UserAuth,
  _ completion: @escaping (RequestError?) -> Void) -> Void {

  let complete = { (entry: UserJournalEntry?,
    error: RequestError?) -> Void in

    guard let entry = entry else {
      return completion(error)
    }
```

```
    if entry.user != user.id {
      return completion(RequestError.forbidden)
    }

    UserJournalEntry.delete(id: id, completion)
  }

  UserJournalEntry.find(id: id, complete)
}
```

Here, you're creating a completion handler, `complete` to delete a `UserJournalEntry` *only* if the entry was created by the same user, who is currently authenticated. Otherwise it responds with "403 Forbidden".

This completion handler is then passed to the `UserJournalEntry.find` method, which makes sure that entry is only deleted if it can be found. That makes sense, right?

You're doing well! Two more of these methods to go.

Next add `update` as follows:

```
func update(id: String, for user: UserAuth, _ completion:
  @escaping (JournalEntry?, RequestError?) -> Void) -> Void {

  // 1
  let findComplete = { (entry: UserJournalEntry?,
    error: RequestError?) -> Void in

    guard let entry = entry else {
      return completion(nil, error)
    }

    if entry.user != user.id {
      return completion(nil, RequestError.forbidden)
    }

    // 2
    let updateComplete = { (entry: UserJournalEntry?,
      error: RequestError?) -> Void in

      guard let entry = entry else {
        return completion(nil, error)
      }

      completion(JournalEntry(entry), error)
    }

    // 3
    UserJournalEntry(self, for: user)
      .update(id: id, updateComplete)
  }

  // 4
  UserJournalEntry.find(id: id, findComplete)
}
```

In this method, you:

1. Create a `findComplete` closure, which checks that the entry exists and was created by the authenticated user before updating the `UserJournalEntry`.

2. Create a nested `updateComplete` closure that returns a `JournalEntry` based on the updated `UserJournalEntry`, if the update was successful.

3. Call the update method on `UserJournalEntry` and pass in `updateComplete` as its completion handler.

4. Fetch the `UserJournalEntry` for the `id` and pass in `findComplete` as its completion handler.

Finally, add the following to implement `find`:

```
static func find(id: String, for user: UserAuth, _ completion:
  @escaping (JournalEntry?, RequestError?) -> Void) -> Void {

  let complete = { (entry: UserJournalEntry?,
    error: RequestError?) -> Void in

    guard let entry = entry else {
      return completion(nil, error)
    }

    if entry.user != user.id {
      return completion(nil, RequestError.forbidden)
    }

    return completion(JournalEntry(entry), nil)
  }

  UserJournalEntry.find(id: id, complete)
}
```

This finds the requested entry, and checks that it is owned by the logged in user before converting it to a `JournalEntry` and responding with it.

This has implemented the multi-user ORM calls. The last step is to update your route handlers in **Sources/Application/Routes/EntryRoutes.swift** to call your new methods that accept `user` parameters:

```swift
func addEntry(user: UserAuth, entry: JournalEntry, completion:
  @escaping (JournalEntry?, RequestError?) -> Void) {

  var savedEntry = entry
  savedEntry.id = UUID().uuidString
  savedEntry.save(for: user, completion)
}

func getEntries(user: UserAuth, query: JournalEntryParams?,
  completion: @escaping ([JournalEntry]?,
  RequestError?) -> Void) -> Void {

  JournalEntry.findAll(matching: query, for: user, completion)
}

func deleteEntry(user: UserAuth, id: String, completion:
  @escaping (RequestError?) -> Void) {

  JournalEntry.delete(id: id, for: user, completion)
}

func modifyEntry(user: UserAuth, id: String,
  entry: JournalEntry, completion:
  @escaping (JournalEntry?, RequestError?) -> Void) {

  entry.update(id: id, for: user, completion)
}

func getOneEntry(user: UserAuth, id: String, completion:
  @escaping (JournalEntry?, RequestError?) -> Void) {

  JournalEntry.find(id: id, for: user, completion)
}
```

Congratulations! You have implemented a fully functional multi-user EmojiJournalServer!

Build and run your project and use the Kitura OpenAPI UI to test that everything is working correctly.

Open a new private browsing window and visit the Kitura OpenAPI UI: http://localhost:8080/openapi/ui.

First, create a new user by selecting the **POST /user** row, clicking on **Try it out** and executing a request with the following input body:

```
{
    "id": "Leia",
    "password": "Organa"
}
```

This should result in a Server response with a Code of "201" for CREATED.

Then create a second new user using the same steps but with the following input body:

```
{
    "id": "Lando",
    "password": "Calrissian"
}
```

Next, create a new entry for Leia by selecting the **POST /entries** row, clicking on **Try it out** and executing a request with the following input body:

```
{
  "emoji":"😄",
  "date": 563725805.57661498
}
```

This causes a log in dialog box to open. Log in with using a Username of **Leia** and a Password of **Organa**.

This should both successfully log in using the Leia user, and create a new journal entry under that user, resulting in a Server response with a Code of "201" for CREATED, and a Response body showing your created entry along with its unique id.

Now verify that you can retrieve the entry by selecting the **GET /entries** row, clicking on **Try it out** and then using the **Execute** button to request all of the logged-in user's entries.

If all is well, this results in a Server response with a Code of "200" for OK and a Response body containing a single element array with your entry inside it.

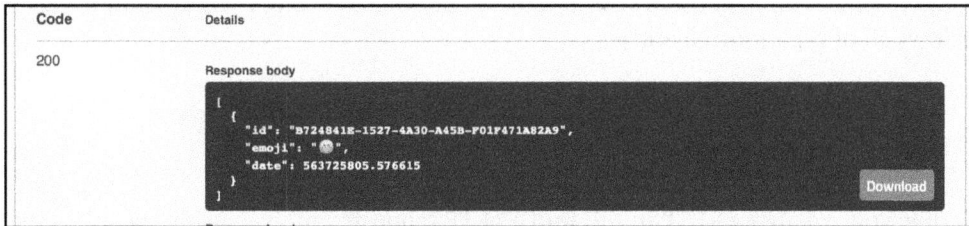

This shows that you have been able to create and retrieve entries against the Leia user. Next, verify that you don't have access to that entry when logged in as Lando.

Open a *new* private browsing window and visit the Kitura OpenAPI UI: http://localhost:8080/openapi/ui.

In the UI, select the **GET /entries** row, click the **Try it out** button followed by **Execute**.

Enter a username of **Lando** and a Password of **Calrissian** into the log in dialog box and click **Log In**.

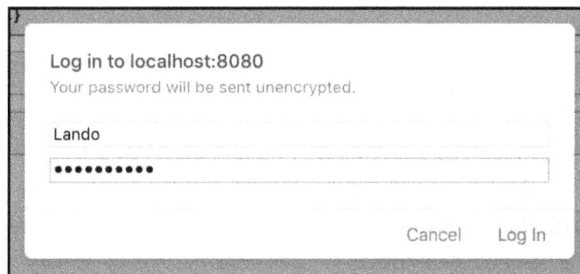

This will retrieve all of Lando's entries, which will be an empty array.

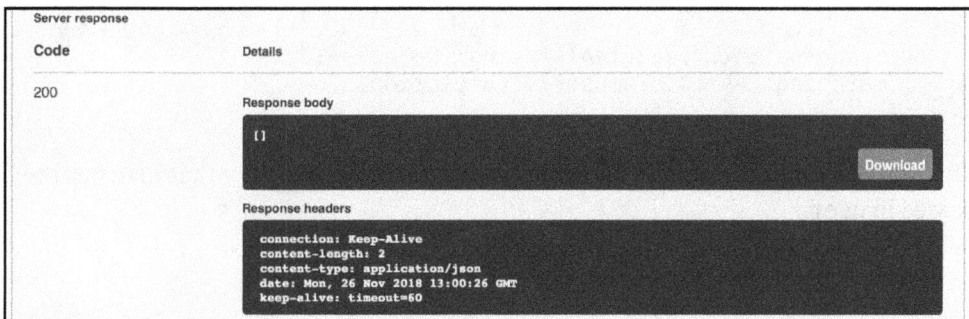

That's it! You have now extended your EmojiJournalServer provide to provide authentication and multi-user support. There is now just one final task: adding support for cleaning up users so that if a user decides to delete their account it also deletes all of their journal entries.

Cleaning up

Earlier, your created a RESTful API for DELETE requests on /user, using the following route handler:

```
func deleteUser(user: UserAuth, id: String, completion:
    @escaping (RequestError?) -> Void) {

  if user.id != id {
    completion(RequestError.forbidden)
  }

  UserAuth.delete(id: id, completion)
}
```

This checks that the authorized user is requesting the deletion of their own account, and then deletes the user from the database. However, it doesn't remove the journal entries for the user, meaning that it leaves unowned entries in the database table. These would waste precious disk space!

In order to ensure that that the journal entries are deleted before the user is removed, you first need to enable deleting all entries for a given user. To do that, open **Sources/Application/Models/JournalEntry.swift** and add the following function to the JournalEntry struct:

```
static func deleteAll(for user: UserAuth, _ completion:
    @escaping (RequestError?) -> Void) -> Void {

  UserJournalEntry.deleteAll(using: Database.default,
    matching: UserQuery(user), completion)
}
```

This makes a request to delete all instances of UserJournalEntry that matches the passed in user.

Next open **Sources/Application/Routes/UserRoutes.swift** and replace the current implementation of `deleteUser` with the following:

```
func deleteUser(user: UserAuth, id: String,
  completion: @escaping (RequestError?) -> Void) {

  if user.id != id {
    completion(RequestError.forbidden)
  }

  JournalEntry.deleteAll(for: user) { error in

    if let error = error {
      return completion(error)
    }

    return UserAuth.delete(id: id, completion)
  }
}
```

This now makes a call to `JournalEntry.deleteAll` before deleting the user, and only deletes the user itself if it successfully deleted the associated journal entries.

Go ahead and test that this is correctly clearing up the entries when you remove a user by deleting your Leia user.

Build and run your project, and then open a private browsing window and visit the Kitura OpenAPI UI: http://localhost:8080/openapi/ui.

Select the **DELETE /user/{id}** row and click the **Try it out** button.

Next enter an id parameter of **Leia** and click **Execute**:

This will cause the log in dialog box to appear. Log in as **Leia** with a password of **Organa** and click **Log In**:

Log in to localhost:8080
Your password will be sent unencrypted.

Leia

••••••

Cancel   Log In

This should then cause the server to respond with a Server response Code of "204" for NO CONTENT:

Server response

Code   Details

204   Response headers
Undocumented

```
connection: Keep-Alive
content-length: 0
date: Mon, 26 Nov 2018 14:36:01 GMT
keep-alive: timeout=60
```

This shows that the Leia user has been successfully removed. The final step is to verify that the journal entries for Leia have also been removed from the database.

You can do that by running a query directly against the PostgreSQL database from the command line.

Open the Terminal app and execute the following command:

```
psql -U postgres -d emojijournal -c 'SELECT * FROM
"UserJournalEntrys"'
```

This uses the `postgres` database user and the `emojijournal` database to run `SELECT * FROM "UserJournalEntrys"`, which requests all data from the "UserJournalEntrys" table.

This should result in an empty set of results:

```
 id | emoji | date | user
----+-------+------+------
(0 rows)
```

As all of the data for Leia has been removed and you are not storing data against any other user.

Expanding user support

You now have the ability for multiple users to have their own emoji journal based on their logins and have ensured that their data is isolated from each other. This has greatly expanded the potential user base for your app.

One way to expand this further is to provide support for users to maintain an emoji journal through a web browser, either in addition to using the mobile app, or as a complete replacement.

In the next chapter, you'll learn how to re-use the same RESTful APIs that you've been using for your iOS app, but to power a new web interface for your emoji journal.

Chapter 11: KituraStencil: Getting Started

David Okun

Right! Think back to the very first chapter of your journey with us, about how Purple Vampire crabs are known for their hard shells. If you have completed each chapter to this point, your Kitura API is now solid as a rock! You learned about some of the different methods of authentication, and you applied a real-life production ready database to your API.

However, to this point, you've just been testing your API with the OpenAPI Explorer, or occasionally with the iOS app. It's totally understandable to want to show this work off to your friends. However, what if they try to log in as Leia Organa through the API Explorer on your machine when you deploy to localhost, and they get annoyed at you for continually asking them to come over? Worse yet... what if they don't have iPhones?!

I know, I know, green bubbles make me leery of people, too — but you want EmojiJournal to be accessible to all! Wouldn't it be nice to have a way for people to use EmojiJournal from a web browser? Well, that's exactly what you're going to do in Chapters 11 and 12!

In this chapter alone, you'll:

- Discover how a web-based frontend is structured.

- Learn how Stencil templating works.

- Set up your basic /client route for accessing EmojiJournal on the web.

By the end of this chapter, you'll have a working web client that still needs some work, but is ready to go out of the box!

Web frontends

This pair of chapters in front of you is going to contain some work in the following languages:

- HTML (HyperText Markup Language)

- JS (JungleScribble... kidding, JavaScript)

Regardless of your experience working with any of these, I humbly ask you to not be alarmed! I might not go into the deepest depths of explaining everything we write in other languages, but I will include a nugget or two of knowledge about everything you add to your project.

If you've been working along, chapter by chapter, this is one of those cases where you'll still need to use the starter project for this chapter. Open the starter project, and navigate to the root directory. Have you found your little surprise yet? You might notice the addition of a new folder — **/public**! Open the folder and look at the structure. It should look like so:

▼ css	Folder	--
emoji.css	CSS	5 KB
emoji.css.map	Document	3 KB
index.css	CSS	2 KB
▼ img	Folder	--
blank.gif	GIF Image	49 bytes
emoji_spritesheet_0.png	PNG image	740 KB
emoji_spritesheet_1.png	PNG image	544 KB
emoji_spritesheet_2.png	PNG image	979 KB
emoji_spritesheet_3.png	PNG image	412 KB
emoji_spritesheet_4.png	PNG image	544 KB
IconsetSmiles_1x.png	PNG image	3 KB
IconsetSmiles.png	PNG image	7 KB
IconsetW_1x.png	PNG image	13 KB
IconsetW.png	PNG image	26 KB
plusSign.jpg	JPEG image	6 KB
▼ js	Folder	--
config.js	JavaScript	129 KB
emoji-picker.coffee	Visual...ocument	3 KB
emoji-picker.js	JavaScript	4 KB
emoji-picker.js.map	Document	3 KB
jquery.emojiarea.js	JavaScript	24 KB
util.js	JavaScript	6 KB

This project will not require you to modify these files in any way, so you can largely leave these alone, but you should at least know what is in each directory:

- **CSS**: This is also known as Cascading Style Sheets. This is how the different HTML components you will be creating will order and position themselves by reference. You have CSS files for both the emoji-picker component and the main page you will format.

- **IMG**: This is short for **images**. This is nothing more than a folder for static image assets that will go on your web client. I am by no means a web designer, so if you see fit to make changes, go nuts!

- **JS**: The scripts that make your web client run as smoothly as it will. If you edit these, to quote npm (Node Package Manager): I hope you know what you're doing.

It is good and common practice to load these into a folder called public on your front end. Typically, you could also put your .html files into their own directory here as well. However, you're going to be working with Stencil, which is a powerful templating library written for Swift, and mostly maintained by Kyle Fuller.

Wait... templating?

When I say templating, I mean the ability to reproduce multiple variables and components in a repeatable manner that you have the power to format.

Take this for example: Let's say you wanted to write a webpage that always tells you the current month. A naïve approach to such a task might look like so in HTML:

```
<!DOCTYPE html>
<html>
  <head>
    <title>The current month is December!</title>
  </head>
</html>
```

Depending on when you are reading this book, this *might* be appropriate, but theres an approximately 8.5% chance it is.

This is hardly sustainable; I wouldn't want to be the web developer responsible for maintaining this! Thanks to Stencil, you now have the ability to pass in a variable, and Stencil will render your template file to spit out the proper date!

Your .stencil file would look like so:

```
<!DOCTYPE html>
<html>
  <head>
    <title>The current month is {{ currentMonth }}!</title>
  </head>
</html>
```

The main difference here is the inclusion of the `{{ currentMonth }}`, but notice the curly braces around each end of the variable. This is the delimiter that Stencil will search for when looking for a place to insert information. Stencil essentially operates on this workflow:

1. Prepare data from your API.

2. Set up a context: a dictionary of key/value pairs.

3. Populate your context with the values you want to display.

4. Render a template in your response, using a context.

If you didn't raise an eyebrow halfway through this list, go back and look at #2. Hopefully, you're thinking, "Wait a minute... all this focus on the `Codable` protocol, and now I have to form a key-value pair dictionary? What gives, David?!" By now, you should know I would never pull one over on you like that — of *course* you can use Codable!

On the Swift side of things, you need to prepare an object that is either `Codable` or an array of homogenous `Codable` objects. You'll cover the whole flow from front to back shortly, but if you wanted to reduce the above sample to a short code snippet, it might look like this:

```
struct CurrentMonth: Codable {
  var month: String
}

try response.render("home.stencil",
  with: CurrentMonth(month: "December"), forKey: "currentMonth")
```

And, then, in your home.stencil file, you would handle this variable like so:

```
<!DOCTYPE html>
<html>
  <head>
    <title>
      The current month is {{ currentMonth.month }}!
    </title>
  </head>
</html>
```

Notice the slight change in the above example. This is because your `Codable` object has a property on it titled `month`. Because `Codable` handles serializing the JSON for you, Stencil gives you an easy way to read stored properties in your .stencil file.

> **Note**: Just like most of Kitura's functionality, if you want to load a raw dictionary of values and keys, you can. Version 1.x APIs still work.

Loops and other operations in Stencil

Just like control flow in most modern programming languages, Stencil has a way to handle looping through an array of objects that you may want to utilize. Using our previous example, say you render an array into your response like so:

```
let birthdays = [CurrentMonth(month: "September"),
                 CurrentMonth(month: "January"),
                 CurrentMonth(month: "March")]

try response.render("home.stencil", with: birthdays,
  forKey: "birthdays")
```

This means you now have a collection of objects available to you in Stencil rather than just a singular object.

Now, you need to make use of one of Stencil's built in template tags with a for loop. Your HTML might look like this:

```
<html>
  <body>
  {% for birthday in birthdays %}
    <li> Month: {{ birthday.month }} </li>
  {% endfor %}
  </body>
</html>
```

https://store.raywenderlich.com/admin/products/17Notice the difference between the {% and the {{ delimiters. As you have already learned, anything inside {{ }} is going to represent as a string inside your rendered HTML document. However, if something is inside the {% %} delimiters, then this is going to apply to a tag that Stencil recognizes. If you've ever written in C before, you're going to be in familiar territory noticing the need for a delimited tag like endif that "ends" the previous command.

This for loop is certainly an example of that, but you can also do this with an if statement in Stencil like so:

```
{% if birthday.month %}
  <li> Month: {{ birthday.month }}</li>
{% else %}
  <li> No month listed. </li>
{% endif %}
```

Here's a partial list of some of the built in tags that Stencil has available for you to use:

• for

• if

• ifnot

• now

• filter

• include

• extends

• block

If you want to check the documentation on how you can use any of these tags in your own website template, visit Kyle's documentation website at <u>https://stencil.fuller.li/</u> <u>en/latest/builtins.html</u>.

> **Note**: Of the tags you can use, the `include` tag is of particular interest, as you can pass a context through to another **.stencil** file in your original file by typing `{% include "secondTemplate.stencil" %}`. You won't use it in this project, but some websites can become a bit cumbersome if you don't split them up — this can be helpful!

Adding Stencil to your project

Open up **Package.swift** in EmojiJournalServer.

First, add the dependency at the bottom of your list of dependencies:

```
.package(url:
"https://github.com/IBM-Swift/Kitura-StencilTemplateEngine.git",
.upToNextMinor(from: "1.11.0")),
```

Make sure the previous line has a **,** at the end, or your **Package.swift** won't compile.

Next, scroll down to the `Application` target, and in the list of dependencies this target has, add `KituraStencil` to the end of the array. It should look like this:

```
.target(name: "Application", dependencies: [ "Kitura",
"CloudEnvironment", "SwiftMetrics", "Health", "KituraOpenAPI",
"SwiftKueryPostgreSQL", "SwiftKueryORM", "CredentialsHTTP",
"KituraStencil"]),
```

Save your file, and wait while Xcode 11 resolves your dependencies. Build your project, and make sure everything runs OK.

Just as you've done for your router with your `JournalEntry` objects and your `UserAuth` management, you're going to add another route for managing connecting to your web client.

In Xcode, navigate to the **Sources/Application/Routes** folder. Create a new file, and name it **WebClientRoutes.swift**.

At the top of this file, import the following libraries:

```
import Foundation
import LoggerAPI
import KituraStencil
import Kitura
import SwiftKueryORM
```

You may be wondering why you need `SwiftKueryORM`; this will be apparent soon! Consider all the work you've done to lock down your API and make it work with PostgreSQL. You don't want to ignore this, so you'll be making use of one of the APIs here, too!

Now, add a function that will help you register a route on your main `Router` object to handle the web client:

```
func initializeWebClientRoutes(app: App) {

  // 1
  app.router.setDefault(templateEngine: StencilTemplateEngine())

  // 2
  app.router.all(middleware: StaticFileServer(path: "./public"))

  // 3
  app.router.get("/client", handler: showClient)

  // 4
  Log.info("Web client routes created")
}
```

Look at each line of this function you've just added:

1. Since you've added the Stencil dependency to your project, you need to tell Kitura that Stencil is going to be the format for templating your HTML. Yes — you do have a choice when it comes to other templating engines, but our team has chosen Stencil!

2. In Chapter 9, you learned about middleware via authentication. Here, you need to tell Kitura that, when searching for static files to serve up (images, etc.) which directory to look in, and this tells Kitura to look in your aptly named `public` directory.

3. Here, you are registering the `/client` route on your router, and you'll handle this route with Stencil and Kitura shortly.

4. Log, log, log your work!

Beneath this function, add the following function signature:

```
func showClient(request: RouterRequest,
    response: RouterResponse, next: @escaping () -> Void) {

}
```

This way, your project can compile, and you've now specified a function to handle your route. From here on out, you're going to write a bunch of Swift code that serves up what you will eventually shape in a Stencil file.

Start by declaring the following object above your `initializeWebClientRoutes` function:

```
struct JournalEntryWeb: Codable {
    var id: String?
    var emoji: String
    var date: Date
    var displayDate: String
    var displayTime: String
    var backgroundColorCode: String
    var user: String
}
```

This might look redundant at first; technically, it is. However, remember our earlier note about how Stencil can only serve stored properties? Stencil cannot handle computed properties of some objects. Notice that this object conforms to `Codable`, too!

Now, you might be thinking: "Wait... my `JournalEntry` object doesn't have any computed properties!" Take a deep breath; it doesn't. However, you're going to extend it here so that it does for the sake of convenience.

Scroll up to the top of this file, but just underneath your imports, and add the following three computed properties to a `fileprivate` `extension` of your object:

```
fileprivate extension UserJournalEntry {
    var displayDate: String {
        get {
            let formatter = DateFormatter()
            formatter.dateStyle = .long
            return formatter.string(from: self.date)
        }
    }

    var displayTime: String {
        get {
            let formatter = DateFormatter()
```

```
      formatter.timeStyle = .long
      return formatter.string(from: self.date)
    }
  }

  var backgroundColorCode: String {
    get {
      guard let substring = id?.suffix(6).uppercased() else {
        return "000000"
      }
      return substring
    }
  }
}
```

A couple of points about what you've just added:

- You want to make sure you are extending `UserJournalEntry`, which will include the user in every object you pass through to your Stencil context. You will handle the authentication context later!

- `displayDate` and `displayTime` are *purely* for convenience. You could absolutely create these variables from the date property you pass to your HTML page, but this allows you to do it with Swift and make your HTML a bit simpler!

- The `backgroundColorCode` is a design decision made in lockstep with your iOS app, based on the ID of a journal entry object. Hey, it works!

Alright, now you've got the object that you're going to pass into the context.

Add the following code to your `showClient` route handler:

```
UserJournalEntry.findAll(using: Database.default) {
  entries, error in

  guard let entries = entries else {
    response.status(.serviceUnavailable).send(json: ["Message":
      "Service unavailable:" +
      "\(String(describing: error?.localizedDescription))"])
    return
  }

  let sortedEntries = entries.sorted(by: {
    $0.date.timeIntervalSince1970 >
    $1.date.timeIntervalSince1970
  })
}
```

Notice that you are making use of the ORM function on `UserJournalEntry` instead of just `JournalEntry`.

This is to override the user authentication on the server side — temporarily, of course! By guarding against a potential issue with the database, you make sure that you protect your web client against unexpected issues.

After you get a handle on your array of `entries`, then you sort them so they are date-descending.

Next, you're going to render the final array of objects that you'll send to your **.stencil** file. Inside the closure for your `UserJournalEntry.findAll` function, but at the very bottom, add the following code:

```
//1
var webEntries = [JournalEntryWeb]()

for entry in sortedEntries {

  // 2
  webEntries.append(JournalEntryWeb(id: entry.id,
    emoji: entry.emoji, date: entry.date,
    displayDate: entry.displayDate,
    displayTime: entry.displayTime,
    backgroundColorCode: entry.backgroundColorCode,
    user: entry.user))
}

// 3
do {
  try response.render("home.stencil", with: webEntries,
    forKey: "entries")
} catch let error {
  response.status(.internalServerError)
    .send(error.localizedDescription)
}
```

With this code, you:

1. Create a buffer array of `JournalEntryWeb` objects to send over.

2. Populate it using a combination of the computed properties from your extension in this file and the stored properties this object already carries.

3. Stuff your `response.render` command into a `do-catch` block, and you're scot free!

Lastly, in Xcode, open **Sources/Application/Application.swift** and go to `postInit`. Right beneath where you call `initializeUserRoutes`, add the following function:

```
initializeWebClientRoutes(app: self)
```

Nice! Now everything is ready to go. Go back to **WebClientRoutes.swift**, set a breakpoint inside `showClient`.

Build and run your server.

Open up a web browser, and visit http://localhost:8080/client. Your breakpoint should trigger; step through the inherent functionality and watch your context build! Depending on whether you've cleaned out your database from checking your work in Chapter 10, you should see some things come through. After you let your breakpoint go and let the route handler finish, check your browser and...

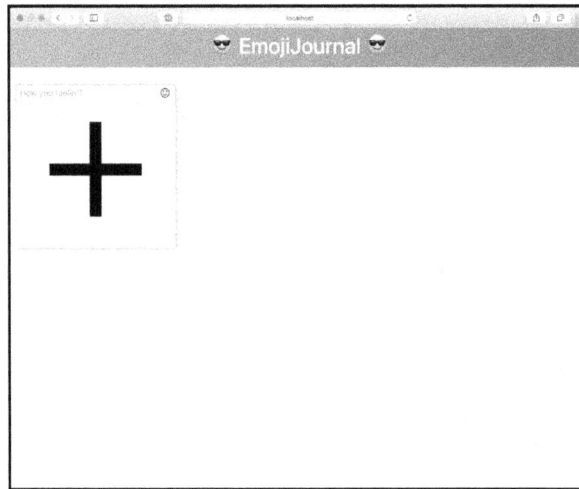

Note: If you don't see this, it's possible you've been following along from chapter to chapter and building this project incrementally — that's awesome! However, this chapter also requires you to use a file called **home.stencil**, which should be in a directory called Views in your root server directory. If you need to add this, do so, then save your project again. If things still aren't cooperating, try running your server from Terminal with `swift build` and `swift run`.

You may want to add a couple of journal entries through the API explorer using what you learned in Chapter 10 if you don't have any already.

From here on out, you're going to be editing your **home.stencil** file and checking the output to see what happens.

In Xcode, go to the Views directory, and open **home.stencil**. Three things to note about this file as you continue.

1. This technically counts as a static file. This means that you can edit this file, save it, and not have to re-run your server to notice the changes! This also means you should build and run your server, and not worry about restarting it for the rest of this chapter.

2. Xcode is... less than desirable as a non-Swift/Objective-C text editor. To make it marginally better, go to the top menu bar, and select Editor ▸ Syntax Coloring ▸ HTML. I won't blame you if you kick the tires on Visual Studio Code or Sublime Text.

3. Take a moment to read through the rest of the code, and peek at the accompanying style in index.css if you want. The web client will use something that looks like a UICollectionView with cards to sort all of the entries.

Ready to edit the template file?

Scroll to line 27, which should read like </article>, and after this line, add the following code snippet:

```
{% for entry in entries %}
<article class="card"
  style="background-color: #{{ entry.backgroundColorCode }};">
<div class="top-content-box">
  <div class="emoji-date">
    <p>{{ entry.displayDate }}<br>{{ entry.displayTime }}</p>
  </div>
  <input id={{ entry.id }} class="delete-button" type="submit"
    value="&#10005;" onClick="deleteEntry(this.id)"
    onEntry="hideEmojiPicker()">
</div>
<p class="emoji-text">{{ entry.emoji }}</p>
</article>
{% endfor %}
```

Here's what you've just done:

- You create an HTML element called an article, which allows you to classify an element with sub-sections called divs. One of the nice things about HTML is that you can override your CSS file with specific style instructions inline; you do that here with the hex code from backgroundColorCode passed through from your context from Stencil!

- Furthermore, you make nice and immediate use of the two computed properties for the date and time.

- You set up an `input` element at the top right-hand corner to delete an entry (Mac vs. Windows holy war participants, don't @ me), but you may notice that you haven't yet written the function to handle this yet — that's OK!

- The main course, obviously, is the particular emoji that you are displaying in the card!

- And all of this wrapped in a for loop across `entries`!

Think about this for a second; you just wrote a way to display however many EmojiJournal entries with one block of HTML, and you did it all with Swift and a little bit of sugar from Stencil!

Reload your browser. Regardless of what user you submitted them under, if you've loaded a couple of journal entries to your database, your website should show them:

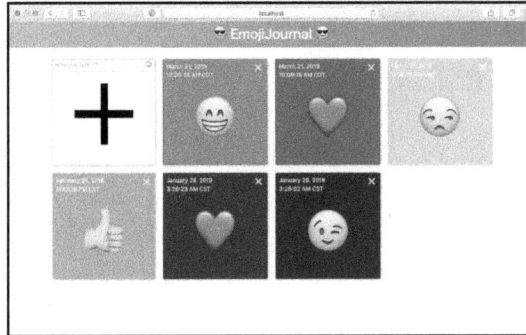

Nice work! Have you ever wanted to slap your Ray-Bans on, cross your arms, and tell Twitter that you're a web developer? Spin up your internet machine — you can now!

By now, you've likely noticed the first card in your collection. Try and click the emoji icon on the right side of the text field in that card. Select an emoji, then click the giant + sign. Nothing happens, right? This is the functionality you'll wire up in the next chapter.

Where to go from here?

Congratulations! You have a working web client now! You aren't done yet, though. In the next chapter, you'll:

- Add authentication to your web client.

- Add the ability to add a new emoji to your account.

- Add the ability to delete an emoji from your account.

Stencil is a very powerful framework for templating, and you should give it a shot on its own. You can check out the GitHub repo for it at https://github.com/stencilproject/Stencil.

Chapter 12: KituraStencil: Authentication, Adding & Deleting

David Okun

At this point, you now have a working web client to view all EmojiJournal entries in a webpage — nice work! Now, it's time to expand on it's capabilities, and do as much work as you can with it using Stencil.

In this chapter, you will:

- Add authentication capabilities to your web client.

- Add the ability to add a new EmojiJournal entry to your account.

- Add the ability to delete an EmojiJournal entry from your account.

To be clear, you aren't going to write a terribly large amount of Swift in this chapter, since you are working with Stencil and a web front end.

As I mentioned in the previous chapter, I won't go deep explaining each concept you use, but I'll make sure that you learn enough about everything you write to understand conceptually how you're using it.

This means that this chapter might feel like a step or two out of your comfort zone. You'll be using:

- **JavaScript**: A programming language capable of running in any web browser.

- **jQuery (jKuery?)**: A JavaScript library used to simplify running scripts in the browser.

> **Note**: Chris thought of the jKuery joke back when we were planning the Table of Contents for the first edition of this book. Do you have any idea how hard it is to sit on a joke for 12 chapters? I hope you laughed.

Don't worry; you will still get to write some Swift. First, let's empower your web client to do a little more!

Finishing your web layout

You're going to start by writing HTML to layout the tools you need for user management.

You can do this with a simple JS pop-up library, and you will write some jQuery to hook up all of the appropriate actions to it.

This is another good time to remind you that you do not have to use Xcode to edit this file; I personally prefer Visual Studio Code, but you can use whatever you'd like (yes, including Xcode if you must!)

Now, open your project, and build and run your server after Xcode resolves your dependencies.

In your web browser, open two tabs with the following addresses:

```
http://localhost:8080/openapi/ui
http://localhost:8080/client
```

You will be adding functionality to your web client to create journal entries from different users. You will also use Stencil to handle viewing journal entries from a specific user. Until then, you will use the Kitura OpenAPI UI to populate the journal with one or two entries from separate users.

In Chapter 10, you likely added a username or two to your database. You are welcome to continue using those throughout this chapter, but I will provide two usernames as separate examples, and to keep the pop-culture references coming.

Click on the **POST /user** route in your Kitura OpenAPI UI, and add the two following users:

```
{
  "id": "bill",
  "password": "excellent"
}
```

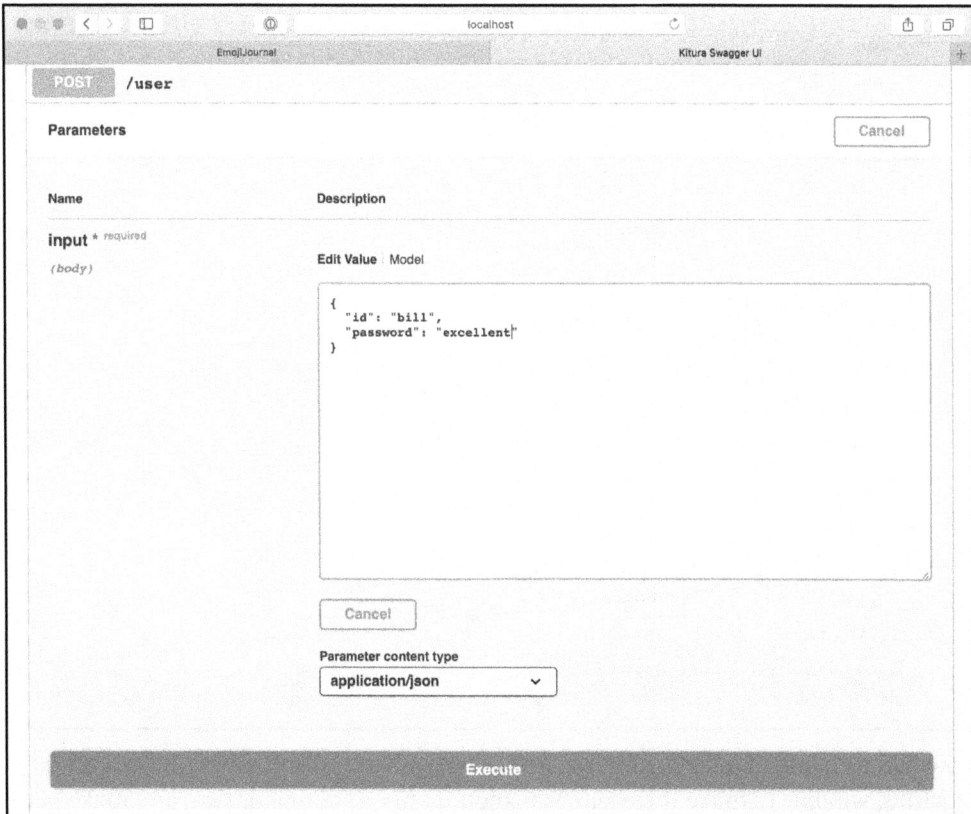

```
{
  "id": "ted",
  "password": "adventure"
}
```

Now, add a couple of journal entries specific to each user (remember to use a private browsing window to make it easier). You should only need one or two, and make sure that the dates are still represented as those wonky large numbers:

```
{
  "emoji":"😱",
  "date": 563725805.57661498
}
```

After you do this once or twice for each of your users, your web client should look like this:

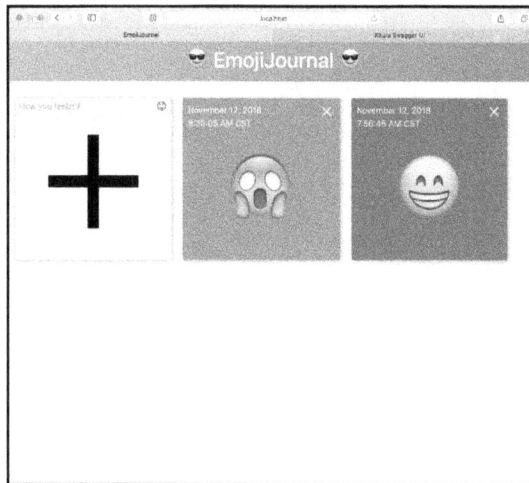

What you can't quite see in your web client is that these entries belong to different users, even if you know, under the hood, that these entries each have a `user` property attributed to them. To ensure that everything is in its right place, put a breakpoint in **Sources/Application/Routes/WebClientRoutes.swift** on the line where you call:

```
try response.render("home.stencil", with: webEntries,
    forKey: "entries")
```

Reload your web client in your browser, and your break point should be triggered. You want to inspect your `webEntries` array and make sure two entries have separate users, like so:

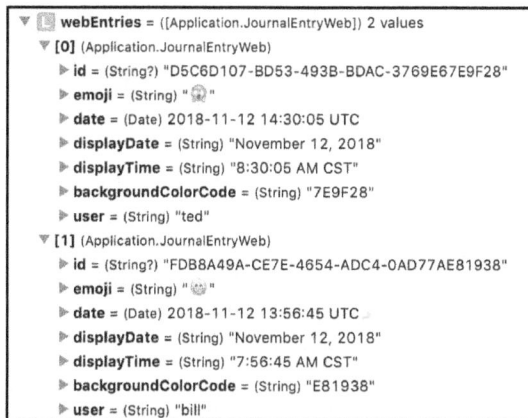

If you're here, or somewhere similar, then you're ready to go. Note that, until I tell you otherwise, you can keep your server running and not have to restart it; you are editing a static file that gets served up uniquely every time you request it from your browser.

Open **Views/home.stencil** in the text editor of your choice. Scroll to line 13, and add the following chunk of code just below `<div class='menu-container'>`:

```
<div id="user-info-popup" style="align-self: auto;">
  <input id="username-field" placeholder="username">
  <br>
  <input id="password-field" type="password"
    placeholder="password">
  <br>
  <button id="cancel-signup-button"
    onclick="cancelButtonTapped()">Cancel</button>
  <button id="signup-button" onclick="createUser()">
    Sign Up
  </button>
  <button id="login-button" onclick="login()">Login</button>
  <button id="logout-button" onClick="logout()">Logout</button>
</div>
```

Refresh your browser. You should see what you just made in the upper left-hand corner — nice!

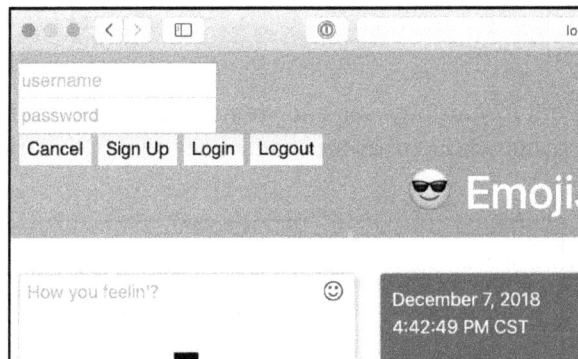

Well... sort of. Sure, it's there, but it doesn't really look that great shoved into the top left-hand corner.

Scroll down to the bottom of your file. Around line 58, you should see a bunch of lines that import JavaScript files, which look like `\<script src="...js"></script>`. Add the following line to the bottom of that list:

```
<script src="https://cdn.rawgit.com/vast-engineering/jquery-
popup-overlay/1.7.13/jquery.popupoverlay.js"></script>
```

Next, go below the first `<script>` tag that you see where you don't explicitly call a URL to import. Add the following block of code above the line that starts with `$(function() {`:

```
$(document).ready(() => {
  $('#user-info-popup').popup({
    color: '#FFF',
    opacity: 0.9
  })
})
```

Refresh your browser, and poof — your login window is gone!

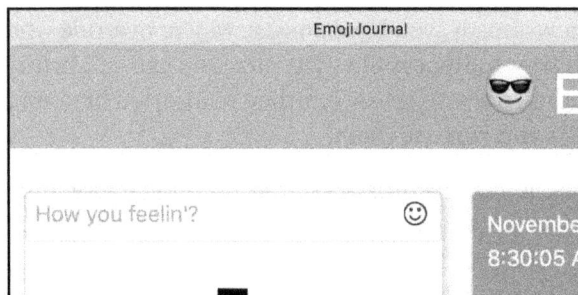

Or... is it?!

In reality, all you've done is declare this HTML element as a popup in jQuery, and now the library will take care of presenting it for you whenever you are ready to do so! In the meantime, it's simply hidden on top of the window, and out of the way until you are ready to invoke it.

Time to come up with a way to invoke your handy-dandy user management pop-up. Back in **home.stencil**, scroll to the top near line 28, and look for a block of code that looks like so:

```
<div class="wrapper">
  <div class='title'><h1>😎 EmojiJournal 😎</h1></div>
</div>
```

Delete this entire block of code, and replace it with this:

```
<div class="wrapper"
  style="display: grid;grid-template-columns: 1fr 1fr 1fr;">
  <div id="logged-in" style=
    "display:flex;margin:0;align-items:center;color:white;">
  </div>
  <div class='title'>
```

```
    <h1>😎 EmojiJournal 😎</h1>
  </div>
  <div class="wrapper"
    style="display: flex;align-items: center;margin: 0;">
    <div class="title-login" onclick="signupClicked()"
      style="margin-left: auto;color: white;">
    User Management
    </div>
  </div>
</div>
```

A couple of notes about what you've just typed:

1. If you didn't know already, you have an easy way to override whatever style rules you've set up in your **index.css** file with what you can call **Inline Style Rules**. It's good practice not to overuse these, but they're inserted here on purpose to demonstrate that **you can** use them.

2. Notice some common characteristics of the code you wrote. An HTML component can be classified as a `div`, and you can assign it properties like `class` and `onClick`. `class` is helpful for referring to HTML documents by name when you are working in jQuery, and `onClick` will specify a JS function to run when you click the element.

3. You might notice some use of the word flex often (weird, but OK) and this is in reference to a popular layout library called Flexbox. You can learn more about this library at http://learnlayout.com/flexbox.html.

Refresh your web browser. You should notice the addition of a white link at the top of your web app that says **User Management**.

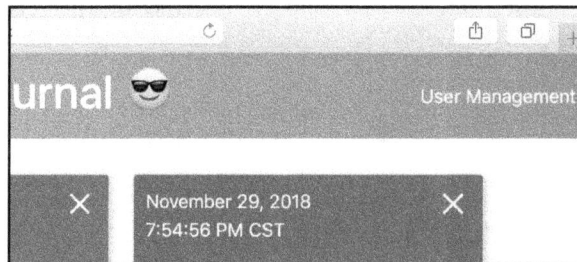

Try clicking it — a whole bunch of nothing should happen. Ahh, almost there! You still need to define your `signupClicked` function.

Scroll to the bottom of the file, and inside your `<script>` block at the bottom, add this function:

```
function signupClicked() {
  $('#user-info-popup').popup('show')
}
```

Refresh your browser, and click **User Management**; you should see something like this:

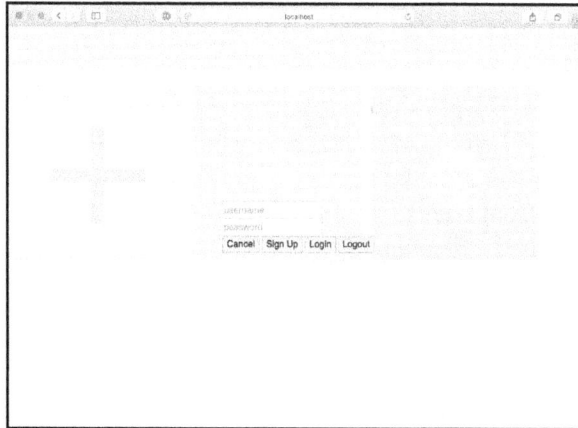

Nice work! In terms of laying out what you need, you've got everything you need here. However, try clicking the **Cancel** button. Shucks, not much to see here. Everyone stand back — you're going to write more JavaScript!

Making the web buttons work

First, you'll add the ability to make your handy new dialog go away. If you scroll back up to the HTML element where you declared the **Cancel** button in the first place, you should notice that the `onClick` function for this button is `cancelButtonTapped`. Scroll down underneath `signupClicked` inside the JavaScript section, and add the following function:

```
function cancelButtonTapped() {
  $('#user-info-popup').popup('hide')
}
```

Save the file, and refresh your browser. Now try clicking on **User Management**, and click the **Cancel** button. Clean as a whistle!

By now, you've likely figured out some of the different things you can call on your popup object in jQuery. Outside of this project, you should play around with it some more https://dev.vast.com/jquery-popup-overlay/!

Next, you're going to start configuring your web client to handle some authentication. To prepare for the implementation of these methods, you are going to add a handler to easily get and set cookies on your browser.

> **Note**: A cookie, in web development, is just a piece of cached information meant to simplify persisting state on your web app. In this tutorial, you are going to store a username and password in a pair of cookies on your web browser. These cookies will be readable on every subsequent request sent to Kitura, which will be helpful later! It is a very bad idea to replicate this practice in production. However, this is a tutorial about Swift on the Server, and not necessarily on the front end, so we will "make this work" in the name of demonstrating Stencil. I recommend you use session-based authentication in the future, where you can store the session token in a cookie when you've authenticated correctly, as opposed to a plaintext username and password.

Beneath `cancelButtonTapped`, add the following two functions:

```
function setCookie(cookiename, cookievalue, hours) {
  var date = new Date();
  date.setTime(date.getTime() + Number(hours) * 3600 * 1000);
  document.cookie = cookiename + "=" + cookievalue +
    "; path=/;expires = " + date.toGMTString();
}

function getCookie(name) {
  var value = "; " + document.cookie;
  var parts = value.split("; " + name + "=");
  if (parts.length == 2) return parts.pop().split(";").shift();
}
```

A browser has the ability to store these cookies for specified amount of times. Think of this like a built-in expiration date. Most websites you visit don't let you stay logged in forever, right? This is because you don't want to feed your services stale cookies... mmmm... cookies.

Scroll up to `signupClicked`, and update it so it looks like this:

```
function signupClicked() {
  $('#username-field').val(getCookie("username"))
  $('#password-field').val(getCookie("password"))
  $('#user-info-popup').popup('show')
}
```

You're adding this so that, whenever your dialog pops up, jQuery will pre-fill your fields with the latest stored cookies. You can choose to omit the password field setting if you'd like. However, at this point, you haven't stored any cookies yet, and that's because you haven't attempted to log in!

Signup and login functionality

You have two methods to write now before you can really do anything of consequence with your `JournalEntry` API. Start with the ability to sign up.

At the bottom of your JavaScript space, add the following function:

```
function createUser() {
  var userID = $('#username-field').val()
  var password = $('#password-field').val()
  var xhr = new XMLHttpRequest()
  xhr.open("POST", "/user")
  xhr.setRequestHeader("Content-Type", "application/json")
  xhr.onreadystatechange = (() => {

  })
  var body = JSON.stringify({"id": userID,
    "password": password})
  xhr.send(body)
}
```

Notice that there is a blank space inside the closure for `xhr.onreadystatechange`. You are going to add code in here soon, but let's cover a little bit about what you've just added.

The most common way to make a HTTP request from a web browser is the XMLHTTPRequest object, which exists on just about every browser.

- First, you are using jQuery syntax to pull your username and password from their respective HTML elements.

- Next, you create a XMLHTTPRequest object to handle your request, and you populate it with some properties that apply to what you are doing. Think back to how you've used the Kitura OpenAPI UI to this point; you can probably follow the logic here and in your use of the explorer.

- Finally, notice that, at the bottom of this block of code, you call xhr.send(body). This works very similarly to a URLSessionTask, in the sense that you have to handle the result of the call asynchronously.

The onreadystatechange property can be completed with a closure, and this is where you essentially handle your response. Inside this closure, add the following code:

```
if (xhr.readyState == XMLHttpRequest.DONE) {
  $('#new-user-popup').popup('hide')
  if (xhr.status == 201) {
    var result =
      confirm(`Created a new user: ${userID} - want to login?`)
    if (result) {
      login()
    }
  } else {
    alert(`There was an error creating this user profile:
      ${xhr.statusText}`)
  }
}
```

You have a couple of different states to check on, but you are most interested in what to do with the completed response and when everything is nice and done; thus, you want to act when your state is .DONE.

Next, you have the ability to check the official HTTP status code of your response with xhr.status, and since a **201** indicates that you have successfully created a new UserAuth object as a result of a POST request, you want to act accordingly. If this is the case, you can prompt the user to log in. This is what you're going to implement next!

You can save your file and refresh your browser if you'd like, but the flow might be easier to check after you implement your next method.

Below `createUser`, and add the following function:

```
function login() {
  var userID = $('#username-field').val()
  var password = $('#password-field').val()
  var xhr = new XMLHttpRequest()
  xhr.open("GET", "/entries")
  xhr.setRequestHeader("Content-Type", "application/json")
  xhr.setRequestHeader("Authorization", "Basic " +
    btoa(userID + ":" + password))
  xhr.onreadystatechange = (() => {

  })
  xhr.send()
}
```

This function should look very similar to `createUser`, but there is a key difference.

Since you have not explicitly written a `login` function on your backend, you need a way to check and see if your username and password credentials are correct. Your GET request on `/entries` requires these credentials, and you will get an appropriately coded response based on the truthiness of your credentials. This means you can essentially throw away the payload of this response, and save your credentials as cookies if you get the right status code! Is this a little bit hacky? Sure! If you are an experienced developer — don't even act like you've never put something marginally hacky into production before!

Before you add response handling code inside the `onreadystatechange` closure, check out the `Authorization` header code in this function. In Chapter 9, you learned about Basic HTTP authentication, and this is how you create that authorization string; the `btoa` function will take your string and create a base64 encoded ASCII string from its contents, which needs to be `username:password`. Server-side, your authentication middleware will "decrypt" this string and check the un-hashed username and password. If you've still wondered why it's called Basic, well, now you know!

Inside the closure for `onreadystatechange`, add the following code:

```
if (xhr.readyState == XMLHttpRequest.DONE) {
  if (xhr.status == 200) {

    // 1
    setCookie("username", userID, 24)
    setCookie("password", password, 24)

    // 2
    $('#user-info-popup').popup('hide')
```

```
    // 3
    alert(`Logged in as ${userID}`)

    // 4
    var loggedInUser = document.getElementById('logged-in')
    loggedInUser.innerHTML = "Logged in as: " + userID
    location.reload()

  } else {
    alert(`Login failed: ${xhr.statusText}`)
  }
}
```

Now, when you get a properly formed response, you:

1. Set the username and password cookie to the properly formed credentials, and you give them 24 hours before they expire.

2. Hide the User Management pop-up.

3. Alert the user that they logged in with the username they requested.

4. Update the **Logged in as:** string with the appropriately titled username.

Save your file, and refresh the webpage. Try to sign up with a new user like so:

```
username: socrates
password: philosophy
```

You should see the following screen if you've wired everything up correctly:

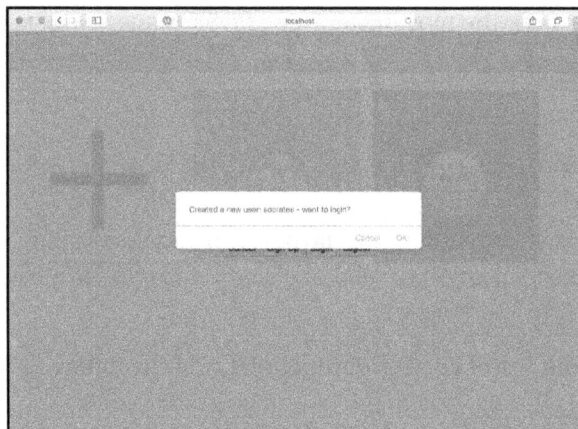

Click **OK** to login, and you should see that you are now logged in as **Socrates**! Nice work! Now, refresh your page, and notice that you should still see the same journal entries you've been seeing all this time.

This makes sense, as you haven't yet added any logic to filter the journal entries by user! You're going to save this for last.Finally, underneath `login`, add the following code:

```
function logout() {
  if (confirm("Are you sure you want to log out?")) {
    setCookie("username", "", 24)
    setCookie("password", "", 24)
    location.reload()
  }
}
```

Scroll up to your function that loads whenever your page loads (right before `signupClicked`), and update it to look like so:

```
$(function() {
  window.emojiPicker = new EmojiPicker({
    emojiable_selector: '[data-emojiable=true]',
    assetsPath: '/img/', popupButtonClasses: 'fa fa-smile-o'});
  window.emojiPicker.discover();
  var loggedInUser = document.getElementById('logged-in')
  loggedInUser.innerHTML = "Logged in as: " +
    getCookie("username")
});
```

Save the file and refresh your browser. Try to log in with any valid credentials you have, and then click **Logout**. When you confirm your intent, the page refreshes and your cookies are wiped out. Now all of your user management buttons are wired up!

Now, it's time to test out the most meaningful POST request you've written so far in this entire project!

Adding a journal entry on the web

Whenever you use the first card in your layout, you should be able to click the giant + button after you select an emoji to send one across the wire. Hook up that button now.

At the bottom of your list of JavaScript functions, add the following function:

```
function addEmoji() {
  var date = new Date();
  var dateString = date.toISOString();
  var emoji = $("#add-new-emoji-field").val()
```

```
    if (emoji == "") {
      alert("You must enter an emoji!");
      return;
    }
  }
```

This code block is incomplete, but it should already set off an alarm in your head. To this point, your API only handles the date property as a Date in Swift, and this is going to create a dateString object for your formed struct.

If you are thinking that this isn't going to work out of the box, well, you're right! We'll get to that in a moment; for now, add the rest of the function at the end, to send this object to the backend:

```
var xhr = new XMLHttpRequest();
xhr.open("POST", "/entries");
xhr.setRequestHeader("Content-Type", "application/json");
xhr.setRequestHeader("Authorization", "Basic " +
  btoa(getCookie("username") + ":" + getCookie("password")))
xhr.onreadystatechange = (() => {
  if (xhr.readyState == XMLHttpRequest.DONE) {
    if (xhr.status == 201) {
      location.reload();
    } else {
      alert(`There was an error adding this emoji:
        ${xhr.statusText}`)
    }
  }
})
var body = JSON.stringify({ "emoji": emoji,
  "date": dateString });
xhr.send(body);
```

Now, you have a way to fully send an object over the wire. If you get a successful **201** status, then you reload the page, and everything should show up successfully.

Save your file and refresh your web browser. Make sure you are still logged in as `socrates`, and try to add a new emoji entry.

I hate to spoil it for you, but you're not going to get a friendly message:

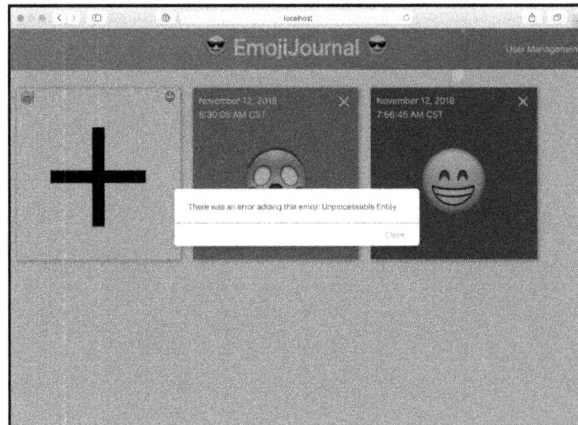

What gives?! Earlier, I alluded to how JavaScript formats dates and, sure enough, it doesn't format dates in a, ahem, Swifty way.

Back in Chapter 4, you learned a little bit about **ISO8601 date formatting**. This is the format that JavaScript has adopted for date formatting in its standard library. Sadly, your Kitura API just isn't ready to handle it, yet!

Instead, Kitura has a great feature that allows you to handle incoming Codable objects and encode/decode them with any custom logic you want!

Stop your server; it's finally time to write some Swift again!

Open **Sources/Application/Routes/EntryRoutes.swift** and scroll to the top of the file underneath your `import` statements. Add the following block of code:

```
enum DateError: String, Error {
  case invalidDate
}

let journalEntryDecoder: () -> BodyDecoder = {
  let decoder = JSONDecoder()
  decoder.dateDecodingStrategy = .custom({ (decoder) -> Date in

  })
  return decoder
}
```

Additionally, you will want to scroll up to the line where you `import Kitura` and change it to the following:

```
import KituraContracts
```

This is because `BodyDecoder` is not included with the base Kitura library, and `KituraContracts` will give you what you need by importing Kitura and extending it with some useful classes — such as `BodyDecoder`!

Because you are working with JSON, you want to ensure that you are using the `JSONDecoder` that Swift supplies you with. Here's where things get interesting. You could easily supply the following line instead of a `custom` date decoding strategy:

```
decoder.dateDecodingStrategy = .iso8601
```

It's nice that Swift packages this for you, but there is an issue with this decoder (as of this writing, this is also an opportunity to contribute to Foundation, if anyone has the bandwidth!) and how it parses proper ISO8601 dates.

The Swift decoder handles dates with no regard for the decimal places, which means that, for the Swift decoder to handle your date properly, your date would have to be formatted like so:

```
2018-11-30T01:42:16+0000
```

Unfortunately for Swift, JavaScript spits out the date string like so:

```
2018-11-30T01:42:16+0000.000
```

This means that you'll have to write some custom logic to handle your dates.

What's more: What if your iOS app still needs to interact with your app? You need to have logic that handles both use cases. This is exactly what Kitura's custom decoder logic was built for.

Inside the `custom` closure, add the following code:

```swift
// 1
let container = try decoder.singleValueContainer()

// 2
let dateNum = try? container.decode(Double.self)

// 3
if let dateNum = dateNum, let timeInterval =
TimeInterval(exactly: dateNum) {
  let dateValue =
    Date(timeIntervalSinceReferenceDate: timeInterval)
  return dateValue
}

// 4
guard let dateStr = try? container.decode(String.self) else {
  throw DateError.invalidDate
}

// 5
let formatter = DateFormatter()
formatter.calendar = Calendar(identifier: .iso8601)
formatter.locale = Locale(identifier: "en_US_POSIX")
formatter.timeZone = TimeZone(secondsFromGMT: 0)
formatter.dateFormat = "yyyy-MM-dd'T'HH:mm:ss.SSSXXXXX"

if let date = formatter.date(from: dateStr) {
  return date
}

formatter.dateFormat = "yyyy-MM-dd'T'HH:mm:ssXXXXX"
```

```
  if let date = formatter.date(from: dateStr) {
    return date
  }

  // 6
  throw DateError.invalidDate
```

With this code, you:

1. Get a handle on your container of variables.

2. Attempt to see if you can decode a variable from your container as a `Double`; if you are sending an iOS formed `Date` over the wire, this will catch it. Don't use `Date.self` here, or you'll end up in an infinite recursive loop!

3. Try to get an actual `Date` from the `Double` you decode from your container using the `TimeInterval` typealias. If this works out, you return the result, and you're home free!

4. Continue on to try and decode a date as a `String`, if this doesn't work.

5. Use custom `DateFormatter` logic to check for the different common amounts of decimal places in your date representation. If you can successfully convert one of these to a date, then you're *really* home free!

6. Throw an error and tell your Codable Router to send back a 422 error — unprocessable entity, if all else failed.

One last thing: Scroll down to `initializeEntryRoutes` and add this line of code at the bottom:

```
  app.router.decoders[.json] = journalEntryDecoder
```

This tells the router to use your custom decoder *practically* as middleware. Now, your custom decoder will attempt to decode any JSON payload that comes across these routes. That's super powerful!

Build and run your server, and open up your web client again. You can set a breakpoint in your custom decoder logic, if you'd like, but try to add a new emoji with your web client, and you should see it pop right up on your screen! Great job!

Deleting a journal entry on the web

You have likely noticed that each card in your layout on the web has a nice big **X** button at the top-right corner; time to make that actually work!

Make sure your server is still running, and go back to **home.stencil**. Add the following code to the bottom of your list of functions:

```
function deleteEntry(entryID) {
    var xhr = new XMLHttpRequest();
    xhr.open("DELETE", "/entries/" + entryID);
    xhr.setRequestHeader("Content-Type", "application/json");
    xhr.setRequestHeader("Authorization", "Basic " +
        btoa(getCookie("username") + ":" + getCookie("password")))
    xhr.onreadystatechange = (() => {
        if (xhr.readyState == XMLHttpRequest.DONE) {
            location.reload();
        }
    })
    xhr.send();
}
```

This function is called from the HTML element, where you declare this **X** button:

```
<input id={{ entry.id }} class="delete-button" type="submit"
    value="&#10005;" onClick="deleteEntry(this.id)"
    onEntry="hideEmojiPicker()">
```

You use Stencil to set the ID of the HTML element to the actual entry.id property, and using JavaScript, you can pass that ID into your function as an argument. This makes it a *lot* easier to specify which entry you want to delete! From there, you should be familiar with how the XMLHTTPRequest object works in your JavaScript function.

Save the file, and refresh your web page.

Try to delete a journal entry; you should notice that you can only delete an entry that you created with the same login you already used!

If this is what happens, then congratulations, you've hooked up everything correctly!

Viewing only your journal entries

Remember you read earlier about how your browser will include all cookies in each request it sends? Since you are managing your user sessions with cookies, you're going to make use of this now!

> **Note**: Again, it is strongly recommended to use token based authentication in the future and to not store usernames and passwords in plaintext with your cookies.

You've already written a bunch of jQuery to handle a lot of your requests. It would be reasonable to write a new jQuery request to GET all of your `JournalEntry` objects, since the GET route on your Kitura API has authentication built in. However, you're already loading all of your journal entries here via the Stencil API, so you're going to make use of your pre-existing cookies to filter out the entries you don't need on the server.

Open **WebClientRoutes.swift** again, and inside the `showClient` route handler, underneath the line of code where you create `sortedEntries`, add the following code:

```
if let username = request.cookies["username"]?.value,
   !username.isEmpty {
   sortedEntries = sortedEntries.filter { $0.user == username }
}
```

Remember, when you log out on your web client, you are setting the username and password to an empty string, so you need to make sure that the username both exists and is meaningful. If you cannot satisfy both of these conditions, then you simply show all journal entries. Otherwise, you can filter out all journal entries that don't match the currently logged-in username!

Before you can build and run, you need to fix a compiler error this code introduced. Xcode is going to complain because `sortedEntries` was previously declared as a constant. Update it to be `var` so that you can properly modify `sortedEntries`.

Build and run you server, and go back to your web browser.

Log in as one user. Voila! You should only see that user's entries now! Add an entry as that user, log out, and log in as another user. Nice work!

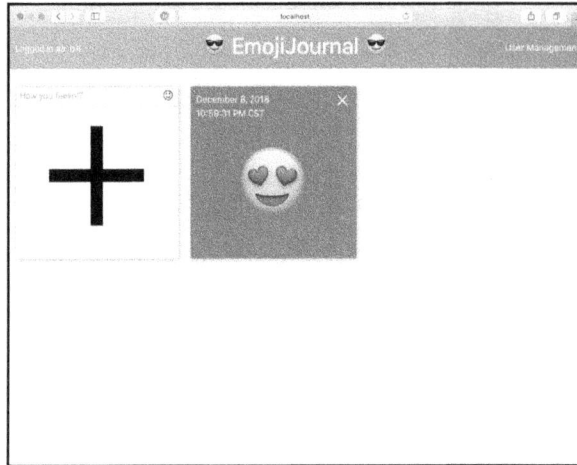

Note: If you've kept your browser running as you've been following along through multiple chapters, and you're not currently using a private browsing window, you may find that previous authentication is conflicting with your currently logged in user. To fix this, restart your browser or use a private browsing window.

Where to go from here?

Whew! How's that for a crash course in jQuery and JavaScript? I bet you feel a bit more powerful and wiser for it, though — at least I hope you do!

Remember that the best way to load your `JournalEntry` objects from this point would be to make a GET request with the right authentication. Since this entirely involves jQuery, and practically entirely sidesteps the need for Stencil, you can try it on your own if you'd like!

In the next chapter, you're going to stay in the domain of the world wide web, but you'll do so from the comfort of your Kitura API and a new framework called SwiftyRequest as you create a mock server!

Chapter 13: Using Other Services

Chris Bailey

Your EmojiJournal app already provides a number of great features, but all of them are ones that you create and manage yourself. In this chapter, you'll learn how to use other services through the use of requests to RESTful APIs in order to extend your app with additional capabilities.

In this chapter, you'll learn how to:

- Access a public API service.

- Build fault tolerance and fallbacks into your use of the service.

- Migrate your data model in your database.

- Build a mock server for the service.

By the end of this chapter, you'll provide an additional capability to your users in the EmojiJournal app, based an on an external third-party service.

The Fortune Cookie API

The Fortune Cookie API service is a simple hosted API that is available at http://yerkee.com/api, where it exposes a GET based API to retrieve a random fortune cookie:

```
GET /api/fortune/{category}
```

This supports categories of **all**, **computers**, **cookie**, **definitions**, **miscellaneous**, **people**, **platitudes**, **politics**, **science**, and **wisdom**.

Try out the following call to the API using curl in a terminal window:

```
curl -X GET "http://yerkee.com/api/fortune/all" -H "accept:
application/json"
```

This returns a JSON response containing a single field called `fortune` along with a wise and cryptic fortune:

```
{"fortune":"Indecision is the true basis for flexibility."}
```

You are going to use this API in your EmojiJournalServer to add a fortune to each journal entry, so the user becomes more enlightened every time they record an entry.

Creating a fortune type

When making a request of the Fortune Cookie API, you ideally want to be able to use Swift's `Codable` capabilities to parse the JSON response and covert it into a Swift data type.

As the response from the Fortune Cookie API is only a single field, that's relatively straightforward to do manually. For more complex responses, this becomes increasingly difficult and time consuming. There are a number of tools that are available that will take an example JSON payload and create the necessary Swift types for you. These include:

- QuickType (Online tool: https://app.quicktype.io)

- JSON Cafe (Online tool: http://www.jsoncafe.com)

- JSON 4 Swift (Online tool: http://www.json4swift.com)

- CuteBaby (macOS App: https://medium.com/@nixzhu/cutebaby-json-swift-f1ea6cc87451)

To create your type for the Fortune Cookie API response, you'll use the **JSON Cafe** tool.

Open your browser to http://www.jsoncafe.com, and make sure the **Model Generator** tab is selected.

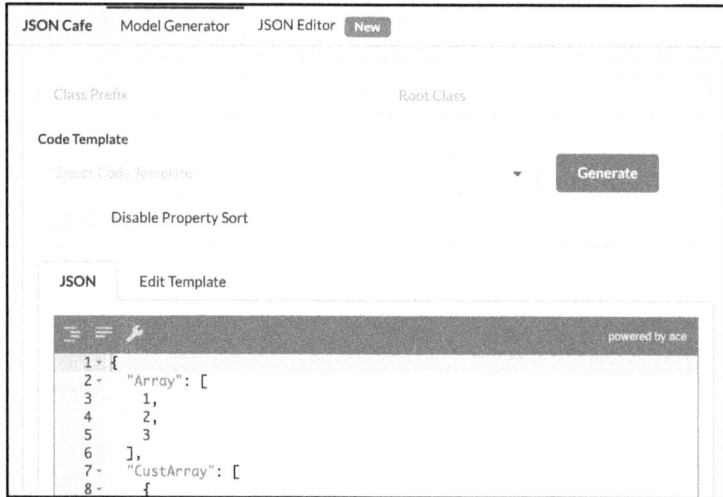

Paste the example JSON response from above into the **JSON** editor window. Then set a Root Class of **Fortune** and a Code Template of **Swift Codable**. Finally, click the **Generate** button.

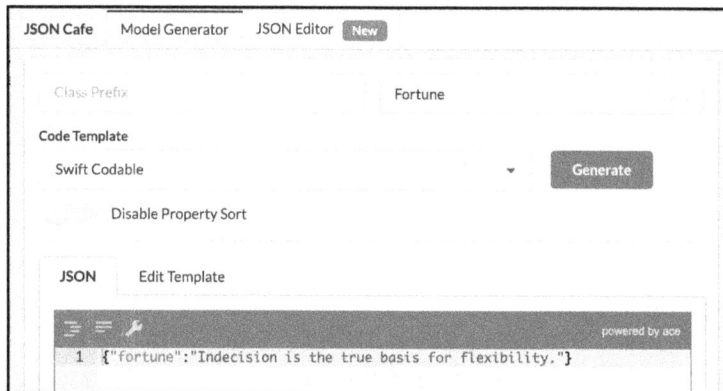

This opens a panel containing a **Fortune.swift** file with a full definition of a Codable type for use with the response from the Fortune Cookie API.

```
Download All        🐦 Enjoying? Tell the world!

Fortune.swift
  2   //  Fortune.swift
  3   //  Model Generated using http://www.jsoncafe.com/
  4   //  Created on November 30, 2018
  5
  6   import Foundation
  7
  8 ▾ struct Fortune : Codable {
  9
 10       let fortune : String?
 11
 12 ▾     enum CodingKeys: String, CodingKey {
 13           case fortune = "fortune"
 14       }
 15
 16 ▾     init(from decoder: Decoder) throws {
 17           let values = try decoder.container(keyedBy: CodingKeys.self)
 18           fortune = try values.decodeIfPresent(String.self, forKey: .fortune)
 19       }
 20

Download
```

Next, you'll need to add that definition into your EmojiJournalServer project. Either download the file from JSON Cafe using the **Download** button, or copy and paste the contents into a new file called **Fortune.swift**. Add this file to **Sources/Application/Models/** in your project.

This provides you with a way to decode and store the fortune data. Next you'll need to use a request library to make requests of the Fortune Cookie API to fetch new fortunes.

Making REST requests with SwiftyRequest

To make calls from EmojiJournalServer to the Fortune Cookie API, you are going to use the SwiftyRequest library, which can be found at https://github.com/ibm-swift/swiftyrequest.

SwiftyRequest is built on top of URLSession from Foundation, but provides two additional features that are useful for making calls from a Swift-based server to other backend services:

1. **Integration with Codable**: SwiftyRequest is able to automatically decode responses received from the requests it makes into Codable types that you request.

2. **Fault Tolerance with Circuit Breaking**: SwiftyRequest enables you to declare a Circuit Breaking policy, which allows your app to gracefully deal with outages of the backend services you're making calls to.

Add a dependency on SwiftyRequest by adding the following in the `dependencies` array in **Package.swift**:

```
.package(url:
    "https://github.com/IBM-Swift/SwiftyRequest.git",
    .upToNextMajor(from: "1.0.0")),
```

And then add `"SwiftyRequest"` to the list of dependencies in the `Application` target so that it becomes:

```
.target(name: "Application", dependencies: [ "Kitura",
"CloudEnvironment","SwiftMetrics","Health","KituraOpenAPI","Swif
tKueryPostgreSQL","SwiftKueryORM","CredentialsHTTP",
"KituraStencil", "SwiftyRequest"]),
```

Save your `Package.swift` file, and watch Xcode resolve your dependencies for you.

Open **Sources/Application/Models/Fortune.swift** and add imports for SwiftyRequest and `LoggerAPI`:

```
import SwiftyRequest
import LoggerAPI
```

Next create a class called `FortuneClient` that you'll use with the Fortune Cookie API:

```
class FortuneClient {

  private static var baseURL: String {
    return "http://yerkee.com"
  }

  private static var fortuneURL: String {
    return "\(baseURL)/api/fortune/all"
  }
}
```

The class contains two static fields: `baseURL` and `fortuneURL`. This makes it easier to handle changes to the location or API path for the Fortune Cookie API service.

Inside the `FortuneClient` class, add a static function called `getFortune` as follows:

```
public static func getFortune(completion: @escaping
    (String?) -> Void) {

  let errorFortune = "No fortune is good fortune"

  // 1
  let request = RestRequest(method: .get, url: fortuneURL)

  // 2
  request.responseObject() {
    (response: RestResponse<Fortune>) in

    // 3
    switch response.result {

    // 4
    case .success(let result):
      let fortune = result.fortune
      return completion(fortune)

    // 5
    case .failure(let error):
      Log.error("FortuneClient request failed with \(error)")
      return completion(errorFortune)
    }
  }
}
```

In this code, you:

1. Set up the `RestRequest`, which will take care of making an API request for you.

2. Invoke a response to your request by calling the `responseObject` method. There are other `response` methods depending on the expected response. For instance, if you expected a `String` as a response instead of a generic `Codable` object, you would call `requestString` instead.

3. Check the `result` field of the returned `response` object to determine whether the request was successful.

4. Extract the `fortune` from the `result`'s associated value and pass it to the completion handler, if the request was successful.

5. Log the error and pass the default fortune to the completion handler, if the request failed.

This provides everything you need to make requests of the Fortune Cookie API and return the fortune message back to the calling code.

Fault tolerance and circuit breaking

Whenever an app makes use of a remote service, another point of failure is introduced into the app. It is important to ensure that, should the remote service suffer from bad performance, respond intermittently, or have outages, your app continues to able to run and service requests. This means ensuring that your app has **Fault Tolerance** capabilities.

As well as making integration with `Codable` to decode the response, SwiftyRequest also provides **Fault Tolerance** using the CircuitBreaker library. You can find the library at https://github.com/ibm-swift/circuitbreaker.

The Circuit Breaker pattern (https://martinfowler.com/bliki/CircuitBreaker.html), which the **CircuitBreaker** library implements, is designed to increase application stability, improve response times and prevent the application from making constant failing requests.

The CircuitBreaker library does this by watching requests to services and monitoring them for failures, including exceeding a defined timeout. Should the rate of failures reach a threshold, the Circuit Breaker **trips** and causes further requests of the service to fail immediately, without the request being made at all. The CircuitBreaker library then allows a **fall back** behavior to be executed instead of making the request that would ultimately timeout or fail.

Finally, the circuit breaker monitors to see if the remote service becomes available again (or more performant) by periodically allowing a request to be made through to the service. If the service is available, the circuit breaker is reset, allowing all calls to go through to the remote service.

To add circuit breaking support to `FortuneClient`, first add the following import to the top of **Fortune.swift**:

```
import CircuitBreaker
```

Next, configure the circuit breaker properties in `getFortune` just above the definition for the `request`:

```
let circuitParameters = CircuitParameters(timeout: 2000,
    maxFailures: 2, rollingWindow: 5000, fallback: errorFallback)
```

This sets a timeout of 2,000 milliseconds (two seconds) before a request will fail — a max number of failures of two and a rolling window of 5,000 milliseconds (five seconds) over which the failures must occur for the circuit to trip.

Additionally, it defines a fallback function to call if the request fails.

You still need to define this function, so add the following code just above the definition for `circuitParameters` you just added:

```
let errorFallback = {
    (error: BreakerError, msg: String) -> Void in

    Log.error("FortuneClient fallback with \(error)")
    return completion(errorFortune)
}
```

This logs an error and calls the completion handler passed to the `getFortune` function with your backup fortune of "No fortune is good fortune". This means that, should there be problems with the Fortune Cookie API, including a full outage, your users will always get a fortune.

While the backup fortune is always the same, the fallback function could be used to make a call of an alternative service that provides fortunes, or to use a local store of backup fortunes.

Finally, just after the line where you define the `request`, add this code:

```
request.circuitParameters = circuitParameters
```

Your complete function should now look as follows:

```
public static func getFortune(completion: @escaping
    (String?) -> Void) {

    let errorFortune = "No fortune is good fortune"

    let errorFallback = {
        (error: BreakerError, msg: String) -> Void in

        Log.error("FortuneClient fallback with \(error)")
        return completion(errorFortune)
    }

    let circuitParameters = CircuitParameters(timeout: 2000,
        maxFailures: 2, rollingWindow: 5000,
        fallback: errorFallback)

    let request = RestRequest(method: .get, url: fortuneURL)
    request.circuitParameters = circuitParameters

    request.responseObject() {
        (response: RestResponse<Fortune>) in
```

```
    switch response.result {

    case .success(let result):
      let fortune = result.fortune
      return completion(fortune)

    case .failure(let error):
      Log.error("FortuneClient request failed with \(error)")
      return completion(errorFortune)
    }
  }
}
```

You now have everything you need to make calls to the Fortune Cookie API to provide your users with fortunes, and handle any failure of the API so that your users are not affected.

Updating the JournalEntry data model

Before you can add the fortunes to the entries and respond with them to your users, you first need to update the `JournalEntry` data model, and the `UserJournalEntry` that's used to store it on a per-user basis in the database.

Open **Sources/Application/Models/JournalEntry.swift** and update the `JournalEntry` model to store an additional `fortune` field:

```
var fortune: String?
```

Also update the `init(_ entry: UserJournalEntry)` constructor to set the new `fortune` field by adding this line at the end:

```
self.fortune = entry.fortune
```

Then make the same two changes to the `UserJournalEntry` model so that it also stores and sets a `fortune` field:

```
struct UserJournalEntry: Model {
  var id: String?
  var emoji: String
  var date: Date
  var user: String
  var fortune: String?

  init(_ journalEntry: JournalEntry, for user: UserAuth) {
    self.id = journalEntry.id
```

```
        self.emoji = journalEntry.emoji
        self.date = journalEntry.date
        self.user = user.id
        self.fortune = journalEntry.fortune
    }
}
```

This updates your data models to store the additional fortune message as a String, but your database is not set up to store the additional field.

This can be handled in two ways. If you don't yet have any users and do not need to preserve the existing data, you can simply reset the database and then create new tables for the new model.

You can do this by running dropdb emojijournal from the command line in the terminal app to remove the database, followed by createdb emojijournal to re-create it.

If, however, you want to preserve your existing data in the database, but add support for the new fortune field, you can do that by manually updating the database.

To do that, open your terminal app and run:

```
psql -U postgres -d emojijournal
```

This opens an interactive session in the terminal to allow you to run commands against the emojijournal database.

Inside the interactive terminal session, run the following command:

```
ALTER TABLE "UserJournalEntrys" ADD COLUMN fortune TEXT;
```

This ALTERs the UserJournalEntrys table to ADD a COLUMN called fortune, which is going to store data of type TEXT, which represents a variable number of characters (i.e., a string).

While this adds the fortune column, it does not set any data for the existing entries in the table. You can add that by running the following UPDATE command in the interactive terminal session:

```
UPDATE "UserJournalEntrys" SET fortune = 'No fortune is good
fortune' WHERE fortune IS NULL;
```

This sets any entry in the fortune column that is currently NULL to a value of No fortune is good fortune — your fallback fortune message.

You can now exit the interactive terminal session using:

```
\q
```

You have now migrated your database to the new structure without losing any data, and added a default value for the existing entries.

Now, you just need to update your app to call getFortune in order to invoke the Fortune API Service to get a fortune message, and add it into the JournalEntry.

Open the **Sources/Application/Routes/EntryRoutes.swift** file and find the addEntry function. Replace it with the following:

```
func addEntry(user: UserAuth, entry: JournalEntry, completion:
    @escaping (JournalEntry?, RequestError?) -> Void) {

    FortuneClient.getFortune() { fortune in
        var savedEntry = entry
        savedEntry.id = UUID().uuidString
        savedEntry.fortune = fortune
        savedEntry.save(for: user, completion)
    }
}
```

This calls FortuneClient.getFortune with a completion handler that adds the returned fortune message string into the savedEntry instance that is being saved into the database.

Notice that, because of your use of the default fortune message, the getFortune call is guaranteed to respond with a message.

Verifying the use of the Fortune Cookie API

You can verify the use of the Fortune Cookie API by creating and retrieving entries through the Kitura OpenAPI UI as you did previously.

Build and run your EmojiJournalServer project and open the Kitura OpenAPI UI http://localhost:8080/openapi/ui.

Note: In a previous chapter, you created a user for John. If you've since deleted that user, or if you didn't follow that chapter, you can create that user now. To do that select the **POST /users** row, click **Try it out** and create a user with an id of **John** and a password of **12345**, which matches the user credentials used by your mobile app.

Select the **POST /entries** row and click on the **Try it out** button. Notice that the Model has been automatically updated with the new fortune field, and that is has been marked as optional.

Click the **Edit Value** tab, enter the following data as the input and click **Execute**:

```
{
  "emoji":"😄",
  "date": "2018-09-18T00:07:01.000Z"
}
```

Once you log in as one of your created users, e.g., John with a password of 12345, you should receive a successful response.

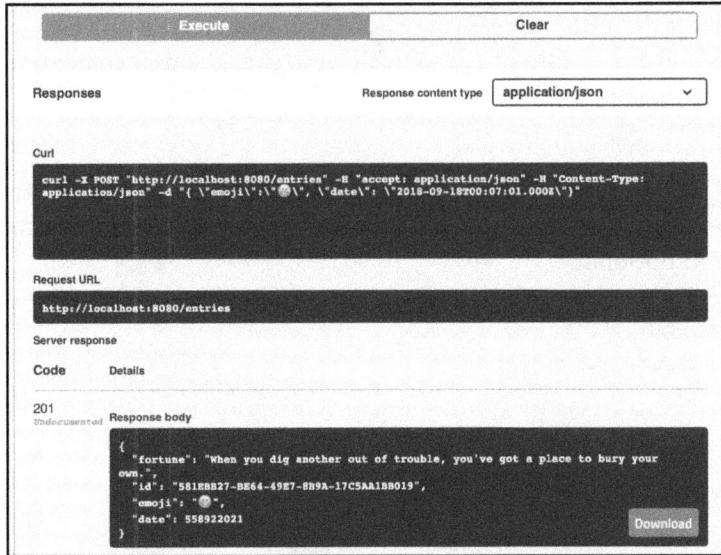

Here, the call has been made to the Fortune Cookie API, which in this case has responded with:

```
When you dig another out of trouble, you've got a place to bury
your own.
```

Congratulations! You have now added fortunes to your EmojiJournalServer app and verified that it is correctly storing fortunes with the user's journal entries.

Building a mock server for the Fortune Cookie API

While you have now verified that the call to the Fortune Cookie API is working using the live Fortune Cookie API, it may not always be suitable to use the live server.

A good example for this is inside your test framework where you:

- Need to test against an API that is guaranteed to be available: Inside your test framework, you ideally want tests to fail only if there is a bug in your app. You don't want to rely on external services that are affected by networking issues or are currently undergoing an outage.

- Need to test error and failure conditions: Inside your test framework, you ideally want to be able to test that your app correctly handles errors being returned from the remote services.

You may also want to minimize using the live server because there is a usage charge associated with each call to it!

One way of resolving these issues is to use a mock server — a server that simulates the behavior of the remote server but that responds with known responses that you specify.

One of the features of Kitura, is that it's easy to provide a mock server — both because you can manually build RESTful APIs in three lines of code, and because the Kitura CLI provides the ability to create a Kitura server that implements a supplied OpenAPI specification. You'll use that second capability to create a mock server for the Fortune Cookie API service.

Below is an OpenAPI specification definition for the Fortune Cookie API, which you can also find in the **fortune-server** directory of the starter project for this chapter:

```
{
  "schemes" : [
    "http"
  ],
  "swagger" : "2.0",
  "info" : {
    "version" : "1.0",
    "title" : "Fortune Cookie API",
    "description" :
      "Returns a random fortune cookie via JSON"
  },
  "paths" : {
    "\/api\/fortune\/{id}" : {
      "get" : {
        "consumes" : [
          "application\/json"
        ],
        "produces" : [
          "application\/json"
        ],
        "responses" : {
          "200" : {
            "schema" : {
              "$ref" : "#\/definitions\/Fortune"
            },
            "description" : "successful response"
          }
        },
        "parameters" : [
```

```
            {
              "in" : "path",
              "name" : "id",
              "required" : true,
              "type" : "string"
            }
          ]
        }
      }
    },
    "definitions": {
      "Fortune": {
        "type": "object",
        "required": ["fortune"],
        "properties": {
          "fortune": {"type":"string"}
        }
      }
    }
  }
}
```

Note: If you didn't use the starter project for this chapter and are working off of your project from the previous chapter, you'll need to copy the **fortune-server** directory from the starter project to your project. It's located at the same level as the EmojiJournalServer and the EmojiJournalMobileApp.

Open Terminal and make sure you're in the **fortune-server** directory. Next use the Kitura CLI, which you installed using **Homebrew** in Chapter 2, with the `create` command to create a new Kitura instance:

```
kitura create
```

After downloading some data, this starts an interactive command console which prompts you to respond to a series or questions and options.

Respond to those prompts as follows:

```
Initialization prompts
? What's the name of your application? server
```

```
? Enter the name of the directory to contain the project: server
```

```
? Select type of project:
> Scaffold a starter
  Generate a CRUD application
```

```
? Select capability presets for application pattern:
> Basic
  Web
  Backend for frontend
```

```
? Select capabilities:
 o Static web file serving
 o Swagger UI
 ● Embedded metrics dashboard
 ● Docker files
>● Kitura OpenAPI
```

```
? Select endpoints to generate:
 o Swagger file serving endpoint
>● Endpoints from swagger file
```

```
? Swagger file to use to create endpoints and companion iOS SDK:
> Custom swagger file
  Example swagger file
```

```
? Provide the path to a swagger file: fortune.json
```

```
? Would you like to generate codable routes, (yes recommended)?
Yes
```

```
Service prompts
? Would you like to generate a Swift server SDK from a Swagger
file? No
```

```
? Generate boilerplate for services: (Press <space> to select,
<a> to toggle all, <i> to inverse selection)
>o Cloudant / CouchDB
 o Redis
 o MongoDB
 o PostgreSQL
 o ElephantSQL
 o Object Storage
 o AppID
```

> **Note**: While the Kitura CLI should manage dependencies for you
> appropriately, you may run into an issue related to events.js throwing an
> unhandled error. If this happens for you, follow these steps to get back on
> track: First, go to https://github.com/nvm-sh/nvm and follow the README.md
> documentation to install NVM, or the Node Version Manager. Then, in
> Terminal, enter the command nvm install 10.16.0. Finally, in Terminal,
> enter the command nvm use 10.16.0.
>
> kitura create should work for you after fixing this.

This creates a new Kitura project in the **server** subdirectory that creates a **Basic**
project with **Embedded metrics dashboard**, **Docker files** and **Kitura OpenAPI**,
generating **Endpoints from swagger file** using the **fortune.json** file.

Additionally, the kitura create command automatically runs swift build to
build the project for you.

Change to the **server** subdirectory, and open the generated Xcode project:

```
cd server
xed .
```

The project structure for the mock fortune server should be familiar as it matches how your EmojiJournalServer is built. Open **Sources/Application/Routes/Api_Routes.swift** to see the RESTful endpoints that have been built for you:

```
import Kitura
import KituraContracts

func initializeApi_Routes(app: App) {
  // Handlers for codable routes are declared below:
  //
  func getOne__api_fortune__handler(id: String,
    completion: (Fortune?, RequestError?) -> Void ) -> Void {

    completion(nil, .notImplemented)
  }

  // Codable routes are declared below:
  //
  app.router.get("/api/fortune/",
    handler: getOne__api_fortune__handler)
}
```

This has registered a single handler on **/api/fortune**, which takes a string identifier and returns a Fortune object. The string identifier matches the Fortune Cookie API service, which allows one of the following categories to be supplied: **all**, **computers**, **cookie**, **definitions**, **miscellaneous**, **people**, **platitudes**, **politics**, **science**, and **wisdom**.

Notice that the getOne__api_fortune__handler function currently calls the completion handler with an error value of .notImplemented which maps to an HTTP status code of **501 Not Implemented**.

Update the handler as follows to respond with a mock Fortune response:

```
func getOne__api_fortune__handler(id: String,
  completion: (Fortune?, RequestError?) -> Void ) -> Void {

  let fortune = Fortune(fortune: "Mock fortunes are fake news.")
  completion(fortune, nil)
}
```

You now have a mock implementation of the Fortune Cookie API that you can use for testing successful responses. As you are going to want to run both your mock Fortune

Cookie API and your EmojiJournalServer at the same time, you are going to want to
run your Fortune Cookie API on a different port.

To do that select **Product ▸ Scheme ▸ Edit Scheme...** in Xcode. With the **Run**
option selected in the left pane, click on the **Arguments** tab. Now, Add an
environment variable with a **Name** of **PORT** and a **Value** of **8081** and click **Close**:

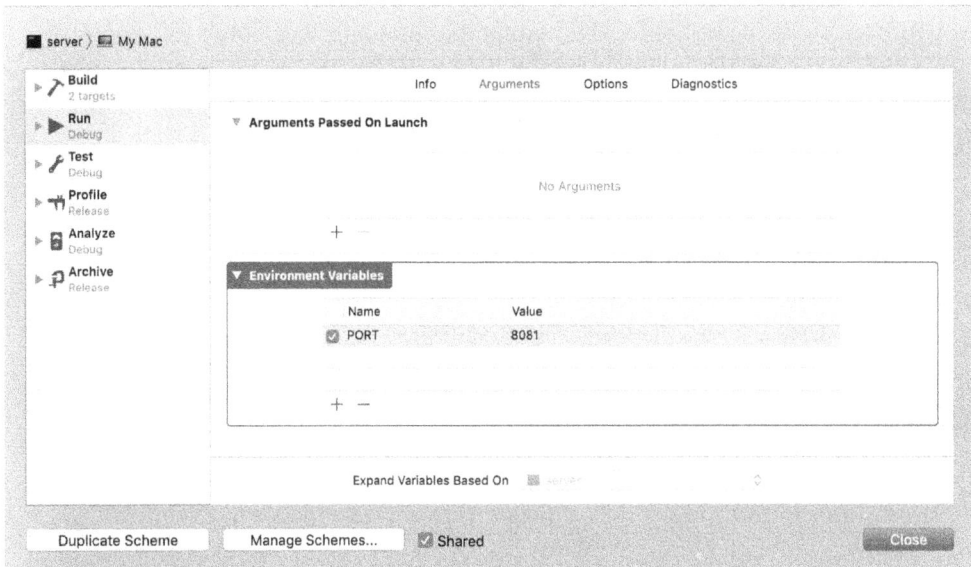

Now, build and run your mock server project, and open the Kitura OpenAPI UI on
port **8081** http://localhost:8081/openapi/ui:

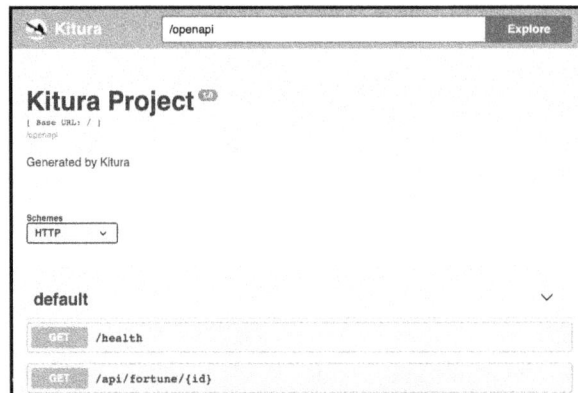

This shows that your generated mock server has both the **/api/fortune/{id}** endpoint
defined by the OpenAPI spec, as well as the **/health** endpoint.

Select the **GET /api/fortune/{id}** row and click **Try it out** to test the mock server

API.

Enter an **id** of **all** and click **Execute**:

This has successfully responded with your mock response!

You will now update your EmojiJournalServer project to use the mock server rather than the real Fortune Cookie API service for testing.

Without closing your mock server project, open your EmojiJournalServer project in Xcode, and open the **Sources/Application/Models/Fortune.swift** file.

The definition for the location of the Fortune Cookie API service is currently as follows:

```
private static var baseURL: String {
  return "http://yerkee.com"
}
```

Because you'll want to be able to dynamically define where the service is located without having to rebuild your app, update the code to be able to also configure the baseURL using an environment variable:

```
private static var baseURL: String {
  return ProcessInfo.processInfo.environment["FORTUNESERVER"]
    ?? "http://yerkee.com"
}
```

This uses a location of `http://yerkee.com` by default, but allows it to be externally set using the `FORTUNESERVER` environment variable.

Next set the environment variable by selecting **Product ▸ Scheme ▸ Edit Scheme...** and adding **FORTUNESERVER** with a value of **http://localhost:8081** to the list of environment variables:

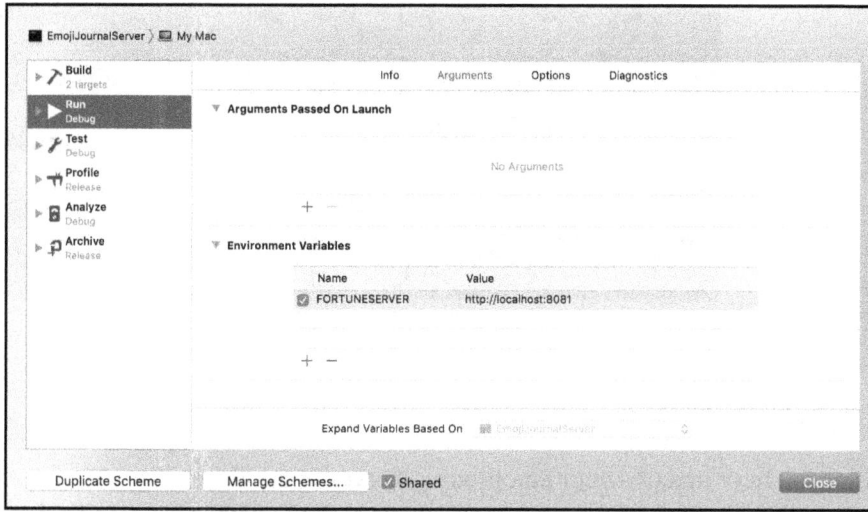

Make sure your mock server is still running. Now, build and run your EmojiJournalServer project, and open the Kitura OpenAPI UI on port 8080 http:// localhost:8080/openapi/ui to test that it's working with the mock server.

Select the **POST /entries** row and click **Try it out**. Next enter the following **input** value and click **Execute**:

```
{
  "emoji":"😎",
  "date": "2018-09-19T00:07:01.000Z"
}
```

This should now respond with a new created entry, including the fortune, **Mock fortunes are fake news,** from your mock server!

Server response

Code   Details

201   Response body
Undocumented
                {
                    "fortune": "Mock fortunes are fake news.",
                    "id": "00C039E9-70A1-4C9C-B6A8-C251EF93D0B7",
                    "emoji": "😂",
                    "date": 559008421
                }   Download

                Response headers

                connection: Keep-Alive
                content-length: 118
                content-type: application/json
                date: Sat, 01 Dec 2018 19:14:51 GMT
                keep-alive: timeout=60

Running it end to end

Now that you have updated your EmojiJournalServer to use the Fortune Cookie API service — either the real one or your mock server — the final step is to verify that it's running successfully in an end to end test. To do that, you're going to again use your EmojiJournalMobileApp to connect to your EmojiJournalServer.

The EmojiJournalMobileApp provided in this chapter has already been updated to work with fortunes. Open `EmojiJournalMobileApp.xcodeproj` in Xcode and open the **EmojiJournalMobileApp/Model/JournalEntry.swift** file. Notice the `fortune` field has been added. Additionally, **Main.storyboard** and **JournalTableViewCell.swift** have been updated to add the fortune messages into the UI.

Build and run your project in the iPhone simulator. You should see a view similar to the following, show journal entries with embedded fortunes being displayed.

Next, click the + button and add a new journal entry with an emoji of your choice. This should now update the UI with your new emoji along with the **Mock fortunes are fake news** fortune, because your EmojiJournalServer is still configured to use your mock server:

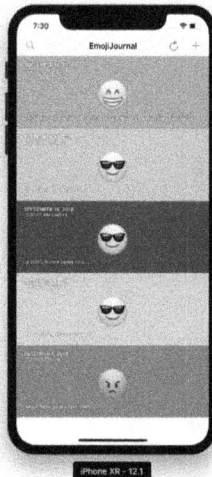

That's it! You've now added a *vital* new feature to your EmojiJournal app, which will surely expand your user base significantly!

Services and the API economy

In recent years, more and more RESTful APIs are being exposed for apps and third parties to use, as part of the **API economy**.

The API economy refers to the exposure and selling of access to useful APIs, usually under a **freemium** model in which low levels of usage are free, with increasing charges as the usage of the APIs increase.

The ability to use API economy services in your app massively increases the scope of what capabilities you can provide. These span a huge range, from being able to retrieve weather or location services information, to being able to carry out image recognition, or sentiment analysis, to using NASA APIs to find out about the number of near earth objects.

This means that the features and functions of your app are not constrained by the data and capabilities available to you, but by the use cases your app is designed to solve.

Chapter 14: HTTPS Certificates

David Okun

Here's a fortune for you: HTTP server without TLS/SSL certificate is like dead fish — cannot stand test of time. Everything you've done to this point has been over the HTTP protocol, and you learned about how to use REST to communicate over HTTP without any issues so far.

If you use the internet in 2019, you have likely seen the use of `https://` in just about any website instead of just plain old `http://`, and this is all in the name of protecting your data!

The only difference between `http` and `https` is that little `s`, which stands for security — however, you'll soon find out that it makes all the difference in the world.

In this chapter, you will:

- Learn the basics about `https` and SSL/TLS.

- Create a self-signed `https` certificate.

- Apply your certificate to your Kitura server.

Additionally, if you continue onto the next chapter, you'll have a couple of resources you can use for a `https` certificate on the internet if you assign a domain to your web application.

This chapter is going to contain a fair amount of theory, and there's no point in side-stepping the issues — security is hard!

This will not be a comprehensive guide to securing a web server, but I hope this chapter gives you enough information to understand what you can do to secure your Kitura server. Technically, this chapter is optional, but I recommend that you at least read this chapter to understand the inherent threats of leaving your server unprotected.

Be afraid, be very afraid

In World War I, the United States worked with a number of Choctaw and Cherokee Native Americans to operate as *Code-Talkers*. They would communicate secret plans and transmissions in their lesser-known native tongues to outsmart the opposition, knowing that they did not understand the language.

The strategy was effective, most notably in the Meuse-Argonne Offensive in France. This practice turned the tide of battle in 24 hours, and the opposition were retreating within 72 hours, rendered unable to anticipate or understand the Allies' moves.

The idea to use *Code-Talkers* came from the Central Powers' forces' intelligence capabilities, and their interception of plans on the battlefield from the Allies. However, once these plans were no longer in a language they could understand, nothing could be done to stop them.

Where am I going with this?

This is a fairly loose example, but imagine if everything you did to interact with any entity on the internet was understood by every entity around it. The best way to see how effective `https` can be is to see how ineffective `http` is at protecting your data.

One tool you can use to illustrate this is a proxy tool called Charles. A free trial is available and you can use it for 30 days. The free trial has a 10 second delay every time you start up the program and will automatically close after 30 minutes. You can download it at https://www.charlesproxy.com/.

After you install Charles, open the program and run it on your machine.

Open a web browser and load a couple of webpages — you should see a flurry of activity that looks like so:

Charles is going to act as a proxy, or an interceptor, for every internet connection on your machine. If you haven't used Charles before, you surely see how powerful a tool like this can be during development! Click on the **Contents** tab in the middle of your screen, and click on a connection that you recognize. In my proxy, I examined a connection with the API of github.com.

Take a look at the contents:

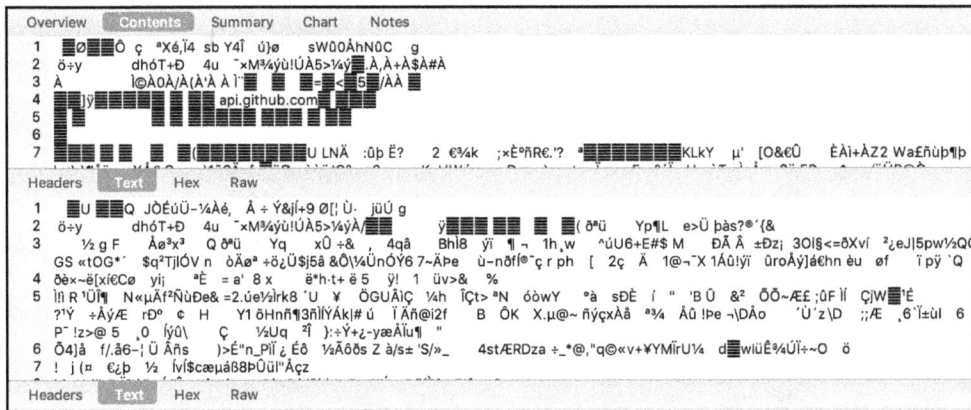

You see how, um, difficult that content is to read? This is on purpose. Of everything that you can see in the body of your request, you can pick out `api.github.com` in plain English. It would make sense for this to be exposed — your RESTful communication mechanism still needs to know where to send this request!

This text can be decrypted — if and only if you have the key and certificate on the `api.github.com` website. If you don't have this key, this is going to sound an awful lot like a Code-Talker to you.

Now, let's see what a regular `http` connection looks like. Open EmojiJournalServer in Xcode by double-clicking **Package.swift**, and wait while Xcode 11 resolves your dependencies.

Build and run your server, and make sure Charles is still running.

> **Note**: If you're not getting any connections for *localhost* in Charles, it means your system is not setup to use proxies for localhost traffic. To get around this, connect to this URL instead: http://localhost.charlesproxy.com:8080/entries. This still points to 127.0.0.1, but forces the traffic to go through Charles.

Open a new tab in your web browser, and navigate to http://localhost:8080/entries. You should have to enter a username and password — if you followed along with Chapter 12, **bill** and **excellent** should be fine credentials!

After you enter those credentials, you should get a result, but then search for your connection in Charles, and look at the contents.

```
 Overview    Contents    Summary    C
▼ Server
   ▼ Basic Authentication
        User ID          bill
        Password         excellent




   Headers    Authentication    Raw

[{
  "fortune": "No fortune is good\nfortun
  "id": "503CAAAE-0322-4EC5-982B-CFAAD81
  "emoji": ⬜⬜" ,
  "date": 0
```

Oh, no. You should feel extremely exposed at this point.

To circle back around to the Code-Talker example — sending a request across http is like screaming across the room (or battlefield) in plain English, and just hoping that no one else hears your plans!

By using Charles to intercept this request, you are basically performing what the L33T H@XX0R5 call a *Man in the Middle* attack.

You should be proud of yourself for your mad skills on display, but if it was this easy to hack into your own server, how easy do you think it would be for someone else that wants your data to do the same thing? Time to lock things down!

SSL/TLS

SSL stands for *Secure Sockets Layer,* a project started by Netscape in 1995 to envelop http communication in an encrypted wrapper. **TLS** stands for *Transport Layer Security,* which is a protocol that encrypts data sent over the internet, and evolved from SSL. For all intents and purposes of this chapter, you can assume that they are essentially different acronyms of the same purpose. We'll stick to referring to this protocol as TLS for the remainder of this chapter to offer you some consistency.

Let's also assume that, for all future examples, your *client* is the browser. When you try to connect with a server, you can send a request over http — this essentially tells the server, "Don't worry about how you give me data, just give me data!" By now, you understand that this is generally unsafe.

However, if you send that same request over https, then you are essentially requesting three things from the server to prove that it can satisfy the requirements of https:

1. A valid server name

2. A valid and recognized **CA**, or *certificate authority*

3. A public encryption key associated with the server name

Assume you've sent a request to https://www.awesomewebsite.com, for example. The public webpage shouldn't require any encryption, so that can be sent over the internet in plain text. However, what if you need to log into that website? Would you want to send that same style of request over plain text? Thanks to Charles, you already know that that is not a good idea.

This is where https comes in handy. Via the public encryption key, you send the body of your request encrypted with that public key, and you rely on the certificate of the server receiving your request to have the private key to **de**-crypt the content of the request. This is where the Code-Talker example comes in — think of the public/private key pair as an understanding of a specific language between the client and the server.

This means that, in order to enable TLS for your server, you have to create a valid certificate for your server. This certificate will implicitly carry a public/private key pair to distribute to clients that make requests of it. Now, you're going to create a *self-signed* version of this kind of certificate.

OpenSSL and self-signed certificates

You are going to enter a series of commands into Terminal shortly, but you first need to read about what you'll create.

Kitura uses the OpenSSL framework on Linux, and Secure Transport on macOS for managing TLS. This means that you'll create all the necessary files you need for Linux first, and then use built-in OpenSSL tools to convert what you create into something that works for macOS.

What works on Linux, and what works on macOS? As of this writing, PKCS#12, or the **.p12** format is accepted for Kitura on macOS.

On Linux, Kitura supports the following formats:

• **PEM**: A Base64-encoded ASCII format of public and private data

• **DER**: A binary blob of the public and private data

• **PKCS#7**: A Base64-encoded ASCII of public data

• **PKCS#12**: A binary blob of both public and private data that can be password encrypted. This is generally one blob that contains both the certificate and the key data

Now, you are going to use OpenSSL to generate a *self-signed* TLS certificate for your server. Your certificate will not be recognized as an *official* CA (certificate authority), but you will mitigate this issue later.

In Terminal, from the root directory of your EmojiJournalServer project, enter the following command:

```
openssl genrsa -out key.pem 2048
```

This lets you generate a 2048 bit RSA (public encryption) key for your certificate. The -out flag means that your generated key will be called **key.pem**. Feel free to type ls into Terminal between each command to see what files you end up with. Next, enter the following command:

```
openssl req -new -sha256 -key key.pem -out cert.csr
```

Answer the prompts about your location, you can enter something made up for the Organization Name, and you can leave the email and challenge password blank.

Here, you create a new **CSR**, or *Certificate Signing Request* using the OpenSSL utility. You create this request using the SHA256 algorithm, which is one of the stronger hashing algorithms in existence right now.

To explain what a hashing algorithm does in a sentence: **it takes plain text and turns it into an encrypted string called a hash.**

You should consider any SHA algorithm to be one way — this is to say that there is no way to extract the original text from a hash.

> **Note**: You may have heard about *hash collisions* before. This is how organizations or people try to figure out ways to invalidate hashing algorithms. An input that passes through a hashing algorithm is supposed to result in a unique output. If someone can come up with two disparate strings of text that result in the same value after passing through the hashing algorithm, then the algorithm is no longer a guaranteed way to promise a unique value on the resultant end. SHA1 was invalidated by Google in 2015 via hash collision, thus SHA2 is the minimum required hashing algorithm for TLS from 2015 on.

Next, in Terminal, enter the following command:

```
openssl req -x509 -sha256 -days 365 -key key.pem \
  -in cert.csr -out certificate.pem
```

This is a mouthful, so let's break it down:

- X.509 is a standard format for public key certificates

- You can specify the number of days that this certificate is valid for — 365 in this example

- You have to use the **key.pem** file you created earlier to hash out the contents of your certificate

- You also need to specify the CSR along with your other payload

- Finally, you get to specify what your final output file looks like with the -out flag

Check the contents of your folder with ls in Terminal. You should have **certificate.pem** sitting there ready for you to use! If you're feeling like you just solved *The Matrix* — you should!

You're doing great! Don't stop now! Enter this final command into Terminal to convert your **.pem** file into a PKCS#12 file, which is acceptable for macOS:

```
openssl pkcs12 -export -out cert.pfx -inkey key.pem \
  -in certificate.pem
```

When it prompts for an **Export Password**, use **emojijournal**.

In short, you've specified a format to convert your certificate file into for macOS, and you've named it what you want it to be. Now, enter the following Terminal commands to put them into a friendly place for your Kitura server to load:

```
mkdir /tmp/Creds
cp cert.pfx certificate.pem key.pem /tmp/Creds/
```

This sets up your certificate files in a convenient place for your Kitura server to pick up. Be advised — when you restart your machine, this directory will be wiped out! It's good practice to keep track of these files somewhere safe as you continue working on your server.

Lastly, you have a slight bit of mystery work to take care of with one of your Docker files. I'll go easy explaining a deep purpose here, as you'll dive into Swift on Linux with Docker in the very next chapter. For now, open `Dockerfile` in any text editor, and find the line that reads:

```
# Bundle application source & binaries
COPY . /swift-project
```

Underneath these lines, add the following:

```
RUN mkdir /tmp/Creds/
COPY cert.pfx certificate.pem key.pem /tmp/Creds/
```

In a sentence, this takes all of the certificate and key files you've just created, and gives your `Dockerfile` a command to add them to a similar directory in your Linux environment. When you get this up and running in the next chapter, you'll want to ensure a safe connection!

Using BlueSSLService

BlueSSLService is a framework written in Swift by IBM to handle setting up TLS for your Kitura server. This comes pre-installed with Kitura, so you don't have to add any more dependencies to your project for Swift Package Manager!

There are two main constructors you need to be concerned with for this library, and you'll use both of them, so you can be ready to load this certificate in the next chapter when you deploy to Docker and Kubernetes! Open EmojiJournalServer in Xcode, open the file **Sources/Application/Application.swift**, scroll to the bottom of the file, and find the `run` function.

Delete the following line of code:

```
Kitura.addHTTPServer(onPort: cloudEnv.port, with: router)
```

You're now going to add code to create a TLS config variable to pass into your Kitura starter. Underneath the line `try postInit()`, add the following block of code:

```
#if os(Linux)
let certificate = "/tmp/Creds/certificate.pem"
let keyFile = "/tmp/Creds/key.pem"
let config = SSLConfig(withCACertificateDirectory: nil,
                        usingCertificateFile: certificate,
                        withKeyFile: keyFile,
                        usingSelfSignedCerts: true)
#else
let certificateKeyFile = "/tmp/Creds/cert.pfx"
let config = SSLConfig(withChainFilePath: certificateKeyFile,
                        withPassword: "emojijournal",
                        usingSelfSignedCerts: true)
#endif
Kitura.addHTTPServer(onPort: cloudEnv.port, with: router,
  withSSL: config)
```

Remember that, in Linux, you can use **.pem** files, but you cannot do this in macOS. This is why you make use of pre-processor directives here — not a practice you want to get used to, but something that is definitely handy when the need arises!

Note one other thing in the above block of code — you specified, in both operating systems, that this certificate is self-signed. I've been alluding to this issue a few times now, and I think, before you run your server, it's time to finally cover what this means.

In TLS/SSL cryptography, a valid CA, or Certificate Authority, will be listed as the signer of a valid certificate. This is a registry that is known to the general public, and this identity is verified when the client makes that original handshake with the server to establish a `https` connection. It's safe to say that, if you sign your TLS certificate yourself, then you are not going to be listed as one of those verified CA's.

This is going to throw a literal red-flag with browsers that try to connect with your server, and you'll see an example of this soon. At the end of this chapter, I will provide you with some resources you can use to set up a properly signed certificate with a deployed version of your server if you would like to do so.

At the bottom of your new block of code, notice that you are passing in the config you are creating to your constructor for starting your Kitura server. This value is, by default, nil, which is why you haven't had to worry about it to this point.

Build and run your server. Open a web browser, and visit `https://localhost:8080` — depending on which one you use, you might have to force your machine to accept the self-signed certificate. However, once you accept the handshake with your certificate, you are cruising in the fast lane with `https`!

If you still have Charles open, and you try to view the request, you should see something much better.

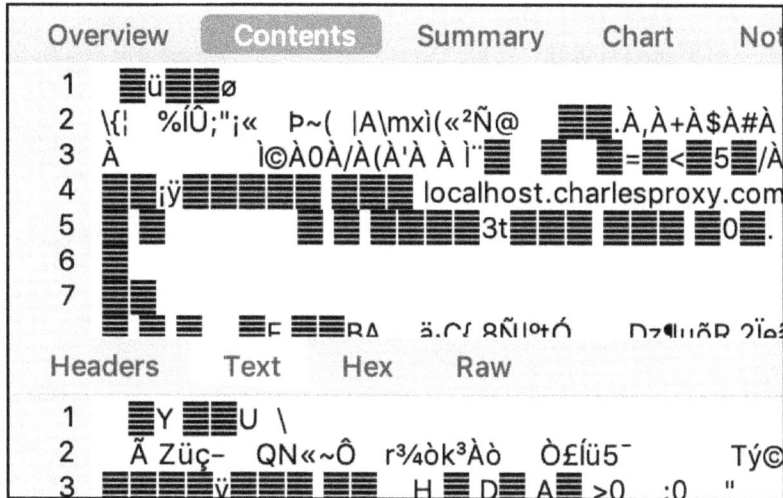

Updating your mobile app

Before you open your EmojiJournal mobile app, quit running your server in macOS, and run your server in Docker using `kitura build` then `kitura run`. At the time of this writing, there is a socket-level issue with OpenSSL, which prevents a macOS build of your server from accepting self-signed certificates. Running your server in Linux via Docker keeps this from happening.

Open your mobile EmojiJournal app. Go to **EmojiClient.swift** and update your `baseURL` to look like so:

```
private static var baseURL: String {
  return "https://localhost:8080"
}
```

Because you are using a self-signed certificate, you need to also let KituraKit know that it's OK to accept such a certificate. Remember, once again, that you have six calls inside this class, all of which have code that looks like this:

```
guard let client = KituraKit(baseURL: baseURL) else {
    return completion(nil, .couldNotCreateClient)
}
```

You can add one parameter to this constructor in each call to force KituraKit to accept your self-signed certificate, so update each instance of the above code snippet to look like this instead:

```
guard let client = KituraKit(baseURL: baseURL,
    containsSelfSignedCert: true) else {
        return completion(nil, .couldNotCreateClient)
}
```

Build and run your app. With your server live, KituraKit handles the self-signed certificate for you, and everything works just fine!

Where to go from here?

In this chapter, you learned about what it takes to lock down your HTTP server with TLS/SSL. You hacked your own server with a proxying tool called Charles, then you created a self-signed certificate in Terminal, and you applied it to your Kitura server for both macOS and Linux. Lastly, you updated your mobile app to accept the self-signed certificate. Now everything is nice and secure!

You might be wondering what Charles looks like if you inspect this traffic — through a series of settings and proxy SSL root certificates, you can get Charles to inspect the contents of this request, but it won't look any different to you than the regular `http` request. This is because you signed your `https` certificate yourself, and that means Charles is able to decipher all of the contents of the traffic, because it has everything it needs to do so! That being said, I recommend you try this on your own to see the difference.

There are tons of resources available to you on the internet to set your website/app up with TLS/SSL, but if you are going to deploy this application to the live internet, then you may want to check out https://letsencrypt.org and https://zerossl.com to get started in setting this up for your own live services.

Speaking of live services… if you've made it this far, you should pat yourself on the back! It's time to put your work into practice, and to take Kitura LIVE!

Chapter 15: Going Live

Chris Bailey

Everything you have built for your emoji journal project has so far run in what is really a development environment: either running locally on macOS or in a Linux-based Docker container on your local macOS machine.

In this chapter, you'll learn about what it takes to **Go Live** with your EmojiJournalServer. You will learn how to deploy your EmojiJournalServer and make it:

- Highly available, so your mobile and browser apps always respond.

- Highly scalable, able to respond to very large numbers of requests.

- Highly observable, providing monitoring for user traffic, performance and resource usage.

By the end of this chapter, you'll be able to deploy a your end-to-end emoji journal app with a backend EmojiJournalServer that is able to scale to thousands of clients.

Deploying Docker with Kubernetes

Kubernetes (https://kubernetes.io) is one of the core projects in the Cloud Native Computing Foundation (https://www.cncf.io) and describes itself as "an open-source system for automating deployment, scaling, and management of containerized applications." What this means is that it provides a platform for the deployment and management of applications, such as your EmojiJournalServer, that have been built into Docker images and can be run in Docker containers.

Kubernetes is designed to allow you to scale your application. You can deploy multiple instances called *replicas* and can even have Kubernetes automatically add and remove replicas based on monitoring data through *Horizontal Pod Autoscaling*.

Kubernetes also provides the ability to automatically restart any replica that has failed based on a liveness or health check, which is why generated Kitura projects include a **/health** endpoint by default. This makes it easier to ensure that your app is always available.

Additionally, the Kubernetes platform is widely supported by the public clouds, which means you can use it with your preferred cloud vendor, and migrate between cloud vendors, if you wish.

You can also run Kubernetes locally on your macOS machine; in fact, it's integrated directly into Docker Desktop, making it very easy to install and use. In this chapter, you'll use Kubernetes as part of Docker Desktop so that you don't have to register for a cloud provider. Don't worry, though; everything you do with your local Kubernetes install will also work with a cloud hosted Kubernetes platform.

Installing Kubernetes in Docker Desktop

In Chapter 2, "Hello, World!", you installed Docker Desktop from https://www.docker.com/products/docker-desktop. Inside Docker Desktop, you can also install and enable Kubernetes support.

To do that, first make sure that Docker is running by choosing the Docker app from the Launchpad. This launches Docker and adds the Docker icon to the menu bar.

Select the Docker icon in the Menu bar and click **Preferences**:

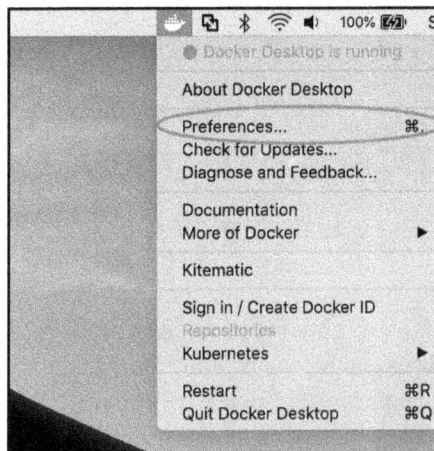

From the Preference window, select the **Kubernetes** tab and select the **Enable Kubernetes** checkbox and click **Apply**:

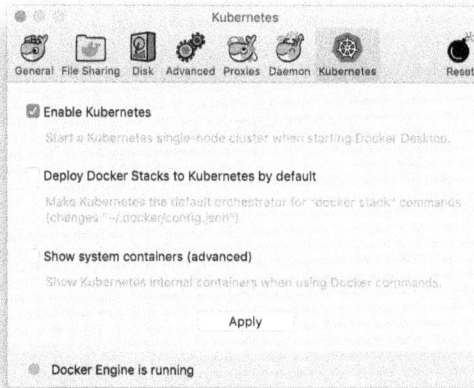

Click **Install** on the dialog box asking, "Install the Kubernetes Cluster now?" to start the install.

This opens the following dialog box:

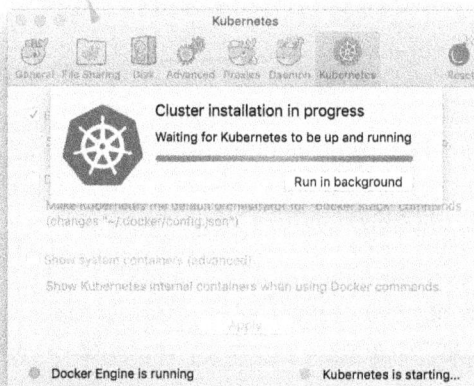

The installation will take a few minutes. When it's complete, the indicator light in the bottom-right corner will turn green:

As well as installing Kubernetes as a platform, this has also installed the kubectl command line tool that lets you interact with Kubernetes.

You'll use kubectl to work with your Kubernetes cluster throughout this chapter, but, before you do that, you'll first install **Helm**.

Helm

Helm describes itself as helping you "define, install, and upgrade even the most complex Kubernetes app." Helm provides you with the ability to package your app along with a number of configuration files into a **Chart**.

Your app's Helm Chart then describes how your app should be deployed and run. This includes configuring the number of replicas of your app to deploy, whether and how to apply horizontal pod autoscaling and how to configure the app.

Helm also provides versioning for your app, enabling you to version your app based on changes in configuration as well as changes to the app code itself.

Helm can be installed locally using Homebrew.

> **Note**: If you've installed Homebrew from previous chapters, you should be set to proceed. If not, first, check to see if you have Homebrew installed by opening your preferred terminal app and running the brew command in a terminal window. If Homebrew is installed, your should see usage information printed to the terminal. If you see an error message, follow the instructions at http://brew.sh to install Homebrew.

Enter the following into your terminal app:

```
brew install kubernetes-helm
```

This installs the Helm CLI for use in the terminal. Next, use the Helm CLI to initialize Helm:

```
helm init
```

This both configures the local Helm client and installs a Helm server component into your Kubernetes cluster called **Tiller**. Tiller interacts with Kubernetes to install, upgrade, rollback, query and remove Kubernetes resources based on behalf of your Helm Chart.

A successful helm init should respond with the following:

```
$HELM_HOME has been configured at /Users/toojuice/.helm.

Tiller (the Helm server-side component) has been installed into your Kubernetes
Cluster.

Please note: by default, Tiller is deployed with an insecure 'allow unauthentica
ted users' policy.
To prevent this, run `helm init` with the --tiller-tls-verify flag.
For more information on securing your installation see: https://docs.helm.sh/usi
ng_helm/#securing-your-helm-installation
Happy Helming!
```

Now that you have the Helm client and the Tiller server installed, you are ready to deploy your first Helm Chart.

> **Note**: You may have noticed a certain nautical naming theme for the tools. In fact, the the theme runs throughout all of the technologies involved in Kubernetes, which itself is *Helmsman* in ancient Greek.

Deploying a Helm Chart

The first Helm Chart you are going to deploy is for your PostgreSQL database, which your EmojiJournalServer will use. Up to now, you've been using a local PostgreSQL install that's been running on your desktop. Once you've moved to a cloud-based deployment that is no-longer an option.

You could use one of the many providers that will run a hosted PostgreSQL instance for you, but you can easily run your own instance in your Kubernetes cluster.

Luckily, a Helm Chart for PostgreSQL already exists, as it does for many different types of software, in the **stable** Helm Chart repository, https://github.com/helm/charts.

First, check that your Helm client is configured with the "stable" repo by running:

```
helm repo list
```

This should return the following:

```
NAME     URL
stable   https://kubernetes-charts.storage.googleapis.com
local    http://127.0.0.1:8879/charts
```

If the stable entry is not present, you can add it using the following:

```
helm repo add stable \
  https://kubernetes-charts.storage.googleapis.com
```

Next, deploy an instance of PostgreSQL using the following:

```
helm install --name postgresql-database \
  --set postgresDatabase=emojijournal stable/postgresql \
  --version 0.17.0
```

This requests that Helm installs the `stable/postgresql` chart as a release called `postgresql-database`. Additionally, it uses `--set` to pass the `postgresDatabase=emojijournal` configuration to the chart, so that it creates a database called `emojijournal`.

By default, the chart will create and use the `postgres` user, and will auto-generate a password.

You can get a full report of the status of your release using:

```
helm status postgresql-database
```

You can also use the Kubernetes `kubectl` command line to query the status of all deployed app instances — called **pods** — using:

```
kubectl get pods
```

This should report:

```
NAME                                  READY    STATUS     RESTARTS    AGE
postgresql-database-59bf99d965-5zcnq   1/1      Running    0           1m
```

This shows that an instance of your PostgreSQL database has been running for one minute and has had zero restarts.

The EmojiJournalServer Helm Chart

The Helm Chart for PostgreSQL was already provided, which means that you only needed to install it. In order to deploy your EmojiJournalServer in the same way, you'll need your own Helm Chart for it.

As you started from a generated Kitura project, you already have a Helm Chart template for your project.

The Helm Chart consists of several configuration files that are stored in the **chart/ {project name}** directory of your project.

For your EmojiJournalServer project, they are stored in **chart/emojijournalserver**.

Open your project in Xcode and take a look at the chart files in the **Project navigator** view:

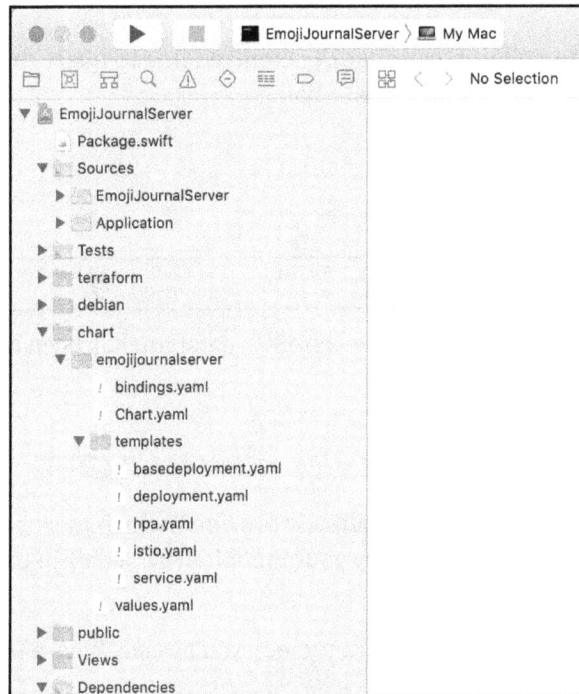

The **chart/emojijournalserver/Chart.yaml** file contains the description and version for your app itself:

```
apiVersion: v1
description: A Helm chart for Kubernetes
name: emojijournalserver
version: 1.0.0
```

This provides a `name`, `description` and `version` for your app, along with the `apiVersion` of Helm that your Chart is for. There are a number of other optional fields that can be added to **Chart.yaml**, including `kubeVersion` for the required version of Kubernetes, `tillerVersion` for the required version of Tiller, and things like `home` and `icon` to set a homepage and icon for the app.

The majority of the configuration carried out by the Helm Chart is in the **chart/emojijournalserver/templates** directory, which contains configuration files for various components and features of Kubernetes. These can largely be ignored because the configurable values from those template files have been centralized into **chart/emojijournalserver/values.yaml**.

Open **values.yaml**, which should contain the following:

```
# This is a YAML-formatted file.
# Declare variables to be passed into your templates.
replicaCount: 1
revisionHistoryLimit: 1
image:
  repository: registry.ng.bluemix.net/replace-me-namespace/
emojijournalserver
  tag: v1.0.0
  pullPolicy: Always
  resources:
    requests:
      cpu: 200m
      memory: 300Mi
livenessProbe:
  initialDelaySeconds: 3000
  periodSeconds: 1000
service:
  name: swift
  type: NodePort
  servicePort: 8080
hpa:
  enabled: false
  minReplicas: 1
  maxReplicas: 2
  metrics:
    cpu:
      targetAverageUtilization: 70
    memory:
      targetAverageUtilization: 70
base:
  enabled: false
  replicaCount: 1
  image:
    tag : v0.9.9
  weight: 100
istio:
  enabled: false
  weight: 100
generatedBindings:
  enabled: true
```

The first value in **values.yaml** is `replicaCount`, which determines the number of instances (pods), that are created when your app is deployed, and `revisionHistoryLimit`, which determines how many old versions of your app are stored in case you need to roll back updates.

The **values.yaml** file is then broken down into sections. The `image` section specifies the `repository`, which denotes the name and location of the Docker image for your app, the `tag` fo the version of your Docker image, the `pullPolicy` for when to pull the version from the repository or use a local cached copy, and the `resources`, which the running app will be able to use.

Update the `image` section as follows:

```
image:
  repository: emojijournalserver-swift-run
  tag: latest
  pullPolicy: IfNotPresent
  resources:
    requests:
      cpu: 200m
      memory: 300Mi
```

This updates the `repository` field to use the name of the **run** Docker image that you can build using the **kitura build** and **kitura run** command lines, and to use the default repository, which is Docker Hub.

This means that the Tiller server in your Kubernetes cluster will try to pull from Docker Hub. You can however configure Tiller to try your local Docker registry first using a `pullPolicy` of `IfNotPresent`, which means that Tiller will only try to pull the image from DockerHub if there is no local version.

Finally, this updates the `tag` field to `latest`. This means that any redeploy of your Helm Chart will pull the most recently build version of your Docker image, which is useful during development. When you are in production this should use a fixed version of your app.

Once your app has been built into a new Docker image, it can now be deployed into Kubernetes; however, there is still one further update that needs to be made. You need to configure your app with the location and credentials for accessing your PostgreSQL database instance.

To do that, open **chart/emojijournalserver/bindings.yaml**. This file describes how to populate a number of environment variables in the environment of your app from **Kubernetes Secrets**, which are configuration values including user names and passwords.

Add the following to the bottom of the **bindings.yaml** file:

```
- name: DBHOST
  value: postgresql-database
- name: DBPASSWORD
  valueFrom:
    secretKeyRef:
      name: postgresql-database
      key: postgres-password
```

This will populate the DBHOST environment variable with postgresql-database, which is the name you used to deploy your PostgreSQL instance, and the DBPASSWORD environment variable with the postgres-password key from the postgresql-database configuration, which was provided by the PostgreSQL Helm Chart when you deployed it.

> **Note**: In Chapter 8, "SwiftKueryORM," you added the DBHOST environment variable into your **Dockerfile** and **Dockerfile-tools** files. This was to allow your EmojiJournalServer to be able to connect out from the Docker container to your PostgreSQL instance running on your Mac. You do not need to remove this; the configuration in the **bindings.yaml** file will be applied last, overwriting anything set in the Docker configuration files.

Deploying your EmojiJournalServer Helm Chart

You are now ready to deploy your EmojiJournalServer to your Kubernetes cluster!

First, build EmojiJournalServer to make sure that it compiles using the following command from the root folder of your project inside Terminal:

```
swift build
```

Next, build a new **run** image for your EmojiJournalServer using the following two Kitura CLI commands inside Terminal:

```
kitura build
kitura run
```

This builds an optimized Docker image for your server and runs it in a Docker container to ensure that it has built successfully. You should see the following printed at the end of the output written to the Terminal:

```
Logs for the emojijournalserver-swift-run container:
[2018-12-09T23:22:55.398Z] [WARNING] [ConfigurationManager.swift:261 load(url:deserializerName:)] Unable to load data from
 URL /swift-project/config/mappings.json
[2018-12-09T23:22:55.499Z] [INFO] [Persistence.swift:53 setUp()] Table UserJournalEntrys already exists
[Sun Dec  9 23:22:55 2018] com.ibm.diagnostics.healthcenter.loader INFO: Swift Application Metrics
[2018-12-09T23:22:55.689Z] [INFO] [Metrics.swift:48 initializeMetrics(router:)] Initialized metrics.
[2018-12-09T23:22:55.695Z] [INFO] [EntryRoutes.swift:74 initializeEntryRoutes(app:)] Journal entry routes created
[2018-12-09T23:22:55.695Z] [INFO] [UserRoutes.swift:36 initializeUserRoutes(app:)] User routes created
[2018-12-09T23:22:55.698Z] [INFO] [WebClientRoutes.swift:77 initializeWebClientRoutes(app:)] Web client routes created
[2018-12-09T23:22:55.698Z] [INFO] [KituraOpenAPI.swift:62 addOpenAPI(to:with:)] Registered OpenAPI definition on /openapi
[2018-12-09T23:22:55.715Z] [INFO] [KituraOpenAPI.swift:105 addSwaggerUI(to:with:)] Registered SwaggerUI on /openapi/ui
[2018-12-09T23:22:55.716Z] [INFO] [HTTPServer.swift:195 listen(on:)] Listening on port 8080
```

Stop the process using **Control-C**, and check that your new image is present in the list of Docker images in your local machine's registry:

```
docker images
```

```
REPOSITORY                          TAG      IMAGE ID       CREATED         SIZE
emojijournalserver-swift-run        latest   480bbe53bc97   2 minutes ago   728MB
emojijournalserver-swift-tools      latest   86f62a59f964   5 minutes ago   1.85GB
```

This should show a newly created **emojijournalserver-swift-run** image with a tag of **latest**, which matches what you have configured in your **chart/emojijournalserver/values.yaml** file.

From here, you can install your Helm Chart using:

```
helm install --name emojijournalserver chart/emojijournalserver
```

This will immediately respond with the following information:

```
NAME:   emojijournalserver
LAST DEPLOYED: Tue Dec 11 06:07:42 2018
NAMESPACE: default
STATUS: DEPLOYED

RESOURCES:
==> v1/Service
NAME                                       TYPE       CLUSTER-IP     EXTERNAL-IP   PORT(S)          AGE
emojijournalserver-application-service     NodePort   10.101.9.32    <none>        8080:32296/TCP   0s

==> v1beta1/Deployment
NAME                             DESIRED   CURRENT   UP-TO-DATE   AVAILABLE   AGE
emojijournalserver-deployment    1         0         0            0           0s

==> v1/Pod(related)
NAME                                            READY   STATUS    RESTARTS   AGE
emojijournalserver-deployment-6f66c5db66-95xw8  0/1     Pending   0          0s
```

This shows that the deployment has a DESIRED count of 1 instance but has a CURRENT value of 0. This is because your app is still starting.

Note: The output shows that you have a **Service**, a **Deployment** and a **Pod**. In Kubernetes, an app is represented as a **Deployment**, which has one or more replicated instances called **Pods**. The deployment itself is then accessed using the IP and port(s) associated with the **Service**.

You can find explanations for more Kubernetes terms in the Kubernetes Glossary found at https://kubernetes.io/docs/reference/glossary/?fundamental=true&networking=true.

Running the `helm status emojijournalserver` command in the terminal window will request the status of the deployed app. This will very quickly start to report:

```
LAST DEPLOYED: Tue Dec 11 06:07:42 2018
NAMESPACE: default
STATUS: DEPLOYED

RESOURCES:
==> v1/Service
NAME                                    TYPE      CLUSTER-IP    EXTERNAL-IP  PORT(S)         AGE
emojijournalserver-application-service  NodePort  10.101.9.32   <none>       8080:32296/TCP  42s

==> v1beta1/Deployment
NAME                           DESIRED  CURRENT  UP-TO-DATE  AVAILABLE  AGE
emojijournalserver-deployment  1        1        1           1          42s

==> v1/Pod(related)
NAME                                            READY  STATUS   RESTARTS  AGE
emojijournalserver-deployment-6f66c5db66-95xw8  1/1    Running  0         42s
```

Showing that the CURRENT count has become 1. In the example above, that instance has a name of emojijournalserver-deployment-6f66c5db66-95xw8 — yours should have a similar name.

Now that everything is up and running, you will test and verify that the app is running successfully using the Kitura OpenAPI UI as you have been previously.

Kubernetes runs on its own network, which both means that multiple app instances can run on the same port, and instances have to be explicitly made externally reachable. To use the Kitura OpenAPI UI with your deployed instance, you first need to map its port to your localhost network.

Run the following command in your terminal window:

```
kubectl port-forward \
    emojijournalserver-deployment-6f66c5db66-95xw8 8080:8080
```

Note: Make sure that you replace emojijournalserver-deployment-6f66c5db66-95xw8 with the name of your instance.

This should respond with:

```
Forwarding from 127.0.0.1:8080 -> 8080
Forwarding from [::1]:8080 -> 8080
```

This will map port 8080 from the instance to `localhost:8080`. Open up the Kitura OpenAPI UI in your browser: https://localhost:8080/openapi/ui

As this is running with a new install of your database, there are no users or Journal entries stored.

First, create a new user with by making a **POST** request on **/user** with a user id of **John** and a password of **12345** and click **Execute**.

POST `/user`	

Parameters   Cancel

Name	**Description**

input * required

(body)

Edit Value   Model

```
{
  "id": "John",
  "password": "12345"
}
```

Cancel

Parameter content type

application/json   ⌄

Execute	Clear

This should respond with a **Code** of **201** for **CREATED**:

Server response	
Code	Details
201 *Undocumented*	Response body

```
{
    "id": "John",
    "password": "12345"
}
```
Download

Next, add a new entry with by making a **POST** request on **/entries** with the following **input** and click **Execute**.

```
{
    "emoji": "😀",
    "date": "2018-11-18T00:07:01.000Z"
}
```

POST /entries		Cancel
Parameters		
Name	Description	
input * required (body)	Edit Value Model	

```
{
    "emoji": "😀",
    "date": "2018-11-18T00:07:01.000Z"
}
```

One you log in using your **Username** of **John** and **Password** of **12345**, your request should respond with:

Server response	
Code	Details
201 *Undocumented*	Response body

```
{
    "id": "41CE197B-399C-464A-8238-D5469351D8ED",
    "fortune": "Doubt is not a pleasant condition, but certainty is absurd.\n\t\t--Voltaire",
    "emoji": "😀",
    "date": 564192421
}
```
Download

This shows an entry was successfully added to the database, including a **fortune** received from the Fortune Cookie API service!

Finally, you'll use your iOS app to check that you can connect to your server.

Open the EmojiJournalMobileApp project in Xcode and build and run it in the iPhone simulator.

Because your app is configured to use the **John** user, this should display the simulator with the emoji journal entries retrieved from your deployed service:

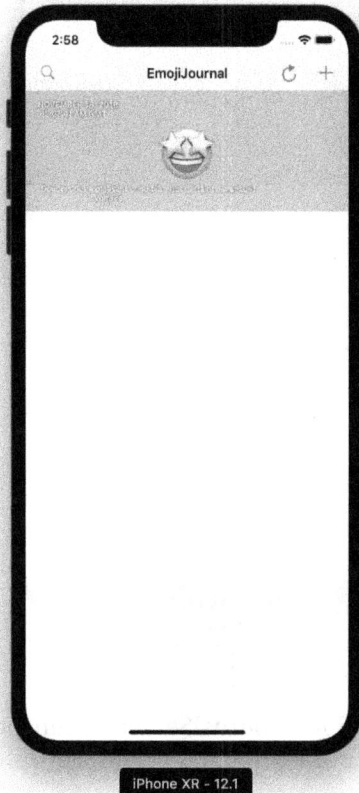

Finally, click the + button, select an emoji of your choice and click **Save** to add a new entry from the app. This should add a new entry, along with a fortune:

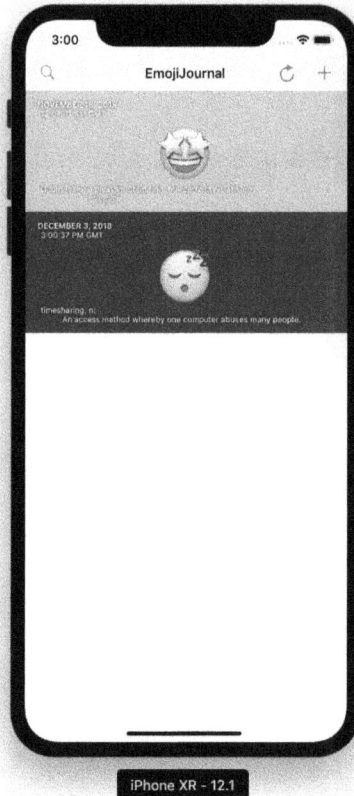

That's it! You now have your EmojiJournalServer running in Kubernetes, and your / **health** endpoint ensures that Kubernetes will automatically restart the instance if it fails.

Adding replicas

Having Kubernetes restart your instance if it fails is great for increasing app availability. If your server instance crashes or becomes unresponsive, it will only be unavailable for a few seconds before it is restarted.

Having additional replicas extends this further, because if there is an outage of one instance, requests can continue to be handled by the other instances. Additionally, having multiple replicas means that you are able to handle larger level of load and therefore more users of your EmojiJournal app.

Increasing the number of replicas requires a very small change to the Helm Chart for your EmojiJournalServer. Open the **charts/emojijournalserver/values.yaml** file, and change the `replicaCount` value at the top of the file to 3:

```
replicaCount: 3
```

Having a minimum of three replicas to provide **triple redundancy** is ideal when deploying for resilience and availability. Should one instance fail, the other two are likely to be able to share the load previously handled by the failed instance. If there are only two instances, should one fail the other may not be able to handle the additional load on its own.

Next, deploy your updated Helm Chart using the following command from the root folder of your EmojiJournalServer project (if `kubectl` is still running to forward the port, use Control + C to stop it):

```
helm upgrade emojijournalserver ./chart/emojijournalserver
```

This will immediately display the following response to the terminal window showing that the upgrade is in progress.

```
Release "emojijournalserver" has been upgraded. Happy Helming!
LAST DEPLOYED: Wed Dec 12 22:43:17 2018
NAMESPACE: default
STATUS: DEPLOYED

RESOURCES:
==> v1/Service
NAME                                        TYPE       CLUSTER-IP      EXTERNAL-IP  PORT(S)          AGE
emojijournalserver-application-service  NodePort   10.109.115.80   <none>       8080:30876/TCP   12m

==> v1beta1/Deployment
NAME                            DESIRED  CURRENT  UP-TO-DATE  AVAILABLE  AGE
emojijournalserver-deployment   3        1        1           1          12m

==> v1/Pod(related)
NAME                                              READY  STATUS            RESTARTS  AGE
emojijournalserver-deployment-6db8d969cb-hchgj    1/1    Running           0         12m
emojijournalserver-deployment-6db8d969cb-qdg62    0/1    ContainerCreating 0         0s
emojijournalserver-deployment-6db8d969cb-tdnmq    0/1    Pending           0         0s
```

As the only change is increasing the `replicaCount` from 1 to 3, your previous instance continues to run, but two more are added.

Running `helm status emojijournalserver` again should then show that all of the three replicas are now running:

```
LAST DEPLOYED: Wed Dec 12 22:43:17 2018
NAMESPACE: default
STATUS: DEPLOYED

RESOURCES:
==> v1beta1/Deployment
NAME                           DESIRED  CURRENT  UP-TO-DATE  AVAILABLE  AGE
emojijournalserver-deployment  3        3        3           3          13m

==> v1/Pod(related)
NAME                                           READY  STATUS   RESTARTS  AGE
emojijournalserver-deployment-6db8d969cb-hchgj  1/1    Running  0         13m
emojijournalserver-deployment-6db8d969cb-qdg62  1/1    Running  0         22s
emojijournalserver-deployment-6db8d969cb-tdnmq  1/1    Running  0         22s

==> v1/Service
NAME                                     TYPE      CLUSTER-IP     EXTERNAL-IP  PORT(S)         AGE
emojijournalserver-application-service   NodePort  10.109.115.80  <none>       8080:30876/TCP  13m
```

Now that there are three replicas running, you cannot simply map port 8080 from one of those instances to your localhost network to expose access to the app — you need a way of load balancing across all three instances.

Adding NGINX as a load balancer

Kubernetes has the concept of an **Ingress Controller**, which is a service that manages external access to the services in a cluster.

Kubernetes provides a simple built-in load balancer that you can use; for production, you'll want to use something like NGINX, which provides a high-performance load balancer and web proxy.

As well as using NGINX as a load balancer, you can also use it as a TLS termination proxy, meaning that it receives the incoming TLS requests and carries out all of the cryptographic processing, forwarding unencrypted requests to your server instances. This both reduces the load on your EmojiJournalServer instances and means that you only need to handle certificate management once, at the load balancer.

This has just the same level of security as you had previously, as none of your EmojiJournalServer instances are directly reachable; all requests must go through the NGINX load balancer.

Just like PostgreSQL, a Helm Chart is provided for NGINX to make it easy to install it into Kubernetes.

As you are going to run it on your local machine and allow the ability to connect using **localhost**, you will need to provide some additional configuration for the Helm

Chart.

First, create an NGINX configuration file called **nginx-values.yaml** anywhere you can run the helm command. Add the following to the file:

```
controller:
  service:
    externalTrafficPolicy: Local
    type: LoadBalancer
    selector:
      app.kubernetes.io/name: ingress-nginx
      app.kubernetes.io/part-of: ingress-nginx
    targetPorts:
      http: http
      https: https
```

This sets an `externalTrafficPolicy` of `Local`, which is required to work with your **localhost** traffic.

Next install the Helm Chart for NGINX with the additional configuration using the following in Terminal:

```
helm install stable/nginx-ingress --name nginx \
  --values nginx-values.yaml
```

This will immediately display a response to the terminal window showing the status of the deployment along with some guidance on registering an **Ingress** with the controller to route traffic to your EmojiJournalServer instances.

This includes the `nginx-nginx-ingress-controller` and `nginx-nginx-ingress-default-backend` services:

```
==> v1/Service
NAME                                    TYPE          CLUSTER-IP       EXTERNAL-IP  PORT(S)                      AGE
nginx-nginx-ingress-controller          LoadBalancer  10.100.131.152   localhost    80:32012/TCP,443:32094/TCP   2m
nginx-nginx-ingress-default-backend     ClusterIP     10.111.241.171   <none>       80/TCP                       2m
```

The `nginx-nginx-ingress-controller` service provides the LoadBalancer, and is exposed on http://localhost:80 and https://localhost:443, which are the default HTTP and HTTPS ports. Conversely, the `nginx-nginx-ingress-default-backend` service provides a default backend to provide error messages for requests that do not have a registered backend service.

Open your browser to https://localhost:443 to see the default message provided by the backend service:

```
default backend - 404
```

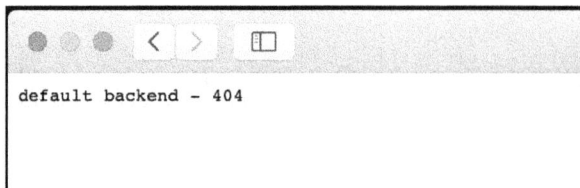

As you want to use the NGINX-based load balancer to carry out TLS termination for your EmojiJournalServer instances, you next need to make the key and certificate you generated available. To do that, run the following command in Terminal from the root folder of your EmojiJournalServer project, where your key and certificate is stored:

```
kubectl create secret tls emojiserver-tls --key key.pem \
    --cert certificate.pem
```

This creates a Kubernetes **secret**, a configuration value similar to the one that the PostgreSQL Helm Chart created to store the database password that can be used by your NGINX based Ingress Controller.

Finally, update your EmojiJournalServer project to remove the use of HTTPS, and update its Helm Chart to register itself with the Ingress Controller.

Open your **Sources/Application/Application.swift** file, and toward the end of the file replace the following line:

```
Kitura.addHTTPServer(onPort: cloudEnv.port, with: router,
    withSSL: config)
```

With:

```
Kitura.addHTTPServer(onPort: cloudEnv.port, with: router)
```

This leaves the certificate and SSL setup code in place in case you want to revert the change in the future, but removes the HTTPS activation.

Next, create a **chart/emojijournalserver/templates/ingress.yaml** file that contains the following:

```
apiVersion: extensions/v1beta1
kind: Ingress
metadata:
  name: emojiserver-ingress
spec:
  tls:
    - hosts:
```

```
        - emojijournal.com
        secretName: emojiserver-tls
    rules:
      - host: emojijournal.com
        http:
          paths:
          - path: /
            backend:
              serviceName: emojijournalserver-application-service
              servicePort: 8080
```

This creates a configuration for the NGINX Ingress Controller to use `tls` for requests to `emojijournal.com` using the `emojiserver-tls` secret you created earlier, and to route requests to all paths to your EmojiJournalServer service.

If you were running your app in a hosted cloud, you would buy the **emojijournal.com** domain name and set the domain name to direct to the external IP for your Ingress Controller so that your EmojiJournalSever is reachable. For testing and development purposes, you can configure your **/etc/hosts** file on your Mac to direct all requests to the **emojijournal.com** domain to any IP you choose, including **127.0.0.1** which is your **localhost**.

Open your Terminal window and run the following command. Note that this will require you to enter your password:

```
echo "127.0.0.1        emojijournal.com" | sudo tee -a /etc/hosts
```

This appends the **echo** statement as a line to the end of your **/etc/hosts** file. To see your updated file, run the following in Terminal:

```
cat /etc/hosts
```

This should return the following:

```
##
# Host Database
#
# localhost is used to configure the loopback interface
# when the system is booting.  Do not change this entry.
##
127.0.0.1       localhost
255.255.255.255 broadcasthost
::1             localhost
127.0.0.1       emojijournal.com
```

This will now redirect all requests to **emojijournal.com** to **127.0.0.1**, which is the internal IP used for **localhost** requests. Now build your updated EmojiJournalServer without HTTPS enabled using the following commands in your terminal window:

```
kitura build
kitura run
```

Once the run command completes, use **Control-C** to stop the server, and deploy the new version of your Helm Chart using the **helm upgrade** command as follows in your terminal window:

```
helm upgrade --recreate-pods emojijournalserver \
    ./chart/emojijournalserver
```

This command includes the additional `--recreate-pods` option, which will cause your instances to restart. This ensures that the new version of your app that you have just built using **kitura build** and **kitura run** becomes deployed.

This has now registered your EmojiJournalServer instances with the NGINX load balancer with TLS termination, so that any HTTPS requests to **emojijournal.com** are handled and decrypted and forwarded to one of your EmojiJournalServer instances based on load. It has also removed the need to specify port 8080 for all of your requests, meaning that it looks like a regular backend server and website!

Now, go back to your EmojiJournalMobileApp and edit **EmojiJournalMobileApp/ Model/EmojiClient.swift** to remove the port number from the `baseURL` in the `EmojiClient` class so that it becomes:

```
private static var baseURL: String {
    return "https://emojijournal.com"
}
```

Now build and run the app in the simulator, and click the + icon to add a new emoji. Again, select an emoji of your choice and click **Save**.

You should again see a new entry displayed!

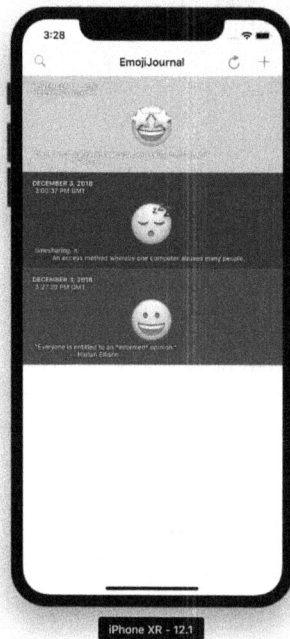

Production Monitoring with Prometheus

You now have a highly available, highly scalable, EmojiJournalServer deployment running in Kubernetes to back your mobile and browser apps.

The final step is to make that deployment highly observable, so you can track user traffic, performance and resource usage data.

Kitura uses the SwiftMetrics module to provide monitoring data, covering metrics like CPU usage, memory usage and HTTP responsiveness.

SwiftMetrics provides APIs for accessing the monitoring data, as well as providing built-in integration with **Prometheus**, https://prometheus.io. Prometheus is an open-source monitoring solution, which is also one of the Cloud Native Computing Foundation projects.

While Prometheus can be run anywhere, it is also designed to integrate easily in a Kubernetes environment, with pre-build configurations to collect data from both Prometheus-compatible apps and from Kubernetes itself.

Just like there was for PostgreSQL, there is already a Helm Chart for Prometheus available from the Stable Helm Chart repository. Use the following command in your terminal window to install Prometheus:

```
helm install stable/prometheus --name prometheus \
    --namespace prometheus
```

This will print the status of the Prometheus Helm Chart to the terminal window, along with some NOTES. This includes the following instructions on how to map the Prometheus server to your localhost network:

```
Get the Prometheus server URL by running these commands in the same shell:
  export POD_NAME=$(kubectl get pods --namespace prometheus -l "app=prometheus,component=server"
-o jsonpath="{.items[0].metadata.name}")
  kubectl --namespace prometheus port-forward $POD_NAME 9090
```

Run those two commands in your terminal window to make the Prometheus server available on port 9090.

```
export POD_NAME=$(kubectl get pods --namespace prometheus \
    -l "app=prometheus,component=server" \
    -o jsonpath="{.items[0].metadata.name}")
```

```
kubectl --namespace prometheus port-forward $POD_NAME 9090
```

The Helm Chart added to generated Kitura projects contains the following entry in **chart/emojijournalserver/templates/service.yaml**:

```
annotations:
    prometheus.io/scrape: 'true'
```

This means that Prometheus is already configured to automatically collect data from your Kitura app, allowing you to create graphs of your data. You can now open your browser to the following address to see the Prometheus dashboard: http://localhost:9090:

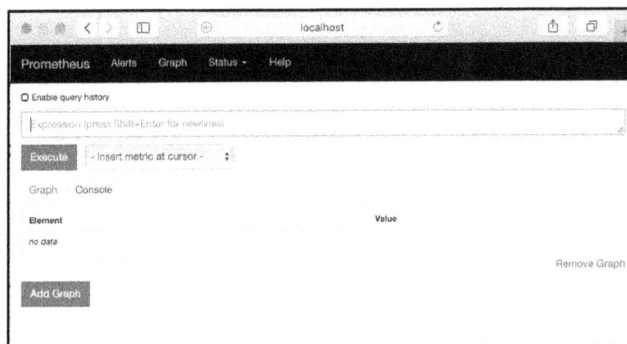

To build your first graph, type `os_cpu_used_ratio` into the **Expression** box and click on the **Graph** tab halfway down the page:

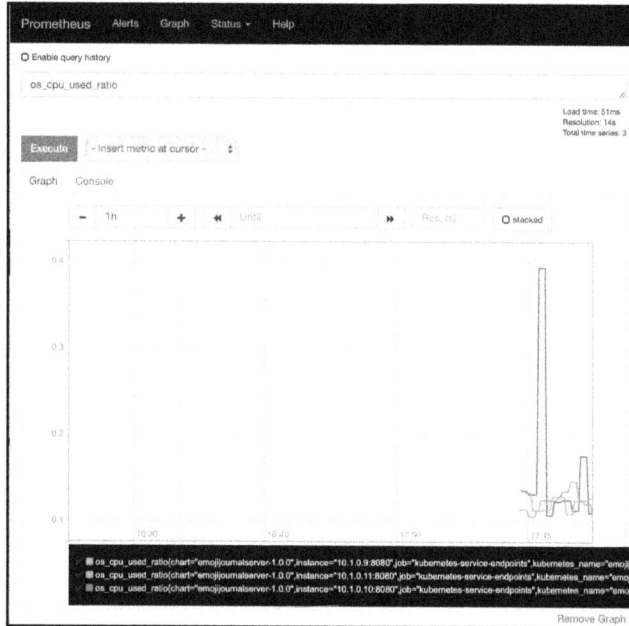

This shows the CPU usage data for all three of your EmojiJournalServer instances.

Prometheus provides the ability to build simple graphs and alerts. However, it is also designed to be used with more advanced graphing and dashboarding solutions. The most frequently used being **Grafana**.

Installing Grafana

Grafana is also available from the Stable Helm Chart repository. Run the following command line in a terminal window to install the chart:

```
helm install stable/grafana --set adminPassword=PASSWORD \
  --name grafana --namespace grafana --version 1.14.3
```

Note that this configures the Grafana Helm Chart to set the password for the admin user to **PASSWORD**.

Running the `helm install` command again causes NOTES to be written to the Terminal, including the following instructions for exposing the Grafana dashboard to your browser:

```
2. The Grafana server can be accessed via port 80 on the following DNS name from within your cluster:

   grafana.grafana.svc.cluster.local

   Get the Grafana URL to visit by running these commands in the same shell:

     export POD_NAME=$(kubectl get pods --namespace grafana -l "app=grafana -o jsonpath="{.items[0].metadata.name}")
     kubectl --namespace grafana port-forward $POD_NAME 3000
```

There is actually a syntax error in the instructions for exporting the POD_NAME in the output written to the Terminal. Instead, run the following commands:

```
export POD_NAME=$(kubectl get pods --namespace grafana \
  -l "app=grafana" -o jsonpath="{.items[0].metadata.name}")
```

```
kubectl --namespace grafana port-forward $POD_NAME 3000
```

Next, open your browser to the Grafana dashboard: http://localhost:3000. This will display a login screen:

Enter a **username** of **admin** and a **password** of **PASSWORD**, which you set when you installed the Grafana Helm Chart, and click **Log In**.

This will then display the **Home Dashboard**:

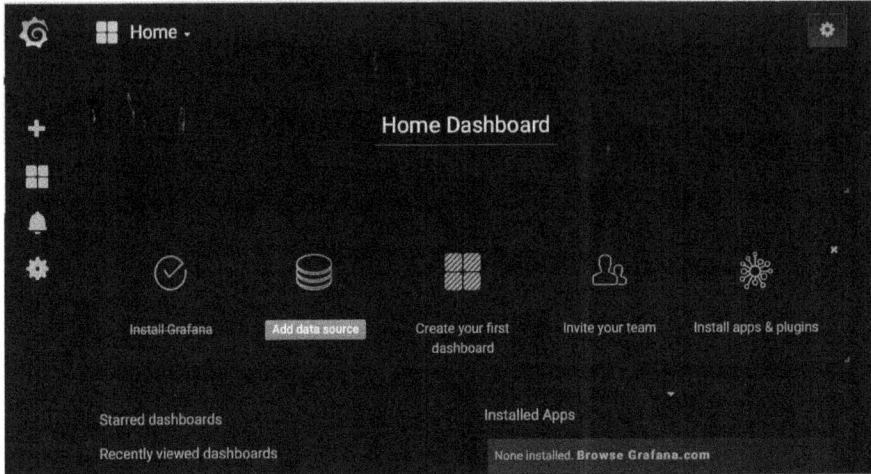

Before you can graph your monitoring data in Grafana, you need to connect Grafana to your Prometheus service. To do that, click on the highlighted **Add data source** icon.

This opens a **Data Sources / New** panel. Set the following options in the panel:

- **Name**: Prometheus

- **Type**: Prometheus

- **URL**: http://prometheus-server.prometheus.svc.cluster.local

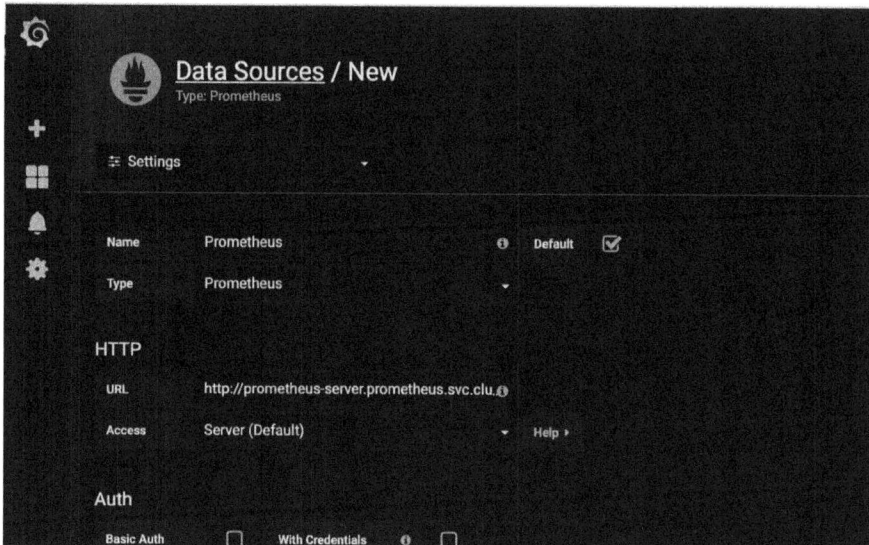

And click **Save & Test** at the bottom of the panel to check the connection to the Prometheus data store and save the Data Source configuration. Then click **Back** to return home.

Grafana now has access to the data from Prometheus!

Building Grafana dashboards

Grafana provides the ability to build custom dashboards and data charts. The Grafana community also provides a large number of pre-created dashboards which are available for download, including some which are designed to display Kubernetes platform data.

To install one of those dashboards, hover your mouse over the + icon (on the left) and select **Import**.

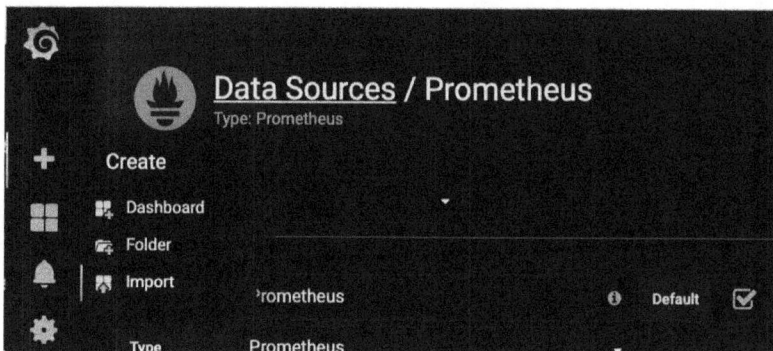

You can explore the dashboards that are available to import in the Dashboards section of the Grafana website, https://grafana.com/dashboards.

As the initial dashboard to monitor your Kubernetes cluster, you're going the install the **Kubernetes cluster monitoring** dashboard, which has an ID of **1621**:

In the **Import** window in Grafana, enter **1621** into the **Grafana.com Dashboard** field in order to import the dashboard and press **Tab**. This then loads the information on dashboard 1621 from *Grafana.com*.

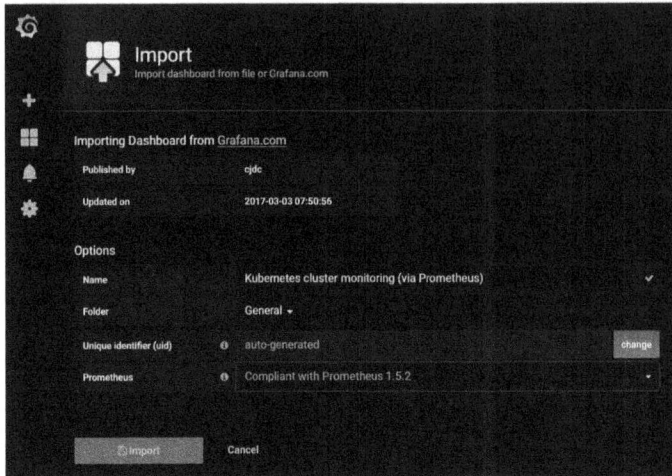

Set the **Prometheus** field to **Prometheus** and click **Import**. This then immediately displays the **Kubernetes cluster monitoring** dashboard:

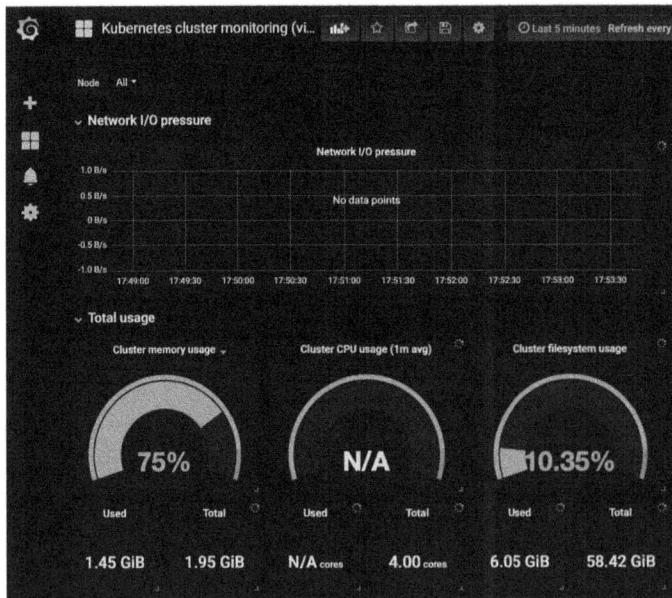

Adding custom charts and graphs

In order to extend the dashboard with your own graphs, click the **Add panel** icon on the top toolbar and select **Graph**.

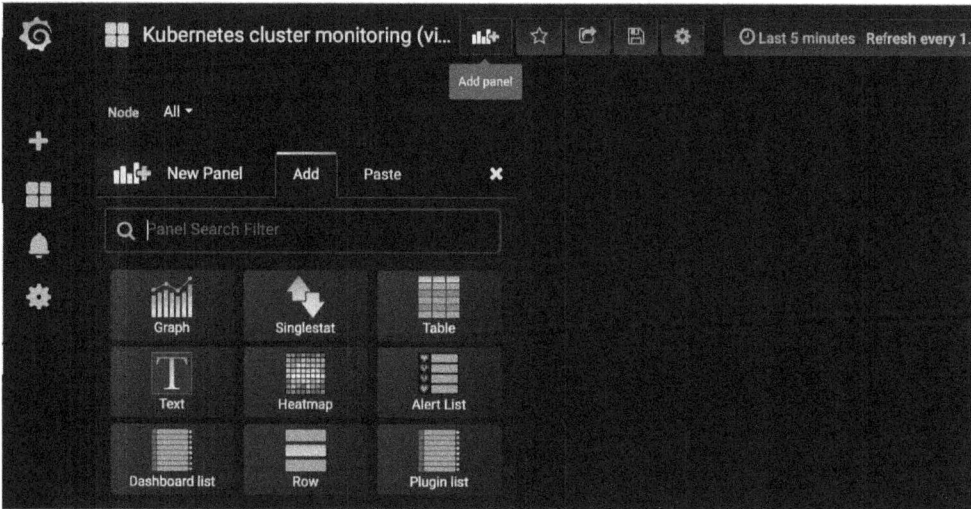

This creates a blank graph. Select the **Panel Title** pull down menu and select **Edit**.

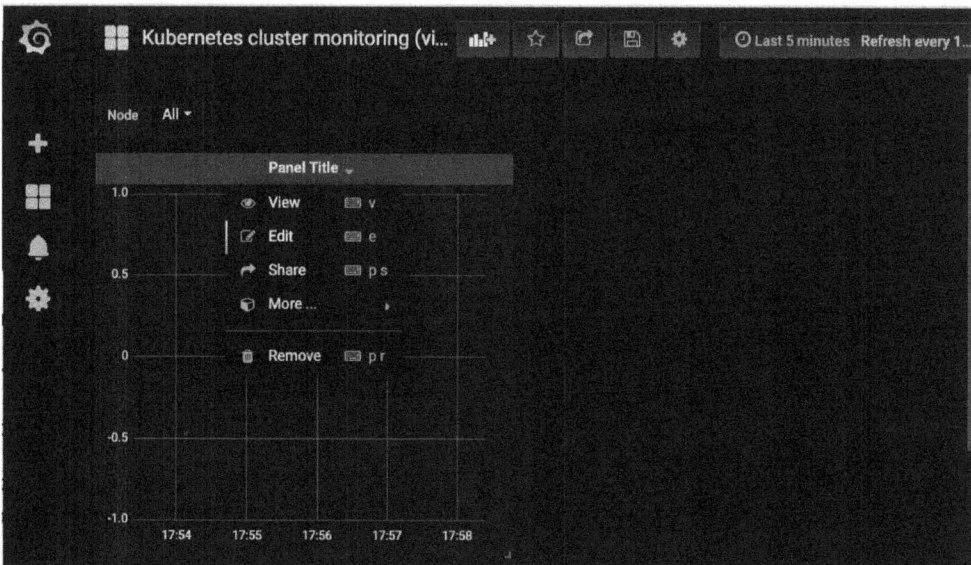

This opens an editor panel, where you can select data that you'd like to graph.

Type `os_cpu_used_ratio` into the data box, and a graph of the CPU used by your three EmojiJournalServer instances will show on the panel.

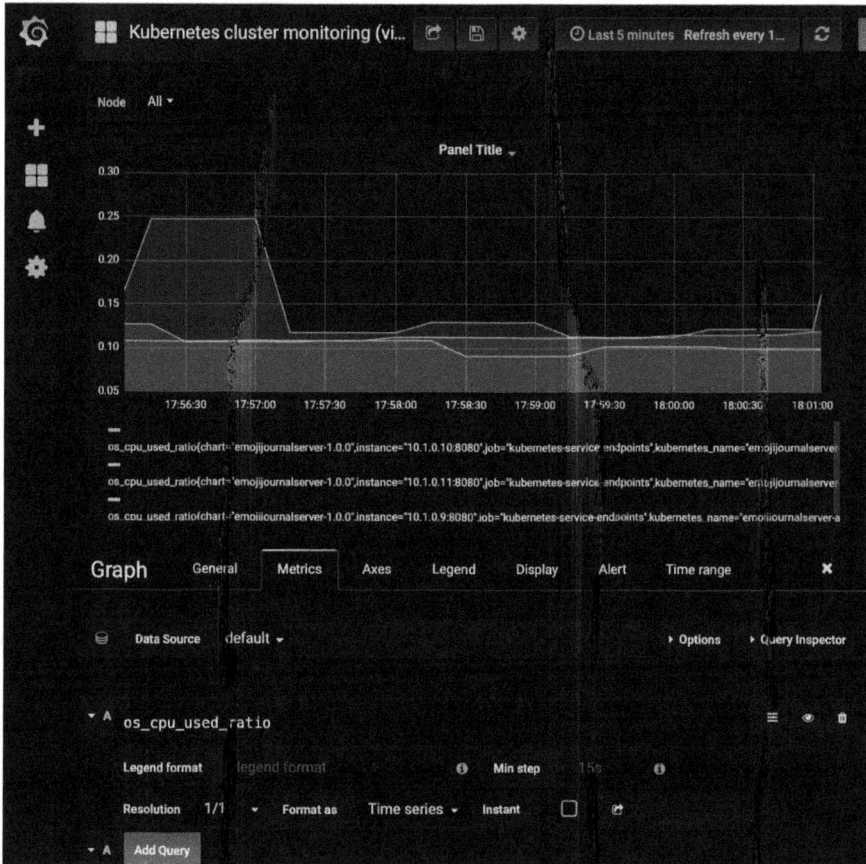

You can create more complex queries and apply filters according to any Kubernetes value.

For example, remove the `os_cpu_used_ratio` entry from the data box and replace it with:

```
http_request_duration_microseconds{chart="emojijournalserver-1.0
.0"}/1000
```

This will display the responsiveness of each of your RESTful endpoints, measured in milliseconds.

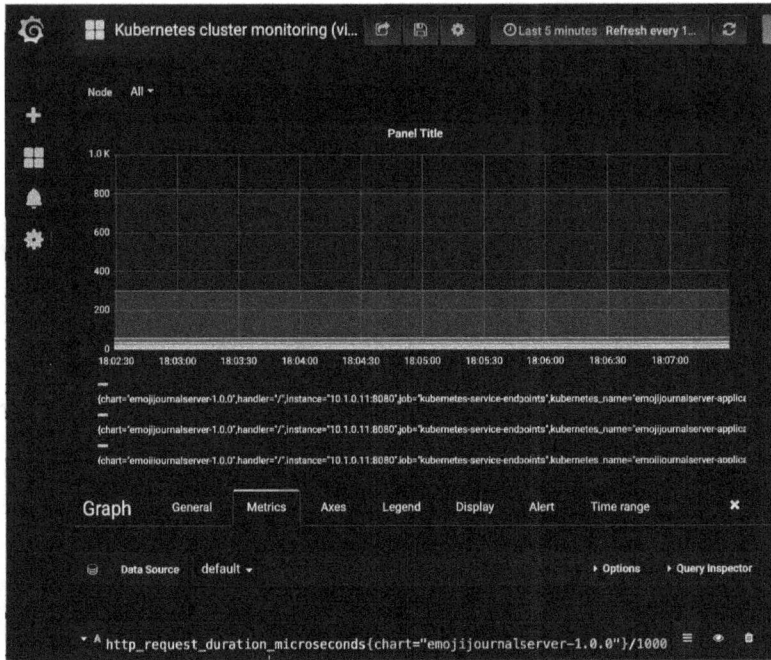

The chart will also provide tooltips that show a detail view by placing your mouse over the lines in the chart:

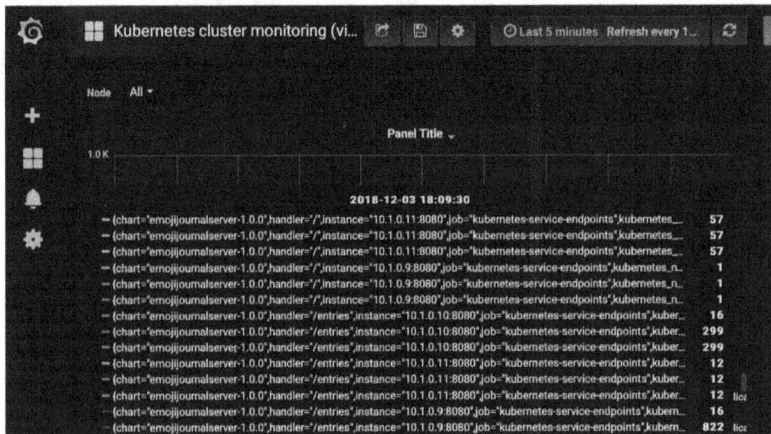

Through the data exposed by **SwiftMetrics** on the **/metrics** endpoint in your app, collected by **Prometheus** and displayed in **Grafana** it's possible to build very rich monitoring dashboard and lets you understand huge amounts about your app.

This is not just limited to performance and resource usage like CPU and memory. It can also be used to track the number of requests and users interacting with your app.

This all means that you can easily gain insight into both your app and your users.

Cleaning up

You've seen how to use `helm install` to deploy your EmojiJournalServer along with Prometheus and Grafana, and how to use `helm upgrade` to update a deployment. There is also the useful `helm list` command to see what you have deployed, and `helm delete` to allow you to remove deployments.

Running `helm list` should show you that you have the following releases deployed:

NAME	REVISION	UPDATED	STATUS	CHART	APP VERSION	NAMESPACE
emojijournalserver	5	Wed Dec 19 09:10:17 2018	DEPLOYED	emojijournalserver-1.0.0		default
grafana	1	Wed Dec 19 10:01:07 2018	DEPLOYED	grafana-1.14.3	5.2.3	grafana
nginx	1	Tue Dec 18 21:56:30 2018	DEPLOYED	nginx-ingress-1.1.0	0.21.0	default
postgresql-database	1	Tue Dec 18 19:15:28 2018	DEPLOYED	postgresql-0.17.0	9.6.2	default
prometheus	1	Wed Dec 19 10:00:34 2018	DEPLOYED	prometheus-8.1.2	2.5.0	prometheus

To remove your EmojiJournalServer deployment you can use the `helm delete emojijournalserver` command, which removes the deployment and the current version of the Helm Chart. As this only removes the current version, you can use `helm rollback emojijournalserver 1` to *undo* the delete and rollback by one version, which you can also do after any `helm upgrade` to rollback the update.

The `delete` command also provides a `--purge` option, which also removes any previous revisions of the Helm Chart. Run that in your terminal window:

```
helm delete --purge emojijournalserver
```

You can repeat this step in your Terminal window to remove your other deployments and their Helm Chart revisions:

```
helm delete --purge grafana
helm delete --purge nginx
helm delete --purge prometheus
helm delete --purge postgresql-database
```

Fully removing the PostgreSQL database also has an additional step. Because your database stores your data, and you need that to persist over restarts or upgrades of the database instance, it uses a **PersistentVolumeClaim** (PVC) bound to a **PersistentVolume** (PV) to provide data persistence.

In order to delete the PersistentVolumeClaim and the associated PersistentVolume, first identify the PVC using the following in your terminal window:

```
kubectl get pvc
```

This should return with output similar to the following:

NAME	STATUS	VOLUME	CAPACITY	ACCESS MODES	STORAGECLASS	AGE
postgresql-database	Bound	pvc-47beebd2-02f9-11e9-971b-025000000001	8Gi	RWO	hostpath	15h

You can now delete the PVC using its **NAME**, in this case postgresql-database:

```
kubectl delete pvc postgresql-database
```

This should respond with persistentvolumeclaim "postgresql-database" deleted.

This has now removed all trace of your deployments.

Where to go from here?

You've just scratched the surface of the capabilities that are provided by Kubernetes, Prometheus and Grafana. In particular, Kubernetes provides scaling features through Horizontal Pod Auto-Scaling and through its integration with Istio, https://istio.io, there is the ability to carry out tasks such as rolling updates during upgrades, and A/B testing by dynamically choosing to direct traffic to different service endpoints.

That's all outside the scope of this chapter, but what you have already achieved is easily enough to take your EmojiJournalServer and deploy it as a live backend for your mobile and web apps!

Conclusion

David Okun

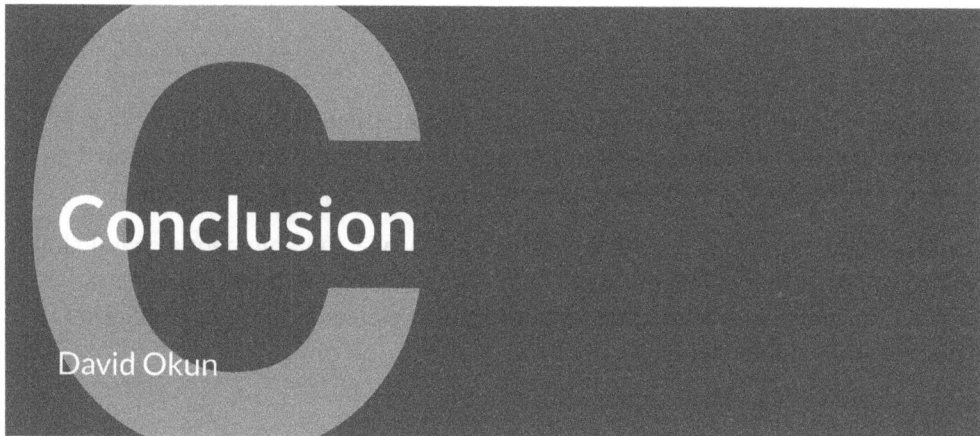

Congratulations on making it to the end! How do you feel? Now, you've got a social network for that!

By completing this book, you have developed EmojiJournal to be a full-fledged app on the server, on iOS and even on the web! In the previous chapter, you learned how to take your server and web app to any cloud with Kubernetes and Docker containers.

The skills you've gained from working on this project should serve you well anywhere you go! If you have a job interview coming up, you should show your interviewer your app, and let them try it. Take a video of their reaction, when you tell them the whole thing is written in Swift, and post it in our forums here:

- https://forums.raywenderlich.com/

As we curated content for this book, there were a few Kitura modules that we didn't get to tell you about. Ultimately, we didn't feel that they fit into the overall look and feel of EmojiJournal, but we still want to tell you a little bit about them.

Kitura WebSockets

The WebSocket protocol gives you a way to upgrade an existing HTTP request to a persisted, full-duplex connection. This means that, if you establish a WebSocket connection between server and client, then you can send messages in either direction from either end of the connection!

If you've ever used a rideshare app, like Lyft or Uber, then you've seen this type of connection in action. When you are waiting on a ride, your car sends location data to the app's server, which then sends a location update to you on your phone.

Another popular use case for the WebSocket protocol is to implement a chat dialog. Maybe you want to implement EmojiChat? If you do, send us your implementation on the forums! You can learn more about Kitura's implementation of WebSockets here:

- https://github.com/IBM-Swift/Kitura-WebSocket

Kitura SMTP

SMTP, or **Simple Mail Transfer Protocol**, allows you to — you guessed it — send an email from your server. Using this protocol, you can specify as much information as you want about an outgoing email, and you can send it off through a REST request.

What if your EmojiJournal users want to get a daily digest of the journal entries that they and their friends post? You could write a function that uses this library to collect entries for the past day, and that constructs an email to send them off to whoever you want! If you want to implement this library, check out the details here:

- https://github.com/IBM-Swift/Swift-SMTP

Kitura CORS

CORS stands for *Cross Origin Resource Sharing*, which is a concept often used for handling other domains that need to get information from your server. If you have a website from another origin separate from where the first request was made, then you would need to enable CORS for your server.

Kitura has a tool that allows you to easily set up middleware on your router, which will enable CORS on your server. You can set it up to simply allow all origins to make validated requests from your server, or you can enact fine-grained controls on who gets what data and from where! If you want to implement this middleware, go to the following resource and add it to your dependecy list:

- https://github.com/IBM-Swift/Kitura-CORS

And many more!

The Kitura community is growing at an amazing rate, and IBM has committed itself to cultivating a vibrant set of libraries for running Swift on the server and for running Swift on Linux. If you'd like to browse all the other offerings it has, visit the following resource to see the organization on GitHub and get a view of what's to come:

- https://github.com/IBM-Swift

Thank you!

We sincerely appreciate that you purchased and read this book. Your support and participation makes our community stronger, and we are excited to see what the future holds in store for Kitura, both in the community and on raywenderlich.com!

Find us in the forums if you have any questions, but we hope you don't stop here — keep making Swift viable everywhere else!

— David, Chris, Brian, Yono, Manda and Jerry